BATTLE OF BRITAIN BROADCASTER

BATTLE OF BRITAIN BROADCASTER

CHARLES GARDNER, RADIO PIONEER AND WWII PILOT

Robert Gardner

AIR WORLD

BATTLE OF BRITAIN BROADCASTER
Charles Gardner, Radio Pioneer and WWII Pilot

First published in Great Britain in 2019 by Air World Books,
an imprint of Pen & Sword Books Ltd, Yorkshire - Philadelphia

Typeset in India by Vman Infotech Private Limited
Printed and bound by TJ International

Pen & Sword Books Ltd incorporates the imprints of Pen & Sword Archaeology,
Air World Books, Atlas, Aviation, Battleground, Discovery, Family History, History,
Maritime, Military, Naval, Politics, Social History, Transport, True Crime, Claymore
Press, Frontline Books, Praetorian Press, Seaforth Publishing and White Owl

For a complete list of Pen & Sword titles please contact:

PEN & SWORD BOOKS LTD
47 Church Street, Barnsley, South Yorkshire, S70 2AS, UK.
E-mail: enquiries@pen-and-sword.co.uk
Website: www.pen-and-sword.co.uk

Or

PEN AND SWORD BOOKS,
1950 Lawrence Road, Havertown, PA 19083, USA
E-mail: Uspen-and-sword@casematepublishers.com
Website: www.penandswordbooks.com

Contents

Acknowledgements

In preparing this book I have been helped by many people to whom I would like to express my sincere thanks. These include, particularly, staff at the BBC Recordings Library, which is part of the British Library, who provided many recordings of my father's broadcasts which have been reproduced in this biography. I am also indebted to the archivists in the BBC Written Archives facility at Caversham Park in Berkshire where I spent many hours researching details of his career. I was often accompanied on these visits by my brother Patrick, who helped in many ways and provided additional information and photographs, many of which have been reproduced in this book. I have also been greatly encouraged and helped by Martin Mace, editor at Pen & Sword, and I have enjoyed the most professional working relationship with sub-editor Alison Flowers. Dr Norman Barfield, who worked both with my father and myself at what was Vickers-Armstrong Aircraft and later BAC at Weybridge, provided a valuable and stimulating appraisal of my father. There were many others, members of the family, particularly my long-suffering wife Charlotte, but finally I would like to express my gratitude to Mike Welsh without whose computer technical skill I would have been exceedingly troubled.

A Message from Richard Dimbleby

I shall not forget those days before the war for a long, long time. You and I together made up the whole of the BBC's reporting staff and did the job for which they now need about 350 people. Of course, although we worked in the same office, we hardly ever saw each other because if I was going north, you were going south and vice versa.

On the basis of absence makes the heart grow fonder, that must be the reason why we got on so well together. There was only one really big battle between us, if I remember, and that was to see who could first produce a child. To this day I can never remember who won. Did your 'Little Umbrage' or my David arrive first? It does not matter anyway – they are both flourishing.

I have the happiest memories of these old days and have watched with the greatest admiration your progress in the aircraft industry. Of course, you always were mad about aeroplanes and this has stood you in good stead . . . While I think of it, you owe me 1/6 for some fish and chips I bought you in the canteen in 1937!

Richard Dimbleby
21 December 1962

Introduction

This is the surprising and significant life-history of Charles Gardner – pioneer broadcaster – whose legendary eyewitness description of an air battle over the Channel in 1940 is still played today. As an RAF pilot in the war, he flew Catalina aircraft on long-distance patrols over the Atlantic and then from Ceylon. His aircraft was the first to spot the position of the invading Japanese navy, report this back, shadow the fleet and return safely to base. He later became a member of Mountbatten's staff tasked with promoting the 'Forgotten Army' in Burma which he did, filing countless stories for broadcast and publication of their heroic feats.

After the war he returned to the BBC as air correspondent. He became known as 'the voice of the air' both on radio and as commentator at the Farnborough Air Show during the burgeoning years of the British aircraft industry.

This book is written both as a matter of historical interest and for the benefit of Charles Gardner's family: his three children – Robert, Patrick and Helen; his grandchildren – Paul, Amelia, Claire, Alexander, Peter, James and Michelle together with their respective spouses; and his great-grandchildren – Chloe, Cameron, Katie, Sian, Evie and Freddie. And for the surviving relatives of my mother's family, together with his many friends and colleagues.

I trust this biography is as engaging as my father's life.

RACG
Leatherhead
March 2019

Chapter One

Dogfight Over the Channel

Standing on top of the Cliffs of Dover on Sunday, 14 July 1940, my father, Charles Gardner, broadcast the first ever eyewitness blow-by-blow account of an early Battle of Britain dogfight over the English Channel. It lasted 9 minutes during which time a squadron of German Junkers 87s dive-bombed a convoy at sea before being chased away by RAF fighters. His enthusiastic description and jubilant shouts as the enemy retreated thrilled many at home but alienated others. Some thought it was in poor taste and others felt it should not be treated as if it were a football match when men's lives were at stake. But by far most people applauded and were uplifted at a time of peril in England.

Gardner, then 28 years old, a pioneer BBC news reporter from 1936, and one of the first war correspondents during the 'phoney war' in France from 1939, would have had no idea that his efforts that fine summer's day would cause such a stir. Nor that it would go down as a classic of the Second World War, to be repeated many times both on the radio, on newsreels and television. It is believed to be the very first eyewitness radio description of any battle, be it on land, sea or air.

As an example of its enduring effect, in 2018 Edward Stourton, BBC journalist and presenter, read extracts on morning radio from his book *Auntie's War*. He devoted much time to my father's contribution to BBC wartime broadcasting and particularly to his account of the air battle. He described it as 'another piece of radio history' adding, 'but this as a live description of an aerial dog-fight was unlike anything the audience had heard before'.

In an earlier television programme in 2015, *The BBC at War*, Jonathan Dimbleby, whose family have contributed so much to the BBC, referred particularly to the Gardner broadcast while standing himself at the top of the Cliffs of Dover and imagining the battle above the Channel in 1940.

He stated that the radio was, 'a crucial means of uniting all those who were fighting Nazi tyranny'. He continued:

> The Battle of Britain was just that, a battle to save the nation from Nazi invasion. But as yet the BBC had only a handful of reporters to cover the drama. One of those was Charles Gardner, like [Richard] Dimbleby, still learning his craft as a radio correspondent in times of war. He was deputed to cover the struggle for the mastery of the skies.

The impact of the broadcast was very well described by John Grehan in the *Britain at War* magazine in 2010:

> There have been a number of live radio broadcast which created major sensations at the time they were delivered and are remembered today. One such live broadcast by a BBC reporter, describing an action in July 1940 was a dramatic account of a combat during the Battle of Britain – but was this reality radio just a little too graphic for the stiff-upper lipped Britons?

The article described how a BBC radio team (including my father) had set itself up in a house overlooking the port of Dover to record the ongoing air attacks by the Germans against British shipping in the Channel.

He continued:

> That afternoon a westbound convoy codenamed Bread was scheduled to pass along the Straight into Dover and the team went to a nearby cliff for a grandstand view of anything that might happen that day. Gardner sat in his car to watch the action with a steel helmet on his head and a mattress strapped to the roof.

My father later described the 'piece of luck' they had to witness the fight in an article in *London Calling*, the overseas journal of the BBC.

He wrote:

> On five or six occasions our recording team – that is Leonard Lewis, Arthur Phillips and myself – had gone to various South-Coast towns in the hope of getting some action. Each time we had been unlucky, but we decided to ask permission to have another

try at Dover. We were there on the Sunday morning, but nothing happened, and so we went for a very hurried lunch. No sooner had we got back to our observation post on the cliff, next door to an AA battery, than the alarm sounded.

A few minutes later we saw about 20 Junkers 87 dive bombers coming from the direction of Calais at about 6,000ft. And above them was an escort of about the same number of Messerschmitts. Lewis immediately started up the recording gear and Phillips and I took the microphone out to watch.

Charles Gardner began by first reading from his prepared script, but as the action began he abandoned his script and 'described what he saw, as it happened in vivid detail'.

But to get the report onto the air waves was not without difficulty. Charles takes up the story in his *London Calling* article. 'As soon as the battle was over we rang up the BBC and told them we were on our way back. Censors (from the Ministry of Information) were good enough to go straight away to Broadcasting House to pass the records, and just over an hour after our return they were being broadcast.'

My father's account differs in one respect from the story he told us. He said his sound engineer that day was Stan Unwin. This was significant for Unwin is now remembered as 'Professor Stan Unwin', who, many years later, became very well-known on BBC comedy programmes, speaking his own muddled but understandable version of the English language which was best described as 'gobbledegook'. Evidence suggests that Stan's recording efforts with the BBC were on another occasion.

Such was the enthusiastic reaction to the Sunday night broadcast that the BBC repeated it on the following Monday and released the recording for overseas transmissions, including and particularly to the United States. *Paramount News* bi-weekly newsreel, which was shown in news theatres and cinemas around the country, had film of the attack and dubbed Gardner's commentary onto it. It is this version which is often seen today on television.

For those who haven't heard the recording – it was later made into a commercial record by Decca with all proceeds donated to the RAF Comfort Fund – I have reproduced parts of it here:

[Charles Gardner:] 'Well, now the Germans are dive-bombing a convoy out at sea. There are one, two, three, four, five, six, seven German dive bombers, Junkers 87s – there is one going down now on its target – bomb – no he's missed the ships – he hasn't hit a single ship – there are about 10 ships in the convoy, but he hasn't hit a single one.

There are about ten German machines . . . I can't see anything . . . but now the British fighters are coming up, here they come. The Germans are coming and they're in an absolute steep dive, and you can see their bombs actually leave their machines and come in the water. You can hear our own (AA) guns going like anything now.

I can hear machine-gun fire but I can't see our Spitfires – they must be somewhere there – oh here's one coming now and there's one coming down in flames – somebody has hit a German and he's coming down with a long streak. He's completely out of control – oh the man's bailed out by parachute, he's a Junkers 87 and he's going slap into the sea – and there he goes – smash! A terrific column of water and there was a Junkers 87.

Now then, oh, there's a terrific mix up over the Channel. It's impossible to tell which are our machines and which are the Germans. . . . there's a fight going on and you can hear the little rattle of the machine-gun bullets.

The sky is absolutely patterned now with bursts of anti-aircraft fire and the sea is covered with smoke where the bombs have burst, but as far as I can see there's not one single ship hit and there is definitely one German machine down.

Well now, everything is peaceful again for the moment. . . . I think the (Germans) have made off as quickly as they can. Oh yes I can see one, two three, four, five, six, seven, eight, nine, ten Germans haring back towards France now for all they can go – and here are our Spitfires coming after them. There's going to be a big fight, I think, out there.

After a pause Gardner sighted another fight going on at about 25,000ft and after a sustained anti-aircraft burst (he was standing close to an AA battery) he exclaims, 'Oh we've just hit a Messerschmitt, Oh, that was beautiful, he's coming right down now, I think definitely that burst got him. Yes, he's come down now – you can hear the crowds –he's finished.'

In a confused situation with machines whirling about high above his head Charles could not follow all the action, 'You can't watch these fights very coherently for long,' he says.

With the rattle of machine guns and anti-aircraft guns clearly audible, he continues:

> Now there's something coming right down on the tail of another – here they go – yes they're being chased home and how they are being chased home. There are three Spitfires chasing three Messerschmitts now. Oh boy look at them going . . . oh that really is grand, there's a Spitfire just behind the first two – he'll get them! Oh yes – oh boy – I've never seen anything so good as this, the RAF fighters have really got these boys taped.

To read the account and not to listen to it only conveys half the impact. And if Charles was over-enthusiastic at times and if the moment got the better of him on occasions, this small air victory did reflect the feelings aroused in this country as the 'unstoppable' Nazis marched ever closer to British shores. Unfortunately some time later it was discovered that the first aircraft shot down was not a German but a Hurricane. The pilot bailed out, as described, but was badly injured. Although he was rescued from the sea, he died later in hospital. Such is the fog of war.

A formal, comprehensive report of the air battle is contained in *Britain at War* magazine. It stated:

> What Gardner actually saw at first was the encounter between the Ju 87s and the Hurricanes of 615 Squadron. As the combat developed they were joined by twelve Supermarine Spitfires from 610 squadron together with even more Hurricanes, seven from 151 squadron and a further six from 615. They engaged the Messerschmitt Bf 109s of 11/JG51 Squadron, which around 30 in number were protecting the Ju 87s that had attacked the convoy.

The report also stated that, 'it was more than likely' that the pilot who bailed out over St Margaret's Bay was Pilot Officer Michael Robert Mundie. He was rescued from the sea but had been badly wounded and died of his injuries in Dover Hospital the following day. It added, 'of the 597 sorties flown by Fighter Command that day Michael Mundie was the only casualty'.

The full impact of Gardner's broadcast, in today's terms, 'went viral'. It was the point of discussion from the man in the street, the women in the factories, to the Minister in the House of Commons and the Director General of the BBC himself. The letters pages of the newspapers were full of comments from 'outrage' to applause and from headlines to editorials and opinion columns. It lasted for some time to come, as we shall see in a later chapter.

Surprisingly, in a broadcast just a fortnight earlier on 1 July, and shortly after the successful evacuation of Dunkirk, Charles Gardner predicted that, 'the air war in this Battle of Britain is likely at any time now to enter its second phase – a phase of concentrated and intensified action'. In a well-argued prognosis of the situation and foreseeing the height of the Battle of Britain to come, he continued: 'This will be no scattered business over a large area as it was in France, but a terrific, unprecedented concentration of aircraft of both sides into one comparatively small space of sky.'[1]

He concluded: 'At Dunkirk our fighters had successes of four to one and I for one had no doubt that in this new and possibly decisive fight between the main forces of the German Air Force and the full fighting strength of the R.A.F. that the figure will be improved upon.'

As a terrifying postscript to his broadcast, my father discovered some years later that he understood that as a result of his dismissive comments about the German pilots' performance his name had been added to the Nazi death list.

Chapter Two

Beginnings

Although Charles Gardner's air battle commentary is probably best remembered, he had, in fact, been a pioneer broadcaster since 1936. For it was then that new voices were heard for the first time on BBC radio news bulletins. Despite opposition, the Corporation appointed their first two full-time correspondents to cover news events and give eyewitness reports. They chose as the first two news broadcasters Richard Dimbleby, whose famous career was to span a lifetime on radio and television, and Charles Gardner. For Charles, it had taken just eight years from indentured 'journalist pupil' on a provincial newspaper to a nationally recognised voice on the BBC. His early beginnings were less promising.

Charles Joseph Thomas Gardner was born in the Warwickshire market town of Nuneaton on 15 April 1912 – the day of the *Titanic* disaster, as he always liked to remind us. Christened Charles, a family name for generations, he was the only child of Joseph Charles Thomas Gardner and his wife Adelaide née Whenham. His parents had been married in 1910 in Marlborough and, as far as we know, there was no family inherited ability for their son to become a writer and journalist, although the writer George Eliot, who was born and lived in Nuneaton, may have been an inspiration.

His father Joseph, known as Joe, came from a farming family background and he had a brother who was a farmer and landowner, although they had little contact with each other. According to 1901 records, Joe worked as a saddler or saddle-maker. His mother, who came from a Wiltshire family, was a trained nurse.

A year after the marriage Joe gave up his saddler job, perhaps because the business did not prosper with the advent of the motor car. They moved to the Chilvers Coton district of Nuneaton and in 1911 they jointly became custodians and partners of a local workhouse. Adelaide as a nurse would have been well suited to this type of work.

With the outbreak of war in 1914 Joe enlisted in the Army and records show that he served as a private, as a medic and stretcher-bearer, but he was invalided out with recurring illness. In the Second World War he was appointed an officer in the Home Guard. An extant photograph shows him in a major's uniform and wearing the First World War campaign medals – 'Pip, Squeak and Wilfred' (1914–15 Star, the British War Medal and the Victory Medal) – together with a Home Guard campaign medal.

His commission suggests that although there was little contact with his farming brother, Joe must have retained an interest in the ownership of the farm to have been eligible for officer rank.

From memory, grandfather Joe was gentle and retiring, while grandmother Adelaide was sharp-witted and clearly the strong voice in the family. Their circumstances at the time of Charles's birth were moderate and not sufficient to send him to a fee-paying school.

Little is known of Charles's early childhood days, but he was clearly bright, bright enough to gain a scholarship entry to King Edward VI Grammar School, Nuneaton. Founded in 1552, the school had long been revered as an establishment of high reputation and learning. Young Charles was a diligent pupil with a love of history, English literature, and science, while on the sports field he fulfilled his ambition and passion for cricket by being selected for the first XI.

In July 1928 at the age of 16 as a member of the classical sixth form, he passed his school certificate with a credit in five subjects – religious knowledge, English, English history, geography, physics and passed with credit in spoken French. This gave him exemption from matriculation so he could study for the higher school certificate. However, his ambition was to become a journalist and writer, and a year later he relinquished the chance to sit further examinations and a likely place at Queen's College, Oxford, when an opportunity arose for a job with the local *Nuneaton Daily Tribune*. Despite entreaties from the headmaster to his father to go to Oxford, Charles decided to forsake a university education, mainly because he could not see it would enhance his journalistic career, believing he would have started at the bottom anyway. Even more to the point, his parents couldn't afford it.

So, in December 1929 at the age of 17 he was formally indentured as a 'journalist pupil' to the proprietors of the *Midland Daily Tribune* Group for a three-year apprenticeship.[1]

My father would probably have started his journalistic career 'learning the job' in the busy environment of a daily provincial newspaper. This

8

would have meant 'holding copy' in the Readers' Room – that is checking the original edited copy against printed proofs; answering the telephone (probably only one in those days), making the tea and sometimes preparing edited versions of contributed stories from local organisations and sports clubs. He would have also had to learn about procedures in the law courts, the council chamber, the law of libel and shorthand writing, essential for reporting court cases and council meetings.

His first efforts in print are unknown and it was not until March 1931 that he felt proud enough of two published stories to enter them into his cuttings book.[2] Both were semi-features drawn from nothing except his keen eye and imagination, and are good examples of a budding talent which are worth reproducing.

In the first, attributed as a 'Tribune Special', Charles fantasised about the possible life story of a local curiosity – a 7ft-high carved wooden statue of a Scottish soldier of the Napoleonic Peninsula War. Known as 'Scotty', it stood in a local tobacconist's shop attracting much customer attention. Gardner wrote: 'Scotty has seen more of the world than Drake, Columbus and Jack Diamond put together. He is nearly a century and a half old and almost since his birth has been in the act of taking a pinch of snuff, which up to the time of going to press has not reached his nose!'

He related how 'Scotty spent his youth as part of a tree in Spain' before he was cut down and carved carefully into a replica of a soldier of the 42nd Regiment and placed proudly on the bow of an English sailing vessel. As such he sailed the seven seas before his ship was dismantled and 'he went into business and entered the tobacco and snuff trade'. Charles concluded, rather poetically: 'Nuneaton is proud to have him, his monetary value is great, his pride is greater but the chapter of our history he represents is even greater still.'

The second article, dated September 1931, is headed 'Nuneaton Town Bridge – A Foreigner's Opinion Regarding It'. Charles tells how an overseas friend, who turned out to be a Mr Van Hock, a noted Dutch journalist on his first visit to the town, admired the bridge. He wrote, 'While strolling over the undistinguished Town Bridge my friend suddenly broke off in mid sentence and waved down at the Anker river trickling along with its mud fresh churned from the Mill walk. What a lovely bridge you have here, it reminds me of Venice,' he said. This surprised the writer who replied, 'I'm afraid I have never noticed it as much as that.'

He assured the readers he had 'no intention of seeking the opinion of architects nor did he wish to start a controversy or a fund for the preservation of the bridge'. He ended: 'you wouldn't believe how hard it has been to stop myself from concluding by quoting "familiarity breeds contempt"'.

The cuttings books (there are two) paint a fascinating picture of life in a provincial town in the early to middle 1930s. They are full of Gardner's news reports of crimes, accidents and events, features of all kinds, dramatic reviews, sports reports and short stories. But for most aspiring journalists a cherished step up the ladder is to have your name in print – 'bylined' – for a story or feature you have written – something which perhaps comes too easily today. And this came first in December 1931 when he wrote a story – not for the *Tribune* – for the *European Herald*, a publication prepared to accept contributed material. Headlined a 'Gipsy Wedding in the Midlands' by Charles J.T. Gardner, it told of the unfortunate ramifications of a young Gipsy girl's 'wrong wedding' in a local Church of England church.

Apparently, Charles was 'an enterprising reporter whose enterprise was shortly to be rewarded' when he described a mix-up of brides at the wedding. The proper bride had missed the ceremony because 'she was delayed through the sudden illness of her father'. By the time she arrived at the church the wedding was over and a substitute bride had taken her vows in her place. The wedding party had by now adjourned to the local pub, where the groom told her that when she didn't turn up and 'thinking she was ill, he had approached the bride's sister and asked her if she would act as a substitute for the intended bride and say the responses'.

Gardner wrote:

> The groom thoroughly believed that the wedding could take place by proxy and he was reduced to tears when the Vicar said that in the eyes of God and man he was married to the wrong girl. The poor groom eventually realised that divorce was his only legal freedom, but brightened when the parson suggested that the best way out of the mess would be to do a little private arrangement all round.

The party then departed and went back to the pub, the Granby Head, and later left the district and 'nothing more has been heard of them'. How and why my father was there, we do not know, perhaps the thought of a Gipsy wedding intrigued him or maybe he happened to be in the pub when it all happened. At least it made a nice feature and clearly he was 'rewarded' in payment.

That it took another publication to give him a byline was because in his own paper, personal identification was frowned on and the writer was usually referred to as 'our own reporter' or 'a Tribune man' or not at all. Such was still the case in December 1932 when he produced a two-page Christmas story for the *Police Chronicle* entitled 'Was it Santa Claus?' and attributed to 'Gordon Crump', a pseudonym no doubt devised to conceal his identity from the Editor of the *Tribune*. Described as 'A charming Christmas story', it told of a brother and a sister arguing about whether Father Christmas existed but when they received their desired presents both began to believe he did. Presumably police funds rose to the occasion while anonymity was assured.

My father loved writing and he loved history and throughout 1932–3 he wrote a string of unsigned local historical features and articles. To mark the fourteenth anniversary of the end of the First World War he produced a special piece headed 'The Great War – what do the younger generation know about it? By One of them'. He wrote:

> We grew up and were educated when everyone was trying to forget. War was a forbidden subject. We wanted to know all about it but no one would tell us. 'Forget and be thankful you were not in it.' Then to our aid came the first war books, 'Peter Jackson' we devoured and in a lesser way 'Shorty Bill.' So this was war we thought, blood, death, hysterical laughter and prowling constant fear.

He concluded, 'We were beginning to be impressed. Battle was losing its mystery and its appeal was fainter in our broadening minds, but nevertheless behind it all was an instinctive pang of sorrow that we had not seen at least something of it.'

Clearly my grandfather, like most veterans of the First World War spoke little or nothing of his experiences. Today, of course, things have changed radically. Almost every school, scout group, cadet corps and many others send groups to the battlefields of the Somme and Ypres, where the daily service under the Menin Memorial is crammed with youngsters from all over the country.

But it was the history of local places that intrigued him most. His first such feature, published in February 1933, was the ghost story associated with the Elizabethan vicarage near his home at Chilvers Coton. In April, not surprisingly, he produced a complete history of his old school, followed by others including the story of the village of Mancetter with its Roman origins, and Atherstone's Friary and its grammar school.

But most notable was an illustrated three-part description of the Battle of Bosworth Field in 1485, when Richard III lost his crown and his life and was unceremoniously interred in the priory at Leicester. Illustrated with maps and photographs of the site, it was a prodigious work. How my father would have enjoyed the remarkable finding and verification of Richard's body in 2011.

But one story in particular was a catalyst for his future career. Headed 'A Flying Lesson – experiences of a Tribune man', he described his first flying lesson sitting in the front open cockpit of a De Havilland Gipsy-Moth biplane. He wrote: 'Flying is delightfully simple, especially when you have a pilot in the rear cockpit telling you what to do!' After circling around, banking, turning and climbing he eventually 'let the rear cockpit do the landing – as a formality!' He added, 'A quite good landing I said condescendingly – after all, pilots like me and Mollison can afford to be polite.'[3]

From personal experience of being flown by my father in the 1950s, he needed to 'be polite'. This was after a rather dodgy landing in a similar Tiger Moth while on our way to the popular Air Races at Lydd in Kent, where he was to do the commentary.

His love of writing was not just confined to his newspaper. We have at home countless short stories and, written in the 1930s, a selection of poems of some merit. One which catches the eye, a ditty, is reproduced here as an example of his light-hearted humour, and because it made me smile.

> If you were but a cup of tea,
> And I a lump of sugar,
> I'd welcome you dissolving me,
> The spooning stir revolving me,
> Were I a lump of sugar.
>
> But if you were a cup of tea,
> I think you'd let me drown,
> Soak cohesion out of me,
> Conduct a melting rout of me,
> Then float me down.
>
> So on the whole, I'd rather be,
> The warm embracing cup of tea.

By now Charles Gardner had come to the notice of other papers in the area. And in January 1934 he left the *Tribune* to move to the county town of Leicester and join the prestigious *Leicester Mercury*, one of the best provincial dailies in the country. His departure from Nuneaton coincided with the termination of his three-year apprenticeship.

We do not know the exact circumstances of Charles's move, other than the usual desire to progress and perhaps disenchantment with the *Tribune*. Whether he was sought out or he actively looked for new employment, normal for most journalists at this stage, is unknown. His cuttings books would certainly have been used to show his ability and would have been scrutinised by the Editor or a senior colleague at the *Mercury* before his appointment.

It did not take him long to make his mark in his new job, and on 29 January 1934 he had his first 'scoop' which was chosen as the lead story for the 6 o'clock edition. Headlined 'Leicester Scientist's Death Ray', it told of a local lecturer who had created an invisible beam which could kill moths, flies and mice, and promised further development 500 times more powerful, which could penetrate metal-lined walls. The story was attributed to an exclusive interview with a 'Leicester Mercury reporter'.

My father was especially pleased with this and told it many times over in later life. He said the scientist had a stall hidden away at the back of a tent at a local fete. Having found nothing to write about and was 'bored', our young reporter 'stumbled across' the inventor and became interested. He asked for a demonstration which was willingly given. Apparently the invention was seriously considered later, but was never developed. But it made a good story at the time.

For the two years Charles was on the *Mercury* he covered the usual run of news stories, as his scrapbook shows. There was a 'fascist' MP who came to Leicester to address a Black Shirt rally. He was described in the paper as 'The central figure in the mace-snatching sensation in the House of Commons.' (Lord Heseltine seems not to have been the first.) However, he 'disappeared' before delivering his promised address in Leicester much to the annoyance of the assembled throng, and a scuffle broke out and the police were called.

Then there was the sinking of a houseboat on the canal due to floods (regrettably no change there) and a bad train crash outside Leicester LMS station. And for the first time he is pictured in a series of photographs wearing a natty double-breasted suit asking people in the street if they knew what day it was – many didn't. Again, even though identified, he is described as 'a Leicester Mercury reporter'.

But, increasingly, Charles's fascination with the fast-growing developments in the air, which first emerged with his flying lesson in Nuneaton, now led to a raft of aviation features. There were stories of many pioneer flights including the long-distance travails of a local MP; the anticipated arrival of the Duke of Windsor in his personal aeroplane; and news of exciting developments at Leicester's main airfield at Braunstone, where scheduled flights both home and abroad were just beginning.[4]

He delved into the world of private flying too, at the Aero Club at Ratcliffe airfield, where club members provided joy rides and where the annual Empire Day air displays were held. The highlight of the 1934 show was the arrival of Amy Mollison herself in her own world-record-breaking Gipsy-Moth.

There was also cricket to write about, another passion since school days. He took every opportunity to report the game at both county and local level with one outstanding opportunity coming in 1934. That year the whole cricket world was aroused by the forthcoming tour of England by the Australian cricket team. This followed the infamous 'Bodyline' series in Australia which had damaged the reputation of the game and almost led to Australia withdrawing from the Commonwealth. Not surprisingly, there was keen anticipation for the Ashes series and locally for a preliminary county match against Leicestershire County Cricket Club.

So my father 'volunteered' to go down to the railway station to see the team arrive and hopefully to meet the legendary batsman Don Bradman. But, as the team made their way off the train, the only one he recognised was the captain Bill Woodfull. He asked for an interview with Woodfull, who had been at the centre of the 'Bodyline' row, but was turned away. He wrote, 'Woodfull told the Leicester Mercury reporter that he could not be interviewed and referred all inquiries to the manager.' Happily, it did not detract from his love of the game which he continued to play into his late 50s.

Unsurprisingly, he contributed heavily to the Sports Section of the *Mercury*, covering all sports especially cricket and later golf, which also became an absorbing interest. Two surviving features in the scrapbook were both, for a change, bylined by C.J.T. Gardner. The first in 1935 was headlined 'Watching Women's Cricket – village maidens get bowling lesson from Leicester'. Today, had he known of the prowess of England's women's team, he might not have been so condescending. The other article was an in-depth feature on Kibworth Golf Club. Whether he played there or not is unknown, but play he certainly did, and continued to do so until into his 70s.

It was about this time that my father met my mother. It happened in unusual circumstances – over the telephone. My mother, Eva Fletcher (usually know as Eve), who lived with her parents in Old Hill, Staffordshire, was also bright, and attended Halesowen Grammar School. The school was well-known in the area for its high academic standards and sporting achievements. Indeed, a contemporary pupil of my mother was the England and Warwickshire spin bowler, Eric Hollies.[5] Eric was her boyfriend then but will ever be remembered for bowling out the great Don Bradman for nought in the final Ashes test at the Oval in 1948, thus depriving him of an average of 100, for which he needed only 4 runs in what was his last appearance for his country. (No batsman has even come close since.)

My mother's good education led to a responsible job in those days as a telephone/copy taker at the Press Association (PA) in Birmingham. This meant she transcribed and made sense of the stories as telephoned to her, before sending the copy up to the News Desk.

The PA, still one of the world's great news agencies, was at that time distributing its material using ticker tape machines throughout the country to newspaper offices. To do this, in addition to its permanent staff, it depended on local and provincial journalists providing news stories on what is called 'lineage' – the method by which the reporter was paid on the number of lines that eventually appeared in the newspapers.

One such regular lineage correspondent was one 'Charles Gardner from Leicester', who phoned in local news stories he thought might have wider appeal and generate extra cash. Apparently he was, according to my mother, 'argumentative and a real pain in the backside'. So much so, after a time, the other girls refused to deal with him and passed him over to her as she was the only one who could cope with him. It should be noted that my father was quick-tempered and downright aggressive to 'fools' such as petty officials and particularly policemen who got in his way. One can imagine his demeanor if confronted with a slow-witted or just slow copy taker at the PA. My mother's calm approach obviously won the day.

Eventually a meeting was arranged and one thing led to another and in September 1935 they were married at Halesowen parish church. A press cutting shows the happy couple after the ceremony, my father wearing a smart, light-coloured, double-breasted suit and the bride 'attired in dark red velvet with halo hat and pink roses'. She was described as a former member of the PA staff, so obviously by then she had given up her job to move to Leicester. His address was given as Shanklin Avenue, Leicester, where the couple set up their first home.

Their time in Leicester did not last long, however. Within just a few months of their marriage their lives were to be completely turned upside down, for in early 1936 my father landed one of the most sought-after jobs in journalism – a job with the BBC in London.

Chapter Three

Dimbleby and Gardner

Charles Gardner at the age of 24 joined the BBC on 20 July 1936. For a grammar school boy without a university education and from a provincial newspaper to be selected would, in those days, be a proud achievement. He must, therefore, have interviewed well and his cuttings book impressed them, confirming his growing reputation in Leicester as a writer with imagination and ingenuity. This was backed up with significant good testimonials from the Editor of the *Mercury* and, surprisingly, from the Chief Constable of Leicester, who wrote: 'I had quite a number of dealings with him, he is very respectable.'

It had been two months earlier in May when my father made his approach to the BBC when he wrote applying for the advertised job as sub-editor in the Radio News Department (there was no television news then). It was written from his address in Shanklin Avenue, Leicester, where he had lived since his marriage. It was good enough to earn him an interview. He outlined his educational qualifications – included playing for the school cricket first X1 – and stated that he had a sound grounding as a reporter and sub-editor, had written a series of historical articles and, in lighter vein, on village cricket in collaboration with a cartoonist for two seasons. He was now also air correspondent and 'descriptive writer' on the paper. He added that he had some wireless experience when he gave a 20-minute descriptive talk on village cricket in the 'Microphone at Play' series.

His interview was on 9 June, and there were ten other candidates, one of particular significance, as we shall see. On 18 June he received a letter from the BBC offering him the job as Home News sub-editor in the News department at £420 pa for a six-month probationary period.[1] Despite this condition, he felt confident enough to take the BBC job which meant resigning from the *Mercury*, and more importantly, especially for my mother, moving to London where they found a suitable flat at 2 Effingham House, Larkhall Estate, Clapham.

Before leaving Leicester, he 'did the rounds' to say goodbye to the many people he knew well in the area. This included the Attenborough family of which father Frederick was Principal of University College, Leicester, and whose sons, Richard and David, were soon to become famous in their respective careers. He also visited his landlady to thank her for her kindness. Apparently he had been paying his rent through an intermediary who, unfortunately, did not pass it on. This went on for some time, unknown to my father, who knew his landlady socially and met her often. Yet, throughout this time, she didn't mention it once. When he eventually found out he asked her why she hadn't tackled him about the rent arrears. She replied she knew he was a struggling young, married man and that the paper didn't pay high wages, but she was confident he would always settle his debts, which he did.

And so they moved to London and a new life. Although he had accepted the job as a sub-editor, it was, he hoped, to be a stepping stone to his real intention to be a reporter again as quickly as possible. This came about even sooner than he imagined. The circumstances of which were unusual and almost entirely due to one young Richard Dimbleby, who was to become a BBC legend both in radio and television and whose broadcasting dynasty survives today through his sons, David and Jonathan.

In May 1936, Dimbleby, then 22 years old and, like Charles, having foregone a university education to work on provincial newspapers, was the Editor of *Advertiser's Weekly* in Fleet Street. Having been unimpressed by BBC news coverage, he wrote an impassioned letter to the Chief News Editor at the BBC, John Coatman. He complained about its dull and impersonal nature with all news stories accredited to the Fleet Street news agencies. For at that time there were no BBC reporters, just radio newsreaders who, despite being unseen, had to read the agency reports dressed in dinner suits and black ties.

He wrote:

> It is my impression, and I find that it is shared by many others that it would be possible to enliven the News to some extent without spoiling the authoritative tone for which it is famed. As a journalist, I think, I know something of the demand which the public makes for a 'News angle,' and how it can be provided. I suggest that a member or members of your staff – they could be called 'BBC reporters, or correspondents' – should be held in readiness, just as are the evening paper men to cover unexpected news for that day.

Dimbleby concluded his well-reasoned letter, 'I do hope that there may be some opportunity for me in your department in the not too distant future, for I really am interested and confident that I should be of use to you.'

When the BBC vacancy arose for a sub-editor, Dimbleby applied and was one of the ten candidates. And, as we know, he didn't get it, no thanks to young Charles Gardner. However, within a few weeks a 'more suitable vacancy' arose and in September Dimbleby was engaged as the first 'Topical Talks Assistant'. Shortly afterwards he was joined by my father, whose sub-editing duties were probably little more than an introduction to the department. Both were now given reportorial assignments.

In Jonathan Dimbleby's excellent biography of his father, published in 1975 after his death, he recalled those days and the passion his father felt for the job and the inspiration he gave to others. He quoted my father who said: 'Richard was the pioneer. There is no doubt about it, that it was he who had the ideas and the driving force to carry them through – the rest of us followed his lead.'

And so, Dimbleby and Gardner effectively became the first full-time BBC news observers under Ralph Murray (later Sir Ralph Murray), who was in charge of the News Talks section and who also contributed reports from the League of Nations.[2] Murray later wrote that the department was a very modest affair with a shoe-string budget – something the two reporters were to test to the limit while bringing a new vibrancy to news coverage. This gave Murray some concern as to the Director General's (DG's) reaction.

For the DG was Sir John Reith, later Lord Reith, the revered founder of the BBC and a man of totalitarian views whose writ ran large across the length and breadth of Broadcasting House. The latter was subsequently described by the well-known American journalist and writer John Gunther as 'his modernist citadel'.

Reith was particularly concerned about retaining the BBC's reputation for impartiality and could see persistent danger in active news reporting violating his code. He preferred the safety of using just contributed agency news stories where blame or political bias could not be attributed directly to the Corporation. He also believed broadcasters should be 'aloof and mysterious', adding: 'In many ways I think this is desirable that they should continue in their comparative obscurity. A place in the stars is more important than one in the sun.'

Jonathan Dimbleby gave a very profound explanation of Reith's doctrine and attitude as it applied to those throughout the Corporation:

> The BBC was the creation of Sir John Reith whose ideals and morality became its own. Reith was a Scot, a son of the Manse into whom the spirit of Calvinism had bitten deep. His outlook was narrow, his principles were rigid, but, as he said, of himself

(with typical modesty and some truth): 'we were vouchsafed a measure of vision. Our responsibility,' he had declared, 'is to carry into the greatest possible number of homes everything that is best in every department of human knowledge, endeavour and achievement and to avoid the things which are, or maybe, hurtful.' Within the BBC his fierce look, his gaunt face , his great height and austere manner made him a formidable, and awesome personality. Few dared cross him: none did so with impunity.

Against such doctrine, one might wonder how both found their way into Broadcasting House. And how they and a few other forward-looking colleagues changed this perception and founded a tradition of immediacy, personality and continued impartiality in the BBC.

This can be in part explained by Charles Gardner in his tribute to Richard Dimbleby, who died in 1965, in a special commemorative booklet published by the BBC. He wrote: 'Reporting was cheerful, good natured, intensely hard-working and bubbling with enthusiasm for each and every story. With hindsight I could really imagine the administration was scared stiff at the possible Trojan Horse they had invited inside the walls of Broadcasting House.'

He added, 'Richard and I were then perhaps too raw, too young or too inexperienced to give these matters of high policy a thought. We were professionally trained reporters, interested only in conveying undisputed facts and not concerned to hold inquests.' Clearly this professionalism and enthusiasm eventually held sway with the hierarchy.

Jonathan Dimbleby provides further insight and tells how the two were 'left much to their own devices'. He continued, 'No-one ordered that they report this or that: they decided between them what they should cover and who should do it. There was however, a tacit understanding that their subjects be non-controversial. It was not a restriction that bothered them.' He described how the two covered almost every conceivable story from 'shipwrecks and fires; they visited lighthouses in distress and crumbling sea walks (it seemed from their reports that Britain was in constant danger of being washed away); they travelled on veteran car rallies and Air Raid Precaution tours; they opened cathedrals and they went down mines. And they explored new methods and new techniques.'

Both were also dedicated to the integrity of their work. Gardner wrote:

Both he and I had to observe one very clear rule of the News Talks Department – there must be no faking. To fake was the unforgivable sin. The bark of a dog that roused the household against a burglar had to be the bark of the dog and not just the bark of any other dog of the same species. We were rather proud of this integrity.

Life within the News Room in those days was, according to Jonathan Dimbleby:

> Quite unlike its sophisticated television successor of forty years later. Where what is absurd and what is tragic becomes a 'story' to be cut, dried, packaged, labeled and then sold in the nation's sitting rooms as the truth. In 1936 the News Room had a casual, leisurely air. Their bulletins were gentle and discursive; and, by the standards of later years, amateurish. R.T. Clark (Home News Editor) ruled with a gentle touch, was exceptionally lazy, devoted to his 'boys' as he called his staff [as we shall see] and incapable of an angry word.

Outside work the two became good friends. By this time Charles and Eve had moved to a new flat on Wandsworth Common and Richard and his wife Dilys lived within reach. They even bought a car together – a Swift – for £10 – with money borrowed from Ralph Murray and re-paid the loan on mileage expenses. Apparently they worked out a system of sharing it at weekends. My father said later that he had forgotten what happened to the Swift but recalled Richard coming up to him 'very excited' to say that MG would give them a new car each – to be changed every year – if they were to inscribe BBC on it somewhere. 'Imagine the temptation, but after a mournful drink, we decided we daren't.'

In December 1936 there was an upheaval within the BBC which could have ended both their careers. Gardner recalled: 'Just before the Abdication [of Edward VIII], Richard and I were parties to one of the BBC's best kept skeletons – the day the BBC News Department threatened to strike.' This was because the newspapers were all full of the divorce of Mrs Wallis Simpson which led to her later marriage to Edward and his abdication. But the BBC was not allowed to carry a word. 'Eventually this became in our view stupid and the staff of BBC News issued an ultimatum: Either that night's bulletin made some reference to the main topic of the day – or there would be no news bulletin at all.'

Both Dimbleby and Gardner gave their general agreement to the strike. Fortunately the matter was not put to the test, for that afternoon the Prime

Minister, Stanley Baldwin, made mention of the matter in the House of Commons which could be freely reported, even by the BBC and the local crisis was averted.

With the New Year came appraisals and in March Charles learned of a modest pay rise from £420 per year to £460 while his grade remained at C, but his full-time staff appointment was ratified. This was confirmed in a memo signed personally by Lord Reith.[3] This 'careful approach' to money ran across the whole of the BBC and both young reporters 'hated the admin' (the administration). They were the 'baddies' who were mean with expenses and mean in providing necessary support and equipment.

In his book, Jonathan Dimbleby amplified the situation and tells how his father's 'unhappy relationship' with the administration had developed – 'to the admiring consternation of Charles Gardner, he spent much of his early career doing for BBC expenses what he had done to the News Service. It did not endear him to a BBC which regarded any expenditure of Corporation money as a mortal sin.'

As an example of BBC pettiness, Johnathan wrote:

> Among their other duties Gardner and Dimbleby were charged with welcoming visiting speakers in the News Talks programme. The BBC maintained a room and a drinks cupboard to help them – though it was a firm (if unwritten) rule that a guest should only be offered one drink before the programme and nothing afterwards. The BBC men were to exercise the same constraint. To enforce compliance with the regulation each bottle was covered with a label on which Dimbleby or Gardner had to mark the new level of the liquor with the name and the date every time they dispensed the Corporation's hospitality.

Jonathan added: 'Charles Gardner remembers that Dimbleby led him in numerous assaults upon the all powerful and much-hated Administration: "They" challenged the need to buy a pint of beer for someone who had helped us. Fighting "them" became the joy of our lives.'

My father described how together they 'made a youthful common cause against the administration.' And in doing so they provoked them whenever possible. He wrote:

> When on a job involving good hotels and a chance of a grander life than either he or I could normally afford (I think we were both under £600 a year) Richard set about making the most of it. I remember him ringing all the bells in sight in one splendid

hotel and ordering a manicure, drinks in the room, and expensive sandwiches – mainly I think to enjoy seeing the shock on my face. On jobs which permitted it, the best was only just good enough for Richard, and I envied the grand manner he assumed to match his temporary opulence. . . . These little assumptions of grandeur were done as a piece of gamesmanship against the BBC administration and always ended in a giggle of anticipation at the reception of the expense sheet.

But of more significance to their news reporting was the use of recording cars necessary for covering breaking news. In those days, without today's mobile devices, stories had to be recorded onto disc in a recording vehicle and then, when London was too far away to be reached by road, despatched by rail – usually 'at the mercy' of the guard – on a London-bound train for collection and transmission. But, there was then only one recording vehicle available, a converted laundry van manned by several recording engineers. The difficulty of allocating this one vehicle against multiple urgent news stories can easily be imagined and both Dimbleby and Gardner had to fight for its use.

Such problems led to both conjuring up many ingenious ways of circumnavigating the system to provide better immediate news, even though they were allocated very little time on the news bulletins. 'It was common to be told that we had only 45 seconds on the 9 o'clock and 2 minutes 15 seconds on the 10 o'clock,' Charles recalled. But Dimbleby, who was 'fascinated by the technique of recordings', came up with a novel idea.

This revealed itself in what Gardner described as 'the affair of the telephone boxes'. It arose after a series of headline news stories had 'annoyingly occurred' in the remoteness of East Anglia – probably the Fen Floods in 1937. Because of the difficulty in getting recorded discs back to London, Richard came up with his telephone-box idea which my father described: 'What was wrong with hitching an amplifier and a BBC microphone to a GPO box and making any telephone kiosk an impromptu Outside Broadcast point – what indeed?' So they wandered about putting in calls to Broadcasting House from telephone boxes and getting them recorded. Unfortunately, the GPO intervened and said it was illegal and 'that was that'. But this did not deter the two. He continued, 'Of course, one ignored the law – and then remembered to remove from the disc the three minute interruptions from the trunk operators – Richard did this several times for straight eyewitness pieces, and so did I. We were never prosecuted.'

Although both were friends 'off the field', on it they were rivals, albeit often hampered by lack of money and resources, as we have seen and as the Sir Tommy Sopwith affair shows. Charles Gardner tells the story:

> We ourselves were permanently broke. I remember the night of 1937 when it became clear to Richard and me that there was potentially big news in the fact that Tommy Sopwith's America's Cup challenger Endeavour, on her return journey across the Atlantic, had broken her tow and was facing full gale conditions. We decided to cover two key places: Southampton, where Sopwith's motor launch had now fetched up without Endeavour hitched on behind; and Plymouth near to which Endeavour must sail if she ever regained our waters.
>
> Richard and I tossed up for destinations. He won and chose Southampton. Then came the little matter of getting railway tickets. An office float cash box existed for such emergencies. It was scheduled to contain £20, we opened the box and found only a shower of IOUs – all of them signed by the News Editor R.T. Clark. So Richard and I turned out our pockets and dunned our colleagues – but the collection fell short by £3. Our next move was to go to Queen's Hall opposite where the BBC was staging the Proms. There we persuaded them to give us £10 each from the till, on note of hand only. Thus did Richard get to Southampton and I to Plymouth that night.

As it happens, Dimbleby drew the short straw. Although he was invited as a guest onto Sopwith's returned luxury motor yacht, 'replete with champagne' and interviewed the man himself, he felt thirsty in the night and drank some doubtful water. He contracted paratyphoid, became seriously ill and was taken to hospital. He was away from work for two months. Gardner, however, 'was getting seasick in Plymouth'. He managed, 'via friendly pilots at the airfield', who had spotted Endeavour from the air, and with the help of a local fisherman, to locate the yacht and went alongside in his boat to interview the skipper, 'while Fleet Street was still arguing the toss in pubs ashore'.

As a postscript he added: 'I returned to London to start my own anti-admin file on the matter of 3s. 6d expended for a bottle of sea-sick remedy. We cleaned up completely on the Endeavour story for a cost of £20 – the newspapers spent hundreds and missed out.'

The two enjoyed their battles with Fleet Street, although, my father wrote, 'We were handicapped by having no money to bribe or buy or to hire aircraft or boats, so we used the magic of the BBC name instead. For some reason people were very willing to talk to us for nothing when they were not so forthcoming to other reporters.'

By now Charles Gardner had established himself, as he hoped, as the BBC specialist in aviation. And there was no shortage of news covering the fast-accelerating efforts of the numerous British aircraft companies – there were twenty-seven of them – now gearing up to the increasing threat from Nazi Germany with new fighters such as the Spitfire and Hurricane. There were developments in civil aviation too, with the introduction of new air services, new longer range airliners and flying boats.

But it was the Vickers Wellesley, a sleek-looking, single-engined, long-range bomber that looked more like a fighter, that allowed Charles Gardner to make his first surviving recorded broadcast. It was at the annual 1937 Hendon Air Pageant that the Wellesley made its public appearance and immediately caught his attention. We still have a copy of his broadcast, recorded on a 78rpm disc, the first of many housed in the BBC Recordings Library. Several others of later date have also been found (by chance) stored in a box in our garage.

For this first recording, there was, unfortunately, very little for my father to say as the Wellesley was very much a 'hush hush' aircraft. 'We can't tell you much about it because we aren't allowed to,' he said. 'The machine on its stand is surrounded by notices saying you must not take photographs or drawings of it.' He added, 'but it looks very fast which undoubtedly it is. It's standing on the edge of the aerodrome now, the engine running . . . there are five men there holding her like mad keeping her down – now she's ready to start.'

Watched by the King and Queen and a vast crowd, he described her taking off, 'flying away at terrific speed into the clouds'. He noted that she was built 'under the new principle of geodetic construction', the Barnes Wallis development which was later applied to the famous Wellington bomber.

A month later in August, away from the military, there was a more pleasurable assignment for Charles, and one which Dimbleby would have approved of. He flew to Paris on the new Armstrong Whitworth Ensign airliner. This impressive-looking, high-winged aircraft was capable of seating forty passengers at speeds of up to 200mph. It was delivered to Imperial Airways to operate the prestigious London to Paris route rivaling the famous Golden Arrow train and ferry service. My father was invited on an early demonstration flight from Croydon to Le Bourget, then the principal international airports of London and Paris.

His recorded observations of the 1-hour, 25-minute flight read more like a description of a delicious lunch than a serious appraisal of the aircraft.

They had hardly set off when Gardner reported, 'It was time for smoked salmon over Eastbourne.' Halfway across the Channel at 14,000ft, came the main course – 'it was Roast Pheasant', and as they crossed the French coast, he declared – 'now for Gorgonzola cheese for dessert and coffee'.

My father did notice, however, when approaching Beauvais, the memorial to the British R101 airship which crashed in 1935 with the loss of forty-eight lives, 'a grim reminder of the disaster,' he said. As they neared Paris, passengers moved forward for a 'smoke and a chat' (my father occupied seat 6) and with a ground speed of 160mph, the Seine was sighted, a 'very smooth' approach was made and the aircraft landed safely.[4] Today's harassed and hounded passengers might read this with envy.

If new Cross-Channel air services were now being introduced the prospect of Trans-Atlantic flights was also being explored. Three days after his Paris trip, Charles was in Ireland to commemorate the first experimental flight from America to Shannon Port by a Pan American Clipper Sikorsky S-42 flying boat. We still have a commemorative menu card signed at the top by the Irish President, Eamon de Valera, and the pilot, Captain H.E. Gray.

Competing with the Sikorsky was the De Havilland Albatross, which he saw on a visit to its home base at Hatfield a little later. 'When you look at her in the air she is obviously a direct descendent of the famous DH Comet, also built especially for the job and you will remember how well she did,' he stated.[5]

This was also a time of popular air races and record attempts. In July 1937 Gardner reported his first of many air races, returning to Hatfield. That year's race for the King's Cup happened to be won by Charles E. Gardner, the 'E' added so as not to confuse with the acting BBC air correspondent. And it was speed again which attracted his attention when he welcomed home the legendary New Zealand pilot Jean Batten, who had just set a new six-day record flight from Australia. 'She was wearing a white helmet, looking very young, very happy, stepping out smiling before a cheering crowd,' he noted. Interviewed later, she said, 'I'm very pleased to have broken the record. . . . but there were storms over Cyprus and I lost all sense of time'.

In the summer of 1937 my father took my mother on an unusual holiday to Germany, not a destination that many would have chosen as tensions rose between the two countries. In his passport, which we still have, is the Visa stamped with the odious swastika. It appears my father had an ulterior motive – to see, if possible, Nazi aviation developments at first hand and photograph them. With his press pass he was no doubt shown what they wanted him to see. Nevertheless it was a risky undertaking and although they had a pleasurable trip to Frankfurt and a cruise on the Rhine, my mother was terrified. She told us many years later how they were inside a church when the doors were flung open and in marched some jack-booted Nazi soldiers looking for a suspect. She was worried they had come for Charles for taking unauthorised pictures. Happily for him it was some other poor soul who they arrested and dragged off.

Safely back home and at work, both my father and Richard Dimbleby still found themselves covering every kind of story and, indeed, it was a pattern of general news reporting which was to last for some time. In October, for instance, Gardner found himself 30ft below ground (for a change) to report the building of an extension to the Highgate to Barnet Tube line. Once again his powers of description were put to the test. To the echoing shouts of 'Mind your backs,' he declared: 'We are practically underneath the existing North East Railway tracks to Barnet. The tube line here has been being built since the beginning of the year. This time last year it was just thick London solid clay.' He added mournfully, 'I've just walked a quarter of a mile of this finished tube, walking along duckboards, slipping around and splashing into the thick mud.'

What we don't know was how he was able to record live from the depth of the tunnel. Either the recording vehicle was able to follow the construction vehicle's route underground or they had an extremely long microphone lead!

By now, with the added use of the recording truck, radio listeners were become familiar with the immediacy and enthusiasm of the new news reporting of Dimbleby, Gardner and others. Everything that Dimbleby had predicted in his letter to Coatman in 1936 about the value of 'getting the news angle' was being fulfilled.

It was to continue and develop through the next two years leading up to the inevitable outbreak of war and another dimension in BBC war broadcasting, such as Gardner's Battle of Britain eyewitness account.

Chapter Four

Threat of War

Towards the end of 1937 my father had not only become a familiar voice on radio but had also established himself within the BBC. A formal assessment for that year stated: 'A really good man who inspires confidence – Mr. Gardner will rise high in the service of the Corporation.' Later R.T. Clark, Home News Editor, wrote to the Director General (probably in support of a new recording vehicle), 'I should like to bring very urgently to your notice Charles Gardner and Richard Dimbleby. For 18 months they have been occupied in News Talks, latterly with the recording van. Here their work has really been admirable.'

So in the late summer of that year, Charles had enough confidence in a long-term career at the BBC to look around for a permanent home near London, but in the country. Their searches brought them to Leatherhead in 'leafy Surrey', 20 miles from London and located among the Surrey Downs between Guildford and Epsom. Here my mother and father found exactly what they wanted, a charming two-bedroom cottage with a nice garden in the nearby village of Fetcham. As an encouraging omen it was called Eaves Cottage because of its roof. It was just 2 miles from Leatherhead town and railway station with a regular 40-minute journey to London Waterloo.

The property was on the market for £400, just within my father's limit and he made an offer to the lady who owned the cottage. But the sale did not go through without an embarrassing hitch. Apparently he mixed up two letters – one was to the owner with a formal offer and the other to the well-know bat-makers Stuart Surridge. The latter was a complaint, as his new cricket bat supplied by them had shattered after only a few games. Thus the 'nice lady' at Eaves Cottage received an outraged complaint while Stuart Surridge was surprised to know that a cheque for a substantial sum was on its way to them. Happily, the matter was soon sorted out when the 'nice lady' showed him the bat letter during their meeting to confirm the sale. Whether he pursued Stuart Surridge or not is unknown.

And so in September they moved into Eaves Cottage on the Lower Road at Fetcham. It was to become the family home for thirty years.

Back in the office, Charles discovered that matters over the recording car had been resolved, perhaps in response to R.T. Clark's memo. The BBC had given way to their insistent demands and those and others to provide a dedicated recording car. This turned out to be a 7-ton truck with a crew of four. David Howarth, a senior recording engineer who travelled with the truck, recalled how, 'they drove like lunatics' to keep up with news stories and 'ahead of Fleet Street'.

Whether it was the 'lunatic' driving or the need for something better we shall not know, but by early 1938 the BBC were able to supply something more suitable and perhaps less dangerous than the 7-ton truck – a new and first recording car. This contained recording equipment which was smaller and lighter and easier to operate. Its introduction in many ways revolutionised news-gathering ability for the reporters. Gardner described the new vehicle as 'an ordinary saloon car with specially designed equipment in the back seat. The whole apparatus is driven from batteries stored in the boot and it is quite possible to get everything out quite quickly and install it in any place that might be desirable.' Richard Dimbleby wrote: 'It is no exaggeration to say that the whole vast network of BBC News recording has developed from the introduction of that solitary vehicle.'

My father found himself busier than ever, especially covering air matters. For now in 1938 the threat of war was very real, although it was to be temporarily averted by Neville Chamberlain's visit to Munich in September. His return to Heston airport waving his bit of paper and declaring 'peace in our time' was, for the first time, recorded for both radio and the new television service. My father always said he was there at Heston and we think we could pick him out in the crowd on the news-reel footage. But we have no evidence he reported on it.

Overseas trips to Europe, however, were still possible. His passport records visits to Cologne in June, to France in October and Lisbon in December. The latter was a three-day proving flight by Imperial Airways of their new Armstrong Whitworth Ensign four-engine airliner, in which he had recorded the demonstration flight to Paris a year earlier. A further trip to Germany was for twelve days in the summer. This was probably another 'working holiday' with Eve.

One small and seemingly unremarkable aside catches the eye when Charles was sent to cover yet more floods, this time on the Norfolk Broads in February 1938. Three hand-written letters by the mysterious A.J. Alan have been carefully preserved. The first is addressed from his home at 46 Clarendon Road, Holland Park W11, dated 23 February, which simply asks my father if he would be kind enough to see if his bungalow at Potter Heigham was safe while he was reporting in the area.[1] A photograph of his bungalow was enclosed. The second and third, both of the same date, thank him for 'such a comprehensive report'. The third, however, is written on Foreign Office notepaper, which gives the clue to why we still have the letters.

Alan, real name Leslie Lambert, described more recently as an 'English magician and intelligence officer', was well-known for his regular broadcast readings of his own intriguing short stories. These were delivered in complete silence – apart from the speaker – to preserve an air of mystery. For Alan was meticulous in the detail, and even found a way of turning the pages of the script without being heard. Apparently he separated each sheet and enclosed them in cellophane covers.

So why have these letters been retained? At the time his real identity was withheld on the radio and in his letters. But the letter from the Foreign Office, which established his real home base, added to my father's long-held belief that Alan was not only a master storyteller, but also a master spy with the Secret Service, and indeed (without evidence) possibly the Head of the Service.

It was at about this time that Charles began a close friendship with another well-know personality, the writer and journalist Hugh de Selincourt whose 1924 book *The Cricket Match* had become a classic. It is unclear how they became acquainted besides each having a passion for the game. But I believe de Selincourt's daughter or niece was married to Michael Balkwill, a senior news sub-editor at the BBC and a personal friend who lived nearby at Oxshott, of whom we shall hear more later. Knowing the mutual enthusiasm for the game perhaps Balkwill had made the introduction.

As a result, a cricket match was arranged at Storrington in Sussex, between de Selincourt's home team and a BBC eleven. 'You can imagine the excitement at the mere thought of having a bang at the broadcasters,' Sellincourt wrote. The result of the match, alas, is not recorded. But many flowery letters from the author to Charles survive. 'Good to have you sharing your delight in that game with me' he wrote. The friendship continued for many years with family visits to the famous Sand Pit House in Storrington, which had become a celebrity gathering point for writers, intellectuals, journalists and cricketers throughout 1930s.

The war-like intentions of the Nazis were now erasing any lingering 'peace in our time' hopes of appeasement. A taste of this became apparent in the Spanish Civil War, when Germany intervened to support the existing Spanish fascist regime bringing new methods of warfare, particularly the use of aerial bombing. Both Dimbleby and Gardner were to have first-hand experience of this war in a long-forgotten engagement, not in Madrid, but in the North Sea off Yarmouth in November.

My father tells the story, which is more like an Agatha Christie detective mystery than a serious and worrying news despatch.[2] It concerned a Spanish warship which fired on and sank a Spanish merchantman, the *Cantabria* – an alleged blockade runner, outside British territorial waters but witnessed from the shore near Yarmouth.

Gardner described what happened:

> I and half of Fleet Street caught a train to Yarmouth. Richard said if I would get the story he would liberate the recording car and join me. I telegraphed ahead and booked the only two station taxis in the majestic name of the BBC, and thus was able to isolate Fleet Street for long enough to sign up an exclusive interview with the Spanish captain (Captain Arguelles who had been rescued by a lifeboat) for £5. I knew that back at the railway station, O'Dowd Gallagher of the Daily Express was willing to offer £100.
>
> I waited ages with my story and the interviewee for Richard to arrive with the recording car mounting guard on the hotel stairs and concealing from our Fleet Street colleagues, who had now arrived, that the principal actors in the drama were upstairs in the same building. Had O'Dowd found out he would certainly have outbid me. Richard eventually showed up (the recording car had been locked up and no one had the key, so he had to break in the garage door) and we all repaired to a back exit to the Post Office where we used our car amplifier to transmit the story and the exclusive interviews. When we had finished I saw a movement behind a pillar in the GPO – it was O'Dowd, notebook in hand taking down our stuff. His office could, of course, have got it direct in London by listening to the radio – and probably did.

My father's general reporting duties at this time were still wide and varied, although that was not to last too long. Among them were reports on a young farmers' meeting, the sale of Ham House in London, London to Brighton walk, Waterloo Bridge reconstruction, the Motor Show, Rat Week, winter sports in London and, most curious of all, 'Hallaton Bottle

Kicking'. Apparently this is an old Leicestershire tradition and as a 'local boy' he would have probably known about it and volunteered to cover the story. Apparently (with apologies to the folk of Leicestershire), it occurs every Easter Monday when the villagers of Hallaton and the villagers of Melbourne, carrying 'large Hare pies, 3inch bottles, and small beer kegs', race and fight each other across a 1-mile course, crossing two streams, ditches, hedges and barbed wire. With origins in the eighteenth century, there were no rules, except there was to be 'no eye gouging, no strangling and no weapons!'. The result was unclear but there is evidence Charles survived and broadcast his findings.

Despite such interruptions, there still were a few civil aircraft stories around for the BBC air expert. In February he travelled to Rochester where the Short company built flying boats, and used the River Medway to launch them.

He and other journalists had been called by the company to witness a strange new machine called the 'Short Mayo Composite', named after Mr Mayo the inventor. What they saw were two flying boats, one, the smaller S.20 Mercury, mounted 'piggy-back' style on the larger Short S.21, a variant of their Empire flying boat. The idea was that the smaller craft, with passengers aboard, would be carried inert by the larger one and then released in mid-air at a convenient location to continue the journey. Thus it would have expended no fuel and on fresh fuel tanks could add an additional 3,000 miles to the combined flight. This was sufficient to cross the Atlantic in one hop from east to west, something no other aircraft could do because of the prevailing head winds.

The company now wished to demonstrate 'the difficult bit' – the airborne separation of the two aircraft as a safe and feasible technique. This must have been quite a sight with the two aircraft flying low enough over the Medway so as to be seen, and then the smaller Mercury detaching itself and climbing away safely from the mother ship to the satisfaction of all those present. A few months later, Charles was able to report its first successful non-stop commercial flight from Ireland to Canada carrying ten passengers in a journey time of then only 20 hours 20 minutes. The idea, however, was short-lived with the cessation of civil Trans-Atlantic flights during the war and afterwards, and with only one built it became obsolete. But, it remains a curious oddity in the history of British aviation.

Meanwhile, other record attempts in the air, particularly over great distances, still registered with the public. It was the conclusion of such an attempt over 26,000 miles from London to New Zealand and back that brought my father to Croydon airport on a foggy day in March. He came to see the return of British pilots Clouston and Ricketts after successfully completing the round trip in their de Havilland Comet. On the way they broke eleven records and their ten-day, 20-hour 15-minute flight was the fastest yet recorded. Ricketts said later he especially remembered seeing the Tasman Sea 'thick with whales and many sharks'. They no doubt prayed that this was not the place to have a break-down.

And it was speed records that drew large crowds to Hatfield for the 1938 King's Cup Air Race. For the second year running Charles was to commentate for the radio and see Alex Henshaw win in the de Havilland Comet at an average speed of 236mph – the fastest yet. Henshaw, a Vickers test pilot, was later to become famous for his development work on the Spitfire during the Second World War.

It was at this time that, as an air correspondent, Charles decided it would add credibility to his job if he were able to fly himself. It would also satisfy a long-held desire to do so. So he began flying lessons at Redhill Aerodrome in Surrey, only a few miles from his home. He already had a basic understanding of how an aircraft flies and was a quick learner so it didn't take him long to qualify as a pilot, which he did in March 1939, for which we have a certificate stating he did so in a ' D.H. Moth, Gipsy 1.85'. He received a pilot's licence from the Air Ministry enabling him to fly all types of landplanes, an Aviator's Certificate issued by the Royal Aero Club in London and a membership card as a flying member of the Redhill Flying Club.[3]

Having been through the flying lesson procedure, he thought it would be a nice idea to make a recording of how a beginner, like himself, was taught. For this purpose he invited a colleague from the BBC to be the pupil. We still have the recording of the less than sparkling dialogue between the anonymous pupil and instructor, a Mr Brown. The result went something like this:

> **Pupil to Instructor**: 'How do you do – I hope you don't mind if I ask you some silly questions – actually I know nothing about flying.'
>
> **Instructor**: 'Now is the time to start, let's go over to this machine, an ordinary club Gypsy Moth.'
>
> **The Instructor now explains the controls**: 'Pull the stick up and you go up. Put the stick down and we go down – move the throttle forward to open and move it back to close . . . Would you like to have a shot?' [at flying it].
>
> **Pupil**: 'All by myself?'
>
> **Instructor**: No, I think I will come up with you.'

If this recording persuaded others to take up flying, which would have been the intention, I would doubt it, but it did no harm.

In November, travelling and work was interrupted by the imminent arrival of Charles and Eve's first child, on the 10th – a boy (me) – at Dorking maternity home. Mother and son were reported to be 'doing well' and I still live to tell the tale. In arriving after Richard Dimbleby's firstborn, David, my father lost a wager as to which one would become a father first.

With the turn of the year and war against Germany becoming more likely, civil aviation stories in 1939 were few and far between. There were RAF displays and a celebration of its 21st birthday, test flying of a new Hampden bomber, royal visits and the usual floods around England to report. But there was one horrifying incident that my father, by chance, became involved in.

It was June 1939 and he had been sent to Catterick Camp in Yorkshire to report the celebrations of the 250th anniversary of the Irish Regiment. On his way back he was diverted to Liverpool Bay where a Royal Navy submarine, HMS *Thetis*, had gone missing on a training exercise.

According to newspaper reports (we still have a copy), Gardner, with two engineering colleagues – Arthur Phillips and 'Lew' Lewis, who were to be with him at the Battle of Britian broadcast and later in France – hired a boat and set out just after dawn to see what they could find. After searching for some miles they saw what looked like a buoy. Closer inspection showed it to be a small part of the stern of a submarine. 'Several times they were to bump or scrape over the submerged obstacle which could have been the Thetis,' it was stated.

Tragically, it was the *Thetis*, and worse still, its escape hatch had been blocked and trapped the men inside. Of the Royal Navy crew of fifty-nine plus technical observers, only three RN men escaped and in all ninety-nine lives were lost. As soon as the BBC realised the scale of the disaster my father's recordings were not used at the time. However, in 1967 the tragedy was remembered and the story re-told.

My father had a much happier assignment later that month which had nothing to do with aeroplanes, but one most reporters would have given their eye teeth for. It was an invitation to go aboard the new Cunard White Star liner the RMS *Mauretania* on her maiden voyage to New York. Several other journalists had also been invited and in newspaper terms it was a 'jolly' to beat all others. Several photos remain of Charles and colleagues thoroughly enjoying themselves.

A well-worn BBC announcer's script of the voyage survives which confirms Charles made at least four broadcasts from the ship, the first being 2 hours out of Liverpool and the last on arrival at New York. The announcer's cue reads: 'The new Mauretania has sailed on her maiden voyage from Liverpool. On board her are our observers Bernard Freestone and Charles Gardner, who are waiting to describe the scene.' Alas we have no record as to what they said only the happy pictures together with White Star tickets and boarding papers.

It had long been Charles Gardner's ambition to broadcast live from the air which had not been done before. In July he actually did so, becoming the first aerial reporter flying as an observer in a De Havilland DH 86, a four-engine passenger aircraft. The prospective flight was featured (bravely) on the front of the *Radio Times*.[4] It stated that 'C.J.T. Gardner will accompany two RAF observer recruits on a navigation test flight, and describe how they got on.' It added that the BBC aerial masts at Brookmans Park are one of the landmarks on the first leg of the course which is shown on the map inside (this outlined the complete route for those who might wish to 'stand and stare' while the live broadcast was in progress).

The broadcast was successfully achieved, although, alas, we do not have the recording, but R.T. Clark, Home News Editor, in the 1941 BBC Handbook in a review of developments in news reporting wrote: 'Charles Gardner's reporting of air events in which [as] an observer actually spoke from an aeroplane for, I think, the first time in this country.' It may have been a first but it was not the last.

By now the inevitability of war would not have been more apparent to my father when he was invited to attend an international air show in Hungary, held at Budapest airport. Significantly an existing air show postcard shows a line-up of old-fashioned Hungarian Air Force biplanes next to a squadron of the Lufwaffe's new Me 109 fighters, there to show-off Nazi air power. Their presence would have been a chilling reminder of German intentions which were soon to be realised across Europe.

Very soon both he and Richard Dimbleby were to be on their way to France to report on the first stages of the Second World War.

Chapter Five

Off to War

On 3 September 1939, Prime Minister Neville Chamberlain made his historic broadcast in which he declared war on Nazi Germany. BBC engineer David Howarth recalled that after Chamberlain's broadcast, he, Richard Dimbleby and Charles Gardner and an engineer named Harvey Sarney, 'went down Regent Street and bought ourselves uniforms at the BBC's expense. It was both emotional and funny when we appeared in them in Broadcasting House.' He added, 'We had our picture (in uniform) on the cover of the Radio Times, looking (it seems to me now) absurdly young and shiny, and we quite expected to die for radio.'

The *Radio Times* photograph, headed, 'Off to the Western Front', showed R.T. Clark saying goodbye to the BBC men who were to act as the first radio war correspondents on the Western Front. Pictured were Dimbleby, Howarth and Sarney together in a BBC office, while Charles Gardner was shown inset. This was because he was on his way to France and was photographed specially outside Broadcasting before being driven to Heston airfield for departure. He was described in the caption as 'the fourth member of the party, who will be specially concerned with the activities of the Royal Air Force'.

A press cutting of this picture has survived, together with a note to my father dated October 1939 from 'Janet' (a colleague in the news room). She wrote, 'I'm so glad they put you in [the photo] with the others.' She added, 'You will also be glad to hear that although we are not having a full Christmas bonus we are to have two thirds of the normal. Not bad as we hardly expected anything at all.'

My father recalled those final civilian days in his tribute to Richard Dimbleby. 'Richard was to go to France with the Army and I, as a qualified pilot, with the RAF. The fun days were over; but for both of us our attitude to broadcasting, to integrity, to non-editorialisation and to careful reporting, whether we knew it or not, was shaped for all time.'

Home News Editor R.T. Clark described how they organised the news team for war coverage in the BBC 1941 Handbook:

> Plans to cover the war were made long before war came. Admittedly we based these plans on the completely wrong idea that from the start there would be, as in 1914, violent action. We lost Murray to government service. Dimbleby was selected to go with the BEF (British Expeditionary Force) wherever it might go, accompanied by a recording unit; Gardner was to cover air activities here when the blitzkrieg came down on us. But all the plans went wrong. There was no blitzkrieg in the air and Gardner actually got to France with the Advanced Air Striking Force [AASF] before Dimbleby was established at G.H.Q.

Charles Gardner also recalled how the BBC had planned for war, which they had done in great detail. He wrote:

> Long before the outbreak of war, the BBC Home News Department under R.T. Clark had laid its plans for what the official memorandum insisted on calling an 'emergency.' There were long discussions with the War Office and with the Air Ministry, and as a result a general arrangement was reached. This was my colleague Richard Dimbleby would report the 'emergency' with any British Expeditionary Force, and that I would cover any RAF detachments which went to France.

Then there was the problem about available recording cars. He wrote:

> Both Dimbleby and I were to have recording cars abroad with us and we relied on getting our discs back to England by any messenger service which was set up. We were given to understand that this service would probably be by air, so that the time lag between the making of the records at the front and their being played in the BBC News Bulletins would be short. That, then, was the rough position when war was declared, but from my point of view there was one snag. We only had two recording cars at the time, and since one had to remain in England to report the 'Home Front' there was only one available to go abroad. This remaining car had been collared by Dimbleby; in fact he had already shipped

it to Paris before war broke out, and it was lying, camouflaged and ready in an underground garage.

My father continued:

At the time, of course, everyone was anticipating instant action on the Western Front, and it was rightly presumed that Dimbleby with the BEF would be able to put the car to better immediate use than I, since he would be surrounded with recordable sound effects – such as guns, rifle and machine-gun fire etc. My stories would, in the main, be interviews with pilots and straightforward descriptions of actions which should, for the time being, be telephoned and read in the News by an announcer in the ordinary way. Richard and I agreed that the recording car could be sent down to me on request, if I had a first class story, but we realised that this was not really a workable plan, and the sooner I had a car of my own, the happier we all would be.

Since he had no allocated car, Charles had no team. He wrote:

But I was hoping when the time came to have Leonard Lewis as engineer and Arthur Phillips from Recorded Programmes, since I had worked with them for several years and we knew each others ways. Lewis had once been in the RAF and Phillips was an 'A' licence pilot, so both of them were useful to have around when covering Air Force stories. I was lucky later on in getting both of them.

Indeed, as we have already seen, they were later to play their part in the Battle of Britain broadcast.

There was then the question of when War Correspondents could go abroad – the first week of October was agreed – and the setting up of an RAF Press Section for getting RAF news at home and for helping correspondents abroad. Gardner continued:

They had mapped out a complete scheme and had appointed official Service Press Officers who had been given Air Force Rank. These officers, all Fleet Street men – were to provide material for the official releases from home commands (to which no reporters were attached) and to help the accredited correspondents abroad with the AASF.

He concluded:

> The arrangements for getting copy back from RAF Headquarters were simple and good. At first there was to be a daily plane, paid for by the Newspapers Proprietors Association, and afterwards there was to be a telephone line which would connect directly with the London newspaper offices and the BBC. This meant, of course, that I would only be able to phone over stories to my office, and that, whenever I wanted to do a broadcast myself, I would have to go Paris to the studios there. R.T. Clark left me to fix all that when I arrived and also to arrange for a broadcasting line, when possible, direct from HQ.

My father's mission was of course, to describe the activities of the RAF in France to radio listeners. At the time of his departure they were still experiencing the so called 'phoney war' with no significant attacks from the Germans and no invasion of France, which was expected. Everyone was awaiting the first move and British forces were deployed in support of the Allies. The RAF, which had been preparing such a move for some two years, had set up its headquarters at Reims and already 179 Fairey 'Battle' medium range fighter/bombers had arrived to strike back.

Thus, at the beginning of October, Charles Gardner, aged 28, was the first BBC man to set off for France, and, according to Edward Stourton, 'Went to war with all the gaiety of a young cavalier.' His first wartime experience began with his departure from London which he recalled in detail in his book *A.A.S.F.*, which was published in the autumn of 1940 and was one of the first – maybe the first – wartime eyewitness accounts to become available in book form.

He wrote: 'My plane for a "destination unknown" was due to leave Heston at 10 in the morning, so I duly elevated myself early at the Langham Hotel to find a Radio Times photographer waiting outside to add my picture to the rogues gallery of War Correspondents.' This was taken opposite Broadcasting House watched only by BBC commissionaires. 'I dutifully draped myself by the car door for the photographer. He took about three pictures, and departed, leaving me grateful that at that hour there could hardly be anyone at Broadcasting House to witness the embarrassment of one temporary officer and gentleman wearing, uncomfortably, his brand new uniform and made to do tricks in the middle of Portland Place.'

The uniform itself which he called 'bogus' had no collar badges of rank, but instead displayed on the shoulders a public notice which read 'British War Correspondent'. The cap was gold and green and had a big 'C' for Correspondent on it. He carried with him an assembly of gear – camp-bed, flea bag, typewriter and other comforts, and in his pocket was documentary evidence of his appointment as British War Correspondent, Licence Number 23. He might have been reminded of William Boot in Evelyn Waugh's *Scoop* (one of his favourite books) who was mistakenly sent to report on a civil war in Africa equipped with everything a London emporium could supply, including six hockey sticks!

Thus he set off. 'The office had allowed me a car to get to Heston airfield,' he wrote, 'But once we started it struck me that I might be unwise in arriving at an alleged secret aerodrome with a civilian chauffeur.' He need not have worried, as everyone in the area knew it was now being used for military transport, including the chauffeur.

On arrival at the terminal building he found that Heston no longer had the appearance of 'an old friend', and he felt a little conspicuous in his uniform. After a long wait he boarded an Imperial Airways Ensign aircraft for Paris. Here he needed to fix up facilities for broadcasting with the French wireless people before travelling to his 'secret' destination which he had now discovered was at Reims, the headquarters of the AASF. Of the flight he said:

> It was quite a pleasant trip – although the only seats were ammunition boxes – and by the time the French coast came in sight I was quite excited and feeling 'Brave New World-ish.' Looking down I kept thinking to myself this is the country where the war is . . . and this is the sky in which our planes are fighting Messerschmitts, but the excitement soon passed and I settled down to the Times crossword puzzle.

In Paris, Gardner was told he could have a broadcasting circuit to London with 2 hours' notice. This pleased him, because he could get from Reims to Paris by road, air and rail – 3 hours by road, 1 hour by plane – so that if a story broke by 4pm he could get to the studio in time to make the 9'oclock bulletin. During his stay he met up with Richard Dimbleby and his technical crew, and saw the much vaunted and camouflaged recording car, which Richard had commandeered and rushed to Paris. He was assured again he could have it, as agreed, to cover any instant news story – particularly if they could record the sound of battle on the spot.

My father later flew on to Reims and was surprised to see the airport buildings 'standing out so large and clear', but with RAF Battles dispersed all around the edge of the airfield and 'cunningly hidden under trees'. He was taken to AASF HQ, where he met the senior RAF officer and the Service Press Officers (SFOs) who had already arrived and would be responsible for controlling and censoring news stories. In the hall he noticed large notices 'warning all and sundry against the dangers of talking in cafes'. These notices were supplemented by 'large drawings of Hitler peeping around a corner with his hand cupped behind his ear under which was a piece of verse beginning:

> He wants to know your unit's name
> He wants to know from whence you came.

Also arrived were other reporters whose office was in a nearby building where the landlord had large stocks of champagne which he sold off cheaply, 'so a good time was had by all'. Among them were American reporters including Ed Murrow, who became an iconic voice of the Second World War for his descriptions from London of a blitz-torn city and later a major broadcasting celebrity in the United States. Many years afterwards, my father was walking along Fifth Avenue in New York when coming towards him was Ed Murrow. My Father greeted his old friend but Murrow walked on with only a cursory glance. A few seconds later there were running footsteps behind and a hand of greeting held out: 'Sorry Charles, how nice to see you again,' Murrow said, 'But I get so many people I don't know stopping me in the street that I have to walk on in self-defence,'

Earlier that day at the headquarters, Gardner had been told he would be billeted at the Lion d'Or Hotel, the largest hotel in the city. He was surprised and delighted to learn that his room had a bath en suite, although with strings attached. For 'such luxury' would entail constant visits from the Press Officers, who were not so lucky. He wrote: 'Having come prepared to live primitively, I think I was a little disappointed at finding the war so comfortable with my now unwanted flea bag and camp-bed like a white knight robbed of his dragon.'

The hotel itself was to be 'home' for most of the British journalists for the next seven months.[1] It was described as being 'typically French of the better class' and was proud of its champagne which 'most RAF officers in the bar seemed to be ordering like beer'. The hotel was also to become a centre for spying and the Swiss manager, who openly stated he hated the French and the British, was less than helpful.

From now on Charles began a constant round of visits to RAF front-line bases, pilot interviews and journeys to Paris to broadcast and file his material during a long period awaiting action. Neither the Germans nor the British wished to bomb each other or invade while some politicians still believed a settlement could be reached. On a visit on 10 October by Sir Kinsley Wood, then Secretary of State for Air, he was asked by the press 'why hadn't the "balloon gone up?" Gardner commented, 'The no bombs order was obviously a political one and this reluctance of ours to take up the offensive was one of the things which gave rise to the many "peace" rumours which were flying around at the time.' Later he interviewed Sir Kingsley for a 4-minute broadcast, but no formal response was forthcoming.

RAF bombers were thus used just for reconnaissance and to drop leaflets on Germany. The only combat action came from the two assigned fighter squadrons, Nos 1 and 73, equipped with Hurricanes. My father described in his book his first broadcast of an encounter with Messerschmitts on 17 October, when three Hurricanes were escorting a flight of Blenheims.

He wrote:

> The Blenheims were out on 'reco' and the Me's came at them. Just as they were going to open fire, however, they saw the Hurricanes – and immediately they turned and ran for home at full throttle. Not a very exciting meeting – but in the light of after events, it was a significant straw in the wind. After all the Me's outnumbered the Hurricanes by two to one – but they still refused to fight. I gave the story to my office, and, since I had been lucky enough to get it on my own, it made a presentable 'exclusive.'

Charles was to spend much time with the Hurricane squadrons, meeting the pilots and relating their stories of 'derring-do', describing their accounts of aerial encounters never heard at home before. But probably the most amazing was a leaflet raid by a squadron of Armstrong-Whitworth Whitleys which became well-known as 'The Ice Flight'. My father devoted a whole chapter to it having observed that, 'for sheer perseverance and determination to do the job it takes some beating'.

The squadron concerned was No. 51 which had been sitting for several days at Villeneuve, a night-flying aerodrome near Epernay. Despite bad weather – it was very cold and damp with low cloud – five aircraft were ordered to go. Just after dark they set off and ran slap into icing conditions. One machine became almost unmanageable and had to turn back right away but the ice kept piling up forcing the bomber down until it was obvious it was going to crash. The order was given to bail out which, despite the low altitude, the crew did while the aircraft went on to crash. What they didn't know was the tail gunner was still inside and the gunner didn't know everyone else had gone. The bomber 'piled up all right' and the rear gunner crawled out just as it caught fire. Although badly shaken, he managed to walk to the nearest village and much later, to his relief, he found the rest of the crew.

Meanwhile the other four Whitleys ploughed on trying to climb above the clouds only to tumble again as the weight of the ice on their wings took away their lift. They reached their target, Munich, with the temperature 30 below and half the crew, except the pilots, lying on the floor crying with agony. They dropped their leaflets and headed home but the aircraft began to stall. Down went one Whitley with 6in of ice on its engine cowling, one engine then caught fire and part of the rudder snapped off to crash-land on a French hillside. All the crew got out safely while the fire immediately spread but they were able to put it out and then sat warming themselves in the embers.

Despite the terrible conditions, two of the other three machines managed to get back while the crew of the other one had to bail out over France. My father wrote, 'We saw these men the next morning. They came into the Lion d'Or half dead with cold and still blue and purple about the hands. Yet, out of all the crews of all five of those planes only one man was an official casualty: he was the tail gunner of the first machine who had a cut head.'

Although Charles's broadcasts were to be ground-breaking, the 'hated' administration at the BBC were more concerned about his expenses. As early as 13 October he received a letter from the Head of Personnel setting out, in meticulous detail, his expense entitlements, this included his subsistence allowance at 30s. per day, and £10 per week for necessary expenses on duty – 'to be accounted for in detail'.

Then there was the question of the purchase of a car. This had arisen because my father had made up his mind to do so as the most economical way of getting round to the airfields and to Paris for his regular broadcasts. He had identified a five-year-old 9hp Mathis with 3,000km on the clock with an estimated price of £30 and requested permission to go ahead. The BBC duly responded by letter detailing the terms and conditions for this. They insisted it be insured by a French company and pointed out that petrol, which he could obtain from the RAF, was already accounted for under 'necessary expenses'. The car was thus acquired and affectionately known as 'Harold'.

Lastly, the letter confirmed his expense claim for £60 10s. and gave instructions on how money was to be forwarded in cash through an agreed arrangement with the Air Ministry. At least in all this, Charles learned he had one admin 'friend at court', a Miss Jane Seymore (a name to conjure with) who processed his expenses. She wrote to him to say he should not be too proud of his book-keeping as she had found two mistakes in which he had 'done himself out of 50 francs', adding, 'However, Aunty Jane is looking after your interests!!!'

But his expenses were not the only source of early problems. A more important letter from his boss R.T. Clark arrived five days later. Clark set out the problems they were having in handling his stuff and outlining what he should do in the future. He wrote, 'The telephoning from Paris like the live broadcasts which both you and Richard have done puts us into considerable embarrassments. For one thing your message today took exactly three quarters of an hour to get down in shorthand. We have neither the staff nor the time to be certain of being able to deal with calls of that time.' He added it also created considerable difficulty with the censor since he had no evidence it had already been cleared and had to be re-submitted and 'the Security people here differed very violently from the Field Censor'.

Clark's solution was that although he recognised that both wanted to get their stories over as quickly as possible, that did not matter so much. He wrote, 'Actually for the moment – although you will curse me for saying it – a time lag is of no importance. The quality of the material and the care with which it is edited are infinitely more important both to the listener and for your own sake, than quantity and quickness.'

He concluded, 'What I would like you to do is to send as much stuff as regularly as you can either by post or plane. We shall then be able to use practically the whole of it in one form or another, and reserve live broadcasts from Paris for a really great occasion.'

His boss had a kindly word at the end: 'Don't let this discourage you, you have done famously so far and we have used practically all your stuff.'

In his letter Clark had touched on the censorship problem In fact this was to be a running issue throughout the campaign, not only for Charles but for all the journalists and at one point later in the campaign provoked a week-long journalists' strike. Edward Stourton, in his book, stated, 'Gardner's memoir boils with his frustration in the face of official censorship. It was not that he was being forced to cover things up – far from it; he thought the censors were missing all sorts of opportunities for morale-boosting propaganda by restricting the way he reported the heroism and skill of our young knights of the skies.'

Clark later reflected on the problems both Gardner and Dimbleby were experiencing in an article in the BBC Handbook of 1941:

> Both soon found wartime reporting very different from peacetime work. Not only was there a whole crop of restrictions of which they had not dreamed when they went out, but there was actually less happening in a month at the Front than used to happen in a week at home. Both of them, none the less, managed to send back, either directly or by record, reports which gave to us a vivid idea of how our troops were faring.

And there was no greater example of the censorship restrictions than his report of the 'Ice Flight', which was held over for some days and then only came out in 'bits and pieces'. Charles wrote, 'Naturally we were all a bit upset at the time as it seemed to us that a first-class piece of propaganda was going to waste.' He quoted the Air Ministry's first official statement 'a masterpiece of understatement' which read: 'More successful reconnaissance flights were carried out by our aircraft last night.'

So what about his stories from the field which were allowed? We have on file some forty original scripts and despatches with handwritten annotations and all cleared for publication by the censor's stamp. We also have actual recordings and there is, of course, his book *A.A.S.F.*, written in a few weeks after he returned to London in June 1940.

I do not, therefore, intend to cover all the engagements but single out a few of note and, particularly, those with a less war-like nature and others which give some 'behind the scenes' reports which help to paint a picture of life in France at the time.

One of the first stories he filed was after a visit with a colleague to an aerodrome at Chalerange, one of the most advanced RAF stations situated halfway to Verdun. He wished to interview a pilot who had forced landed on the Maginot Line and had been given the 'Maginot Medal' by the French.[2] The pilot, who had been flying a Fairey Battle on a leaflet drop, was attacked by Messerchmitts and with his navigator injured, and his engine failing, made a crash-landing near one of the forts which had so stoutly repelled the Germans in the First World War. As the pilot struggled from his aircraft, a French soldier ran towards him and shouted in recognisable Cockney slang: 'Blimey governor, you're bloody lucky.' Having pulled out the wounded navigator, the Frenchman explained his 'command of English' came from living in Chelsea for many years. 'Poor old Chelsea,' Charles wrote.

Of the mission he stated, 'Imagine what everyone had said would be the bloodiest, most indescribable war the world had ever know, that two British war correspondents would drive about 60 miles out and back to get a story from a man who had been presented with a badge by some Frenchman!'

Another very early report revealed an unsung but quite remarkable air supply operation to the first RAF units scattered around France. This was carried out by civil aircraft only and without significant road, rail and sea support. It was probably the first of its kind and possibly would have gone unnoticed had it not been for Charles's interview with Sir Kingsley Wood on 10 October. Sir Kingsley said that in the course of the first days or so of the war, 'the Air Force in France was served completely by air'.

Charles wrote:

Now it doesn't need much imagination to see that behind a piece of work like that there must be a story worth telling, especially when you have seen, as I have, the loads of stuff an isolated air wing out here needs. Food, clothes, blankets, signalling equipment, searchlights, picks, shovels, tents, aeroplane spares, telephones and heaven knows what else.

So yesterday I went out to one of our remoter aerodromes to find out how this enormous job of air transportation had been done. Getting the bombers out here was reasonably easy – they flew over with their crews. Then the civil machines took over. They were already the bigger machines off the Paris run, and also the smaller transport planes gathered in from internal routes. Backwards and forwards they shuttled, bringing men and materials for ten days or a fortnight without ever failing to deliver the goods. The result was there was never a lag of more than 24 hours between a request being made out at a lonely French village and its fulfillment via its home base in England.

When you think that most of the equipment for all these aerodromes in remote and difficult places to find, was flown over ten days, and without – as far as I can find out – a single accident. You have got to hand it to the general organisation and particularly to those civil pilots who did the job.

I wonder if he remembered all this when in 1948, he broadcast and flew on the Berlin Air Lift?

A few days later he described another new development. This was what he called, 'the first wireless running commentary in the middle of an air battle'. This time it was not an RAF pilot but a Frenchman who was responsible during an encounter with Messerschmitts of the crack Richtofen/Goering squadron.

But all was not quite as it seemed, as Gardner recalled:

> What happened was the French fighter pilot who had led his plane to the attack, had, by accident, left his communications microphone on. Back at headquarters, French officials heard the pilot talking to himself as he manoeuvered and fought. They heard him swear as a Messerschmitt twisted away just as he was going to fire and they heard him shout when he shot one of the enemy down.

Of course, it wasn't long before Charles, with the expert aid of BBC engineers, set up a real live broadcast with Flight Lieutenant 'Cobber' Kain from the cockpit of his Hurricane while on patrol. (We shall hear much more of 'Cobber' later.) Unfortunately on that day, very unusually, no enemy were sighted making the recording very unexciting.

Sir Kingsley Wood was back again a week after his first visit and was seen 'wading through thick mud and in persistent rain' to see RAF machines and talk to the pilots on their 'secret aerodromes'. But one of his visits was out of the ordinary, as Charles described:

> This morning, all the war correspondents went with Sir Kingsley to a small French village, which is now one of the most important store parks in France. It is the sort of place where you open the door of an ordinary barn in a very muddy farmyard to find inside – not a couple of hens and some hay – but rows of aeroplane parts guarded by RAF sentries. And there, the last thing you expect in a stable of horses but much more likely aeroplane wings. And almost every cottage opens on to some branch of Air Force activity.

One of their biggest problems he discovered, was trying to conceal their activities from German spies and aircraft, 'particularly the disposal of supply lorries, because nothing is a surer give-away of a store park than a transport convoy'. And so the lorries were now all camouflaged and parked in nearby spinneys and woods.

The Minister also inspected the kitchens and the cooking arrangements and found that everyone had, what Charles called, 'the ubiquitous dart board – which you find in almost every barn, if it is only chalked on the door'. Sir Kingsley then looked in at the medical centre, the sleeping arrangements in a very large barn (with dart board on the door) and the sizeable bath house. He was told that 'every man was supposed to have a bath at least once a week and that a book was kept to make sure they did'. My father commented, 'I don't know if the existence of that book at all is a compliment to the Service – but I was told there had been no trouble so far.'

By late October still very little was happening. 'As far as I can discover here not a single bomb has yet been dropped on this front by either side.' So Charles visited one of the 'carefully hidden' aerodromes which had been chosen before the war. He wrote:

> The aerodromes themselves are just large fields with no prepared landing surface, or, in fact, anything except for the camouflaged machines to distinguish it from the surrounding stretches of flat agricultural land. All its tents and small huts were cunningly hidden in a nearby spinney, while every single piece of equipment which had to be in the open was shadow shaded. Since the squadrons operating from here are all billeted in the villages, there are only a minimum number of store huts etc which need to be near the aerodrome at all.

Although some of these reports were never broadcast or published, they do provide a useful picture of life in France at the beginning of the campaign. But it was his stories of the pilots and their experiences which were to capture the public's imagination in those early days. It was not long, however, before these almost pleasant, peaceful days were transformed and the worst fears of the skeptics about this being the 'most indescribable war' were to be realised.

Chapter Six

'Cobber' Kain and Pilots' Tales

Charles Gardner first met Flying Officer E.J. 'Cobber' Kain on a visit to No. 73 Hurricane Squadron at Rouvres airfield, near Verdun, towards the end of October. 'Cobber' was a 21-year-old New Zealander who came to England in 1936 and was commissioned in the RAF a year later. He had already made a name for himself as an aerobatic pilot in England; now he was doing the same as a fighter pilot in France.

Gardner recalled that first encounter at Rouvres:

> A flight of Hurricanes happened to come in over the field after one of their routine patrols along the frontier. The squadron leader was standing with us, and as the Hurricanes circled round he said, 'now watch this lot.' We did and were given one of the best aerobatic shows I had ever seen short of the Gladiators at the last Hendon display. I noticed at the time the particularly fine handling of the leader's machine – there was a firmness and a precision about the flying of that plane which stood out – so much so that I asked who the pilot was. 'That's Cobber Kain,' said the officer, 'you'll be hearing some more about this lad before the war is much older.' He had already shot down at least 20 German fighters, for which he was later to be awarded the DFC.

My father and 'Cobber' were soon to become good friends and he became the source of several stories about his many air combat encounters. It was one of these – an aggressive and dangerous 'dogfight' with a Messerschmitt – which was recorded. It was probably the first such account by an RAF pilot to be broadcast and describes the fight and his miraculous escape. The recording has been preserved and the following extract is a vivid example of Cobber's courage and the danger he faced.

Charles Gardner:

Last week many of you probably heard or read about a fight which took place between two Hurricanes and two Messerschmitts. It was one of the most adventurous fights we have reported and it took place over 20,000ft and 30 miles on the German side of the line. Tonight I want to introduce to you the young New Zealand pilot who was mainly concerned in this fight. I can't tell you his name but he is known in the squadron as 'Cobber' which is New Zealand for pal. [His name was eventually released to the press after representations from the press and from New Zealand.]

'Cobber' Kain, in a rather English voice with only a small trace of his heritage, then described how he and a second Hurricane flown by a sergeant pilot, were on patrol when they encountered seven Heinkels:

As we approached they turned towards our lines and we gave chase, they put their noses down to go like stink and we went after them. . . . I was going flat out and hardly dared take my eyes off them . . . after about a three minute chase I gave a quick glance to the left to see if my Sergeant was with me and noticed a machine about 100 yards behind. I thought it was my Sergeant and I was just going to call him on the wireless for him to close in, when I heard him yell – 'look out something is on your tail.' The machine I presumed to be my old friend the Messerschmitt.

The next thing I knew was 'whang' and I saw the tip of my wing disappear into the blue. It had been hit by a shot from his cannon. I immediately made a steep turn to the right and saw the Hun was climbing up for another attack. I managed to get a short burst into him and he dived down. At the same time I was hit again from the rear by a second Messerschmitt, and I found out afterwards he had already shot down my Sergeant just after he had yelled at me. Luckily he got away with it and managed to make a landing on our side of the line.

Then started a general free-for-all. Me chasing one and the other chasing me. It was while making a climb and flattening out at the top that I managed to get a longish burst in from behind and sent him down giving out black smoke and later he burst into flames.

Meanwhile, the other got behind me and that was when he got my engine with another cannon shot which made a big hole in it. Oil and fumes poured into the cockpit and went all over the windscreen and the instruments. The Messerschmitt went down under me and I stuck my nose down hoping to get him into my sights, but my plane was too sluggish to get him into my sights.

After that I expected him to come back and teach me to 'play the harp,' but either he had used up all his ammunition or thought I was finished, because he didn't make another attack. I was then about 30 miles on the wrong side of the line but with the help of a very strong wind blowing me towards France at 20,000ft, I managed to glide over French territory. Then the flames began to lick back from the engine and the fumes almost suffocated me. So I opened the hood, undid my safety harness preparing to jump. Then I looked down and saw my parachute strap was off my shoulder, it had slipped so I got back again. Just after that the flames went out and I managed, after a long glide, to pull off a forced landing on the edge of the aerodrome. I climbed out of the cockpit and more or less passed out because of the fumes.

He was rescued by the French and taken to the sick quarters, 'where they gave me the once over and a lot of brandy. Later a French pilot, who had also been forced to land, decided to celebrate with me. After that I felt grand,' he said.

Although such pilot stories were soon to become familiar during the Battle of Britain, just a few months away, Kain's account, given in a 'matter of fact' way, would have brought home the continual danger and bravery of RAF aircrew, currently facing overwhelming odds in France.

For my family, the 'Cobber' Kain story did not end there. For one of our treasured souvenirs, now taking pride of place in my room, is a mounted altimeter with a smashed glass face from the first German aircraft shot down over France by No. 73 Squadron. This came into our possession after a visit by my father to the crash site of the aircraft, a Dornier DO 17 in October. He was accompanied by three journalists – Peter Masefield of *Aeroplane* magazine (who as Sir Peter was to become one of the leading figures in Britain's postwar aviation industry), H.F. King of *Flight* magazine and Lord Donegal of the *Sunday Dispatch*.

Apparently there had been a dogfight overhead at the airfield and the Dornier had been shot down by a Hurricane and crashed in a nearby village, miraculously without killing anybody on the ground. The wreckage was described by Charles as 'a horrible sight'. The fight, it appeared, was unique in itself, having been fought at the extreme altitude of 27,000ft.

After examining the wreckage my father retrieved the damaged altimeter and its German description plaque from the aircraft and entrusted it to Lord Donegal, who was leaving shortly for England. A letter from Donegal addressed to my mother on 10 November survives. In it he says the altimeter and plaque that father had lent him would be reproduced in the next *Sunday Dispatch*. He added, 'Charles did not give me any particular news but seems very well and happy. He is certainly doing a good job. If you kindly do not pass the information on I can tell you that he is at present at Reims and is living at the Hotel du Lion.'

And the pilot of the Hurricane who shot down the Dornier – Flying Officer 'Cobber' Kain.

The crashed Dornier story came hard on the heels of AASF's earlier success when a No. 1 Squadron Hurricane downed another Dornier and on 23 November the two fighter squadrons had 'the best day of the war' when they shot down seven aircraft – five Dorniers and two Heinkels. Charles sent the story over the telephone and it made the lead on the 9 o'clock news – a small fillip in an otherwise gloomy war situation.

After the immediate excitement of the seven victories had died down, Charles discovered another 'first class story' about an encounter between a Hurricane of No. 1 squadron and a Dornier, which had a surprising end.

It appears that the Hurricane was chasing a Dornier and 'got home so many good bursts' that the German gunner and observer would have to take to their parachutes. So, seeing the Dornier go down, the Hurricane pilot pulled alongside but found the German pilot huddled over the wheel, he was obviously dead or wounded, so he jubilantly opened up the throttles and pulled ahead. But the German was not dead or wounded but only foxing. As soon as the Hurricane opened up in front of him, he stood up, reached for the front gun and shot it up so badly that the Hurricane had to land.

There followed one of those amazing stories of mutual respect that still existed between pilots, friend or foe. The German pilot shortly after the encounter with the Hurricane lost his second engine, crash-landed and was taken prisoner. On hearing this, No. 1 Squadron asked the French to let him out on parole for an evening, and threw a party for him in their mess 'because he had put up such a good show'. The German arrived and was astonished at his welcome. He then broke down and began to cry. Two of the RAF officer, one of them the very pilot he had forced down, asked him what was the matter. The German replied that for most of his 31 years he had been taught to hate the British and believed that if he was caught he would be tortured and killed. To find instead that he was treated as an honoured guest was too much.

PART ONE

The earliest known photograph of Charles Gardner as a boy, probably aged 7 with his parents Adelaide and Joseph (Jo). Adelaide, a trained nurse, was the driving force in the family, while Jo, a saddle-maker by trade, was gentle and retiring. Neither had any background in creative writing or journalism, nor was there any known history in the wider family, so it is unknown where Charles got his inspiration to become outstanding at both – though it was possibly a master at his school, Edward VI Grammar School.

Jo Gardner (seated left) fought in the First World War as a stretcher-bearer but was subsequently invalided out. During the Second World War he was appointed an officer in the local yeomanry, which was when this picture was taken. Jo's family had a farming background and he retained a part ownership in his brother's farm which made him eligible for officer rank.

As a young man Charles had decided not to go to Oxford University, despite entreaties by his Headmaster to do so, preferring to go into journalism as a trainee on the local *Nuneaton Tribune* daily newspaper.

Charles did well on the *Nuneaton Tribune* and in 1934 moved to the more prestigious *Leicester Mercury*; he is seen here at his typewriter in the News Room. He soon made a name for himself as a creative writer particularly specialising in the growing field of aviation, which was to become his abiding interest.

Charles met Eva (Eve) Fletcher in 1934 while she was working for the Press Association in Birmingham. At that time Gardner frequently telephoned news to the PA which he thought were of wider national interest. Apparently, he was short-tempered and difficult with the copy takers and Eve was the only one who could cope with him. The following year they were married at her local parish church at Halesowen, Staffordshire. They became a devoted couple for the rest of their lives.

In 1936 Charles Gardner joined the BBC and became, with Richard Dimbleby, one of their first ever news reporters. To be near London, Charles and Eve acquired Eaves Cottage in Fetcham, near Leatherhead, in 1937. Situated in 'leafy Surrey' 20 miles from London, it became the family home for more than forty years. This photograph shows the pleasant garden that was much to the delight of Eve. Charles soon joined the local cricket and golf clubs and the house was also close to Redhill airfield where he learned to fly.

Charles at the microphone, at an unknown location, though probably commentating on one of the air races that had become very popular in the 1930s. He began his public address commentaries in 1937 at the annual King's Cup Air Race at Hatfield and continued to do so for the next forty years, including at the Farnborough Air Show.

It was not surprising that Charles wanted to learn to fly – his first experience of open-cockpit flight came while he was on the *Nuneaton Tribune* when he was given a flying lesson, which he duly reported in the paper. In 1939 he qualified as a pilot at Redhill and is seen here leaving his Gipsy-Moth after his first successful solo. This photograph was later used in the *Radio Times* to illustrate his forthcoming (and successful) first live air to ground broadcast.

With the outbreak of war with Germany in 1939, Charles became one of the first war correspondents and was posted to France to follow the RAF. In December of that year King George VI, together with the Duke of Gloucester, visited the area where RAF squadrons and troops were stationed. Gardner followed the tour and is seen here far right.

The New Zealand ace pilot 'Cobber' Kain, whose heroics caught the public imagination. Charles interviewed him many times and they became good friends. He is seen here with colleagues the morning after he escaped by parachute from a burning Hurricane having shot down at least one, but possibly two, Germans. He is reading a telegram of congratulations from the AOC-in C, Air Marshal Sir Arthur Barratt.

The use of the precious and only recording car in France was a constant problem for the BBC observers. But here Gardner had the benefit of it when recording an interview with Squadron Leader Dodds. The recording engineer in the car is Harvey Garney.

The men in charge of the Advanced Air Striking Force in France were Air Marshal Sir Arthur Barratt, AOC-in-C (left), and Air Vice-Marshal (later Air Marshal) Sir Patrick Playfair, AOC. The history of the AASF from 1939 to the blitzkrieg in May 1940 was written by Charles and released later that year. It is believed to be the first eyewitness Second World War book to be published.

The crew of a Whitley bomber which, after an 11-hour leaflet drop over Germany, was caught in strong headwinds that forced them to land. Unfortunately, by mistake, it was on German soil – but thanks to a helpful local man they escaped. Charles covered the story in full, but the Censor deprived him of interviewing crew members minutes before they were to go on air.

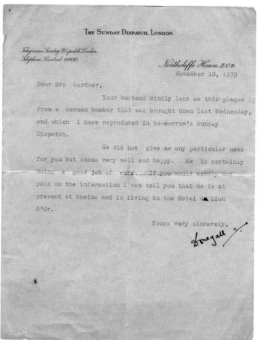

A crashed Dornier Do 17 that was shot down by 'Cobber' Kain being inspected by several war correspondents, including Charles who 'rescued' the aircraft's altimeter. This was returned to the UK by Lord Donegal of the *Sunday Dispatch* before he sent it on to Eve at home with a letter (below right) which also informed her that her husband was well. A press cutting about the Dornier and the altimeter (below left) subsequently appeared in the *Sunday Dispatch*. The altimeter has survived and remains in the author's possession.

Although there were to be further air combat encounters, and more long-range bomber sorties – just to drop leaflets over Germany, there was still relative calm as the 'phoney war' proceeded. Unsurprisingly this led to further increasing speculation among the air crews and journalists as to when and if a real war would start. The question had been raised before, but still without resolve or explanation. So when a harsh winter arrived and the temperature dropped, the focus was on maintaining the fighters and bombers which was giving ground crews problems in servicing their aircraft.

A good example was the cause of a lucky escape of a Heinkel bomber. Charles reported:

> Somewhere in Germany there is a crew of a Heinkel bomber who don't know how lucky they are to be alive. Apparently a young but unnamed New Zealand pilot had been sitting on the tail of the German with the raider well in his sights when he pressed the firing button of his Hurricane. But nothing happened, his guns were silent. The German must have been astonished at his reprieve.
>
> In the British fighter the pilot continued to press his firing switch hoping his guns would start up. He remained in this attacking position for so long that enemy bullets were now ripping their way into his plane and several came through the cockpit just missing his body. By this time the New Zealander was so furious, to use his own words – he felt like 'ramming the Heinkel.'
>
> Having resisted the ramming idea, he landed safely and when he examined his guns he found that an excess of oil on parts of the mechanism had frozen up. It is a good illustration of the problems RAF ground crews have throughout this long cold winter.

Despite the cold weather, the lack of activity encouraged those in France to look forward to Christmas and a host of goodwill visits from royalty, politicians, RAF chiefs and to popular acclaim, the singer and entertainer Gracie Fields, who was then probably the best known 'star' in the land.

Chapter Seven

Visits, a Row and His Own Studio

Morale in France was raised by a visit by King George VI in December. We have the recording made by my father who followed the royal party. In a very guarded report, because of security concerns, he told how the King, accompanied by the Duke of Gloucester, had been to see the 'Royal Air Force in the field'.

His broadcast began:

> His Majesty was in the uniform of Marshal of the Royal Air Force and on the left breast of his tunic – above the ribbons of great honour – he wore the most democratic award the Air Force gives – it has always been closely guarded – the pilots wings. These the King earned in the only way they can be earned – when he himself became a qualified service pilot in the last war.

By leading with this observation of the King, I can only assume my father didn't know that he was a qualified service pilot. But, then, many others were unaware of this achievement – mainly because he was then the Duke of York and not the heir to the throne, or much in the public eye.

The King had come to Reims after visiting the BEF, and spent the night in his train in the siding before arriving at Reims station in the morning. His first visit was to the stores park which had been elaborately camouflaged, as it would have been a prime target for German bombers. Then on to Villeneuve airfield, where he met crews of Whitley bombers, which were going on a pamphlet raid that night, and then drove round rows of parked Fairey Battles.

Gardner continued, 'French soldiers lined the first part of the route . . . in the fields men stopped working to watch the cars go by'. Later he noted that a 14-year-old girl, Jeanette, had tried to present the King with a bunch of autumn flowers. 'But she chose to stand in the wrong place and the Royal car was not supposed to stop there, so it continued while Jeanette sadly watched the car go by.' However, two French policemen travelling in an official car saw what happened and, 'revived her day by promising they would try to see they reached the King later' (which they did and were given to him just before lunch).

At another airfield the King made the first gallantry awards in the field since the start of the war. Later, Gardner reported that, 'His Majesty was received by a Group Captain who had been his senior officer at Cranwell in 1918. As he shook hands with him the King said, "It's been a long time since Cranwell hasn't it?"' (no further dialogue was recorded so we do not know how the Group Captain appraised the then Duke or how his student regarded him, except that he passed out successfully with his wings on his chest).

The King continued his tour, including a drive through Epernay where, he observed, 'British nurses lined the famous champagne street. Actually, HQ had taken extra precautions in Epernay, which was always thought to be a big spy centre. The drive passed off without incident.'

Back at Reims, the King took great interest when shown recent reconnaissance photos taken by the RAF of the Siegfried Line and other locations and was presented with an album of the photos 'to his great delight'. He later took a train to Metz to inspect the Maginot Line. Gardner, who did not travel to Metz, later recorded that, 'While the King was in the Maginot Line he saw the French General Gamelin present the Croix de Guerre to a young British Sergeant pilot whose courage saved what might have been a large loss of life in a French Village'. The pilot was, in fact, the first British serviceman to receive the award in this war.

Charles related:

> Apparently he had been chasing some Messerschmitts in his Hurricane when his petrol tanks were punctured and he saw the first flick of flames. He was about to jump out when he saw he was heading for the village. Almost suffocating, he hung on to his controls with the Hurricane coming down so fast it would be too late to jump. Then, when it was almost too late he jumped – and his parachute opened just in time to break the fall . . . the machine crashed in another field not far away.

Gardner, concluding his report, noted, 'All through this tour two flights of bombers circled above guarding the Royal car from any possible attack from the air and high above the bombers keeping a look out in the hazy grey sky were three fighters'.

Another visitor in December was the Chief of Air Staff, Air Chief Marshal Sir Cyril Newall, who was interviewed by my father about 'the State of the Nation in France' in which he was asked to compare the RAF fighters with the Germans. Sir Cyril unexpectedly replied:

Whenever a Spitfire or a Hurricane gets in touch with a German machine it fills it so full of holes that it looks like a colander! Our eight-gun fighters have fully come up to expectation and the pilots have already learned valuable lessons from their flights. All my men have got their tails right up and long to have a crack at the enemy – in fact there are few things they would like better.

He concluded, retaining his humorous theme, by paying tribute to the French for their kindly welcome, 'Our men are making good progress with the language. Only the other day one of them said a coup de grace was a lawn mower!'

Some of my father's reports filed at this time contain personal 'service messages' to his boss R.T. Clark. He did so at the end of his interview with the Air Chief Marshal. Again the vexed question of the recording car came up when he wrote:

What are the arrangements for broadcasting from here at Christmas? Do you want anything – if so how are the line negotiations going between Air Ministry and General Julian in Paris? If no line, how about a recorded feature – but I would need a second (recording) car to make it as Bumble (Richard Dimbleby) will want his for Christmas with the Army. Please let me know your wishes as soon as possible.

Alas, we have no record of Clark's response, but Charles did record a Christmas piece, as we shall see.

On another despatch about a visit by the then Chancellor of the Exchequer, Sir John Simon, he wrote appealingly at the bottom of his routine visit report: 'I have no money, am flat broke!' Although the BBC were known to be less than generous over pay and conditions, as we know, I don't think my father would have been left penniless too long.

Nine days after the King's tour, the Prime Minister, Neville Chamberlain, visited and Charles accompanied him throughout. 'This was a much more informal affair. He came down and had a drink with all the correspondents and chatted freely with us for a long time.' He added, 'throughout the day he was as spry as a turkey. He hopped in and out of aeroplanes, jumped down gun-pits and generally showed amazing vitality for his age'.

On a more serious note, the Prime Minister examined the crashed Dornier which my father had visited earlier. 'He was very interested in the self-sealing petrol tanks, which were made of rubber and fibre. He looked at them for a long time and said, "we must have some of these."' (This was an issue which Charles and others had taken up before the war.)

But perhaps the most popular visit at this time was from the fabled singer, actress and entertainer Gracie Fields, the 'Lass from Lancashire', who appeared at what was described as a 'memorable concert' in the cinema at Reims. My father wrote, with regret, that he was unable to attend, but she is pictured in his AASF book signing Christmas cards for the men.

For Christmas, Charles was delighted to receive parcels from home and a 'charming' letter from Hugh de Sellincourt describing 'Umbrage's' (me) adventures on an afternoon when he and his wife had visited the cottage in Fetcham.[1] 'The letter was a lovely piece of descriptive writing,' he wrote. 'Umbrage was a very big boy then – one year and two months – and he had already staggered his friends by swearing.'

And he did put together his promised Christmas feature describing some of the festivities around the bases (with or without the recording car):

> Even Headquarters are going gay. Holly and paper chains around the doors – though there is a suggestion that in their most secret rooms there should be a sentry on duty to see that no Santa Claus of foreign origin comes down the chimney! . . . The senior officers not on duty will visit the men at dinner time – and in some officers' messes they are arranging to have their Christmas dinner on Christmas Eve so that the mess servants will have free time next day.

By New Year 1940, things were so relaxed that even the censors were able to give the men a welcome lift.

Charles wrote:

> From today wives and sweethearts of the men out here will be able to get letters from the front which will not have on them the official label 'Opened by the Censor.' The green envelope – familiar to the troops of the last war – has been introduced again and in it the men can post personal notes of their private affairs knowing that no third person will read what they say.

By mid-January, Charles was sending 'chatty pieces' in a regular 15-minute weekly slot 'Despatches from the Front' now allocated to him and Richard Dimbleby. He spoke about people falling down in the snow, engines not starting at 25 °F, and more speculation as to why the war hadn't started properly. He even had a light-hearted swipe at his many Scottish friends and wrote in his diary: 'Everywhere in England is snow-bound and Scotland cut off! That distressed me not at all – indeed I had often advocated it.' (Had he known that his granddaughter Claire would marry a Scotsman, BBC political correspondent Glenn Campbell, and live in Scotland he might have thought twice about this 'tongue in cheek' remark aimed at his many Scottish friends.)

Things remained so quiet and with so little to report, that my father was able to return to England with the intention of covering the RAF at home. His efforts to visit air bases and interview pilots were, however, thwarted by the Air Ministry who refused to let him go on his own. All they could offer were two organised press trips. One was to Digby to see a fighter squadron which, Charles observed, 'was on the normal lines – we talked to the pilots and watched them shoot up the aerodrome'. The second visit was to Mount Batten (Plymouth) – 'an old hunting ground of mine', which he surprisingly described as 'great fun' after flying on a very early (3am) patrol in a Sunderland flying boat of Coastal Command. It was extremely cold in the cabin and a 'very bumpy four-hour trip which made him feel sick'. As soon as the Mount Batten flight was over he decided there was nothing useful he could do at home and returned to France.

On arrival back with the ASSF, he found there had been little change with little to report. But something which did catch his eye was the unusual delivery of 'Boys Toys' to RAF fighter pilots. On investigation he found they were not toys and had serious intent.

Charles wrote:

> Special toy models of German aeroplanes are now part of the equipment for all the squadrons here. They were built to Air Ministry specifications and mounted on swivels and small lamps mark the position of enemy guns. These throw a beam which represents the field of fire on all know German types, and from a study of them British pilots are able to work out their plan of attack.

In the air, in operations, the RAF was still flying missions deep into Germany and Hurricanes were still engaging the enemy with great success.

Stories were still there for the telling, but this was to cause Charles to be caught in the middle of a serious row with Fleet Street.

The problem was that his stories, be they telephoned or direct broadcasts, were always ahead of the newspapers, who were now complaining to the authorities and the BBC that this was unfair to them. Their objections coincided that month with a visit by the new Director General of the BBC, F.W. Ogilvie, whom my father accompanied during his time in France. After much consideration it was agreed that telephone stories would be held over until 8am the following day, but Ogilvie backed Gardner in broadcasting his recorded stories as soon as received that night. Thereafter Charles abandoned the telephone as much as he could and broadcast his reports, which were processed at the BBC studios at Maida Vale and the record sent post-haste to the News Editor for the 9 o'clock news.

On a lighter note, Ogilvie asked what the troops in France wanted from BBC radio. Charles, pre-warned, had already arranged a quick survey. He reported his findings, which were for 'short French lessons, short thrilling plays – but not long ones, and above all new songs'. He was told the 1940 Army was rather tired of 1914–18 songs like 'Tipperary' and wanted 'Rollout the Barrel' instead. (There were no disc jockeys or Radio One in those days.)

It was shortly after the Ogilvie visit that my father became ill and had to go to bed. No doubt his illness brought feelings of remorse, frustration and sadness which he confided to his diary.

He wrote:

> I feel like lying here forever – and just letting the war happen around me. Maybe the first glimpse of sunshine will put me right. In fact, I have tried to imagine it. I shut my eyes and thought hard that I was going to play cricket this afternoon. That Eve had put my flannels out – that my shoes were drying out in the loggia – that there was a gentle sun and that the flowers were out in the garden.
>
> I have tried to imagine all the things that make me get up enthusiastically – an aeroplane ticking over on a windless morning – waiting for me to fly it – the office ringing me up with a first class story. And yet I still open my eyes, and want to stay in bed.

Charles's depression did not last long, but just as he was feeling 'reasonably fit', his eyes started to give him trouble and he returned home to see the doctor.[2] But the doctor 'did not take too bad a view of it'. So he took the chance to go to the office and fix up the final details of his own and at last promised a recording car. Leonard Lewis had been chosen as his recording engineer and Arthur Phillips as the recording programmes man, as he had hoped. 'This cheered me up a lot. I had worked with them both for three years and more and had been to America with them.' (This was on the *Mauretania*'s maiden voyage to New York.)

His efforts to speed up his broadcasts were also pursued as soon as he got back to Reims. For some time he had been seeking a room at HQ which could be equipped and used as a remote studio for direct transmissions, thus saving the delay caused by trips to Paris. Now a room had become available which had previously been occupied by Wing Commander Bishop. 'I busied myself fitting up a studio ready for my long-delayed permanent microphone in Bishop's office,' he wrote. He bought a desk, table, chairs and a clock, 'second hand to keep the costs down and thoroughly enjoyed myself'.

But it was not until 16 March that it became fully operational, when Leonard Lewis arrived 'with a lot of gear' and with the help of Eric Lycett, who had come out to look after BBC Outside Broadcasts, that they got the studio working. His first broadcast was an interview with an RAF parson, Squadron Leader the Revd J.H.W. Haswell in the continuing weekly 15-minute 'Despatches from the Front' series. To celebrate they threw a champagne party to which all the correspondents and senior Press Officers were invited. But in the middle of it, the Revd Haswell had to do his piece. 'We all stood quietly round, taking great care not to clink the glasses while he spoke . . . We were like children with a new toy.'

It was soon after the opening of the studio that Charles made his first and last visit to the BEF in Arras, where he met up with Richard Dimbleby and recorded interviews with some Blenheim pilots. He discovered they were 'having a hell of a time' having lost twelve aircraft from one squadron including the CO. Richard, who he hadn't seen since arriving in Paris in October, told him 'lots of stories' about the BEF and particularly the problems they were having with German spies in the area. In Lille, seven had been arrested and shot by the French. There was also a large British spy organisation based there but, according to Dimbleby, they hadn't yet lost an agent.

On the last evening at Arras, he was asked to take part in a general knowledge broadcast that Richard Dimbleby had organised. He and a colleague, David Howarth, were invited to think up questions. 'The best question I could think of was: "What is the French for cul-de-sac?"'

And still on a lighter note, was a story about a German parachute drop with a difference.

Charles reported:

> I can now reveal that some time ago two girl parachute spies were dropped behind our lines and that they were captured in a village where they were moving about among our airmen in the disguise of pedlars. The presence of spies was first suspected when a German aeroplane was heard flying near one of the aerodromes at night. A thorough search led to the finding of two opened parachutes – both in black silk. This was not a female thing, but had obviously been made for night use. But there was one peculiar thing, the harnesses were much smaller than usual. . . .
>
> Immediately a questionnaire was sent round the units asking if anyone had seen two strange women in the district. There was a quick reply that airmen had noticed two girls selling picture postcards and stationery in the village. Both were dressed in short leather jackets and lace-up boots. One girl spoke French well enough the other was not heard speaking at all.

They were apprehended and their gallant, if ill-prepared mission came quickly to an end.

Intermittent action by the RAF continued throwing up many individual stories. My father recorded how one Whitley bomber on a leaflet 'raid' flew over 1,000 miles first over Munich, which was blacked out, then Vienna, which was a 'blaze of light' and on to Prague, Bilsen and Bruno. 'There were so many planes over the impregnable Reich that it was a wonder there wasn't a traffic jam,' he said. 'But they were held in search-light beams but not shot at.'

One piece of good news came from a telephone call to his friend Michael Balkwill in London. Balkwill told him that Hugh Dalton, the former First World War flying ace and now a Minister in the Air Ministry, had nice things to say about him in Parliament in the Air Estimates Debate. 'For which I was very grateful but a little amazed.'

Balkwill was appointed as a News Sub-editor from the beginning, and his contribution to the BBC's news reporting should not go without mention. He was a winner of the Newdigate Poetry prize at Oxford and was described by Jonathan Dimbleby in his book,' as a man of rare ability who chose to spend his entire BBC career in the News Room and who was to be responsible for more BBC radio (and then television) bulletins than anyone else'. His friendship with my family continued long beyond BBC days and I personally remember him fondly for trying to teach me Latin for my school exams.

A remarkable story which caught Charles's attention at this time was about 'a very fine show' by the crew of a Whitley bomber of No. 51 Squadron on a leaflet raid over Poland. For over 11 hours they had been flying on dead reckoning when a strong headwind on the return forced them to land. Unfortunately and unknowingly they had put down in German territory. After landing they unloaded the aircraft's guns and stopped the engines. The pilots, a flying officer and a pilot officer, got out and were met by 'a group of peasants' advancing towards them from 200yd away. 'C'est France, n'est pas?' the flying officer asked, but the man shook his head. They tried again to which another man replied, very politely in a strong German accent, 'C'est l'Allemagne, la frontier est a vingt kilometres,' and obligingly pointed out the direction in which France lay.

'Like one man we turned and bolted for the machine,' the pilots said. But remembering it was some 200 yards away with the engines stopped, they sprinted back 'in about even time' and, 'saying something for British engines', they started right away. As they did so, another more hostile group were running towards them from the other end of the field. 'Our plane just roared out of that field without stopping to say thank you to the peasants,' they added. Luckily shots from the ground missed the aircraft and no damage was done.

Fortunately, the Flying Officer said later, they had enough petrol to make the 25km to the frontier, but before landing they made very sure they were over French territory. This was confirmed when they spotted a lighted hoarding advertising a popular French drink. Even so, after putting down four of the crew remained with the aircraft with engines running and guns loaded while the Flying Officer went to make sure. It had been the longest night flight in the war.

But that was not the end of the story. It took a day-and-a-half for it to be released and it was not until 8.40pm the following day that Charles had permission to phone the story through, although he just missed the 9 o'clock news. The next day he was allowed to interview the pilots for broadcasting. The Whitley captain, Flight Lieutenant Tomlin, was already sitting down at the microphone when 'someone at H.Q. banned the broadcast'. In the end he reported it himself.

No doubt enraged by the suppression of this story and the many other frustrations with the censors, the correspondents in France, including my father, went on strike. 'There was plenty of justification in our attitude,' he wrote. The strike brought to a head many long-standing grievances. These were settled for a time in March, but by May 'further incidents' resulted in the recall of all reporters with the AASF. This was only broken by the outbreak of real war – the blitzkrieg.

For the first industrial strike in March, my father and colleagues enjoyed a week of glorious weather and played golf at the Reims Golf Club. Gardner wrote, 'The only work I did in this period was to write a letter to the Radio Times describing our new studio and to record a piece which had nothing to do with France at all.' Because it had nothing to do with AASF the Strike Committee allowed it to be broadcast.

His letter first described proudly his new studio and how they had set it up for their first broadcast.

He wrote:

> We have taken over a top room in a house which used to belong to a French General. It's a very nice house too, and our window looks over a large garden and a summer house. We have some nice pictures of French aeroplanes, a visitors' book, a map of the front, a bottle of ink and some essentials like amplifiers, telephones, and batteries which the engineers have grouped very neatly around one wall. An RAF orderly has painted 'Silence, BBC on the Air' above one of the doorways.

He added, mischievously, 'we have even run to an outside warning light, so all we want is a commissionaire outside and a daily memorandum from somebody about the waste of paper-clips to make us think we are back in Portland Place'.

On a more serious note, he gave an example of the speed of delivering material from the studio. On one occasion they did a recording at an hour's notice. 'The lines had been asked for at eleven, they were over by twelve, and the report I made was in the news at one o'clock.' He concluded, thinking the worst:

> Our only fear now, having settled in so nicely here is THAT MAN will start something somewhere and we'll all have to move. In that case we'll probably fit the whole works up inside Harold [his little car] – and put a mast on the roof. Poor studio – I hope the Germans will treat the furniture well – we'll get it back one day.

A few weeks later his letter to the *Radio Times* was published alongside two photographs of him at work in the studio.[3]

Charles's recorded piece was concerned mostly with the controversy over the use of the cannon machine gun based on a recent speech by Harold Balfour, Under Secretary of State for Air. Charles's conclusion was that it would depend on the type of new aircraft but 'all the indications are in favour of the cannon'.

By 26 March the strike was called off, and having heard 'Cobber' Kain had succumbed to a measles epidemic, my father and other correspondents motored down to No. 73 Squadron at Rouvres to see what was happening. They soon discovered that Cobber (measles over) had shot down two Messerschmitts, but had been shot down and wounded. 'He had managed to bail out ; landed in No man's-land and then he had to bolt for the French Lines with a bit of shrapnel in his knee,' he wrote. They found him, 'hobbling about on a stick; his face all burned (his plane had caught fire) and his hand bandaged. He had just been awarded the DFC.'[4]

Gardner found that No. 73 Squadron had been involved in three or four different flights that day and had shot down seven Germans with no loss except for 'Cobber's' Hurricane. 'It was their busiest – and most successful day of the war.' He managed to get two pilots who were involved, Flying Officer Orton, who was shortly to be awarded a DFC, and Pilot Officer Perry, to go back with him to the studio in Reims where he broadcast a lengthy interview with them about the battle. Unfortunately Perry was killed the following day.

The day after this broadcast my father found 'a storm broke around my head and around the head of the BBC in London'. The press were again complaining of the advantage the BBC had by breaking news, particularly on the 9 o'clock bulletin which 'took the cream off any action before the pages of the morning papers were even made up'.

Gardner responded vigorously in his AASF book, defending the BBC and wrote a compelling reason why Fleet Street should not fight them on competitive grounds as though they were another newspaper:

> I, perhaps naturally, think they are barking up the wrong tree . . . no matter if the BBC were churning out 'hot' news all day, people would still buy papers. The spoken word is too fleet – it cannot be held, lingered over tasted and re-tasted. . . . a newspaper can be handled; preserved; discussed; re-read. It has a permanence which is, now, its greatest asset.

His deeply thought conviction still has relevance today despite the advance of numerous and instant Internet services.

Chapter Eight

Blitzkrieg

It was during another lull in RAF activities that, with tensions eased, some correspondents and a few RAF officers decided to bring their wives over to France, believing that the threatened spring offensive by the Germans was so overdue that it was probably postponed indefinitely. This included Charles's good friend Noel Monks of the *Daily Mail* and his 'petite and completely charming' American wife Mary Welsh, who gave up her then job on the *Daily Express* to move over to France.[1]

This was also time for frivolity, and my father tells of an escapade with 'Harold', his tiny car, and 'Cobber' Kain when, after a very good night in Paris, they tried to drive 'Harold' into the Hotel Gallia, where they were staying. 'We drove him up to the main door but the hall porter wouldn't undo the latch to let us take the car into the foyer. I said I always slept with Harold and Cobb backed me up, so there was a long discussion while Harold's headlights shone longingly into the hotel lounge.' In the end, they had to reverse the car back onto the roadway.

It was almost appropriate that an Air Ministry order unwittingly reflected the times. It stated: 'Despite the lull in air activity there is still a threat of a sudden German air attack on a big scale. And as a consequence in future gas masks were always to be carried and anti-gas clothing were to be kept at hand at work.' My father described the order as 'rather shattering'.

But how serious was the threat? Gardner talked to a French Air Ministry official about the possibility of a full-scale war and the likelihood of the bombing of their factories, towns and railways. The official responded, 'why do you think the Germans have abandoned for these last seven months the methods of land terror which they have always used up to now? Why haven't they bombed our open towns and factories? I'll tell you, it's the same with us as it is with you British – they are frightened of reprisals from the French Air Force.' Although the Armée de l'Air had been built up rapidly, it was, in Charles's words, 'as good as anything of their class in the world'. Unfortunately the French official was soon to be proved wrong.

By Easter the mood in Paris was still jolly and a group of friends including Mary Welsh, Noel and Charles held a ceremonial dinner complete with 'a violinist who played Chopin'. He recalled, 'This brought waves of nostalgia gulfing over me and the thought I, too, was about to commit, what proved to be an elementary mistake, by bringing my wife and infant over to Paris added too, rather than damned, the rush of home-yearning which that evening brought.'

And a mistake it proved to be which my father would have realised almost as soon as he had made a quick trip to London to fix passports for Eve and 'Umbrage'. For no sooner had he made the necessary arrangements, the Germans on 9 April invaded Denmark and Norway and the whole well-being of Western Europe was brought into doubt. But it was too late and there was still no certainty the Germans would continue to advance. And so it was on 13 April, an auspicious day, my mother and I flew to France arriving at Le Bourget airport together with the wife and child of colleague 'Groucho' Roland of the Exchange Telegraph press agency.

The arrival was not without difficulty and delay as Charles and 'Groucho' waited for their families while a procession of Imperial Airways planes arrived without them.

He wrote later:

> Then a second Dewoitine [arrived] and the first thing I saw through its windows was 'Umbrage's' little red pixie hat, perkily bobbing about. Our wives, both well and very happy were disgorged – and it appeared that neither infant had been sick or naughty. Umbrage in fact had so taken to the aeroplane that he kicked up a hell of a fuss when we had to get him out. He walked across the tarmac all by himself – carrying a tiny attaché case – and then turned back to the Dewoitine and clutched at it – I had to drag him away.[2]

The party then drove to Le Tremblay near Versailles where Groucho's aunts, who ran a shop in Paris, had a cottage where they had been invited to stay until they could fix up permanent accommodation. 'The aunts' cottage was a dream,' Charles wrote, 'whitewashed walls, beautiful lawns and loggias, flowers and lovely old furniture. Eve could hardly speak for happiness and excitement, while Umbrage wandered around and made noises.'

Meanwhile there had been further air combat activity involving No. 1 Squadron. Gardner was unable to persuade any of the pilots to be interviewed so he described it in his own words. 'The Royal Air Force on the Western Front have for the second time this week, beaten three times their own number of Messerschmitts. The most important thing about the encounters was that one of the enemy fighters shot down was a twin-engined Messerschmitt 110, the first to be shot down on the front.'

There were further stories of RAF success as described by several pilots. One sergeant pilot in a Hurricane told him how he found a Messerschmitt 110 on his tail and 'did such a steep turn that I blacked out'. When he came to again he had spun down to 2,000 or 3,000ft. The fight began again this time with two Me 110s on his tail and one in front. Despite being fired on and having taken 'violent evasive action', he got some shots in but wasn't hit although he thought he got one of them. After that all the other 110s turned away and put their noses towards home.

As a result of this successful period of air combat, Air Marshal Barratt, Commander-in Chief, flew down to the fighter squadrons to congratulate the pilots and ground crews personally. His visit was kept secret from the press, because the RAF were concerned about personal publicity for their pilots and officers which was not approved by the Service. On this occasion, by chance, Monks and Roland were at Rouvres when the Air Marshal arrived and he reluctantly agreed to be interviewed, but was not drawn on the reason for secrecy.

However, the whole issue of identifying and praising individual pilots for their gallantry was still a controversial subject. This was emphasised by a visit by 'Cobber' Kain, who was passing through Reims on his way for leave and to receive his DFC.

My father wrote:

He looked tired and ill and was obviously nervous. I felt very sorry for Cobb because apart from the strain of his experiences and daily patrols, he was the football in a 'higher policy' row about individual publicity which was no fault of his at all. If anyone was to blame, we were, because the correspondents were writing some sort of story about him every day. Naturally this annoyed other pilots who were doing just as much work (which they probably were) and poor Cob got the kicks.

As far as the invasion of Norway and Denmark was concerned, Gardner observed that once the Germans had established air bases in Norway, 'it became obvious there was little we could do'. This was because there were no suitable long-range fighters and all they could get out there was a squadron of Gladiators (biplanes). 'Although,' he stated, 'The work of that squadron makes one of the finest chapters in RAF history. They flew and fought until only one machine was fit to take to the air.'

Having left the family at Le Tremblay, 'Groucho' and Charles drove back to Reims where there was a 'flap on' in anticipation of deployment by aircraft and journalists to Norway. But this soon died down and the two fighter squadrons returned to their frontier duties. He was pleased to receive his promised recording gear which had been brought out by Arthur Phillips, but it was to be used only once.

The RAF were now engaged in more air combat encounters, which were growing steadily. 'RAF fighters on the Western Front have for the second time this week beaten three times their own number of Messerchmitts,' he reported and then gave further details of individual actions and dogfights including the first air combat to be seen over Reims. 'In our stories of this time can be seen the seed of that fighting superiority which was to flower at Dunkirk,' he wrote. 'The Hurricanes were proving themselves to be the most formidable fighting weapon which had ever taken to French skies.'

During this time my father and 'Groucho' were still managing to get back to Le Tremblay for weekends.

He wrote:

> We were having a happy time taking our wives and children to Paris. Those were the happiest days of the war for us because both Groucho and I knew at the back of our minds that the storm was coming. We hung pathetically on to those last days of sunshine. We mowed the lawns at the cottage, walked up to the farm to get milk, we wore grey flannels, and did all the escapist things which men do when they don't want to stop and think.

But back at Reims they now found they were facing a major problem. New censor conditions had been brought in which demanded that news could only be obtained through the RAF Press Officers. Visits to airfields and interviews with pilots would only be allowed under strict supervision. Such was the feeling of the correspondents against these restrictions that strike action was again taken and news coverage ceased.

Most of the journalists were recalled and Gardner returned to London to report on the impasse which effectively prevented him filing any stories. He secured a promise from the BBC that they would never require him or any of their correspondents to work under these conditions. Even so, he returned to France on 8 May, ready to help move his family to a flat he had taken at Versailles. Most of the other correspondents stayed in London to take up the censorship restrictions with the government.

But events overtook all such discussion. On 10 May the Germans invaded Holland, Luxembourg and Belgium and began moving towards France. It was the day Winston Churchill took office as Prime Minister. The feared blitzkrieg had begun and the 'phoney war' was over.

Now everything was to change, and these must have been fearful times for my parents. After just two days my father had to leave the flat, which was still surrounded by half unpacked luggage, say goodbye to his wife, whom he might not see again:

> Poor Eve – she was tearful – yet very brave. Her glorious week had vanished and instead she was just a lonely and deserted wife in a strange foreign town. I wouldn't let her come downstairs to see me off – and instead she leaned through the window and waved. I stood on the pavement and said 'good-bye.' An old French woman who was passing turned round and said in English, 'Ah – there are so many good-byes being said today – so many. Good luck young man.'

From now on Charles decided to reproduce in his AASF book his personal daily diary entries giving a blow-by-blow account of those first few terrifying days of the blitzkrieg. This would give 'a better reflection of the changing picture of the war than I could possibly write now in the after-knowledge of the fall of France,' he wrote. He added that his diary had many shortcomings, 'The worst of which is they cover only the things of which I had personal knowledge.'

Returning from Versailles to Reims on that fateful May day, he found the town had already been bombed, the aerodrome raided and other damage caused in the area. Significantly all the 'secret aerodromes' had been pinpointed and bombed. Although news was confused, the RAF had sustained no casualties and only a few planes damaged.

That night Gardner did his first 'real war' broadcast during a raid wearing a tin hat. 'Just as I started recording the siren went for the "all clear" so I took the mike over the window and got the noise and effects in on my piece. It was broadcast at nine o'clock, in the news and I could hear the sirens coming through very well.'

The fighter squadrons were now being bombed on the aerodrome. 'Cobber' told him they were just taking off when the Germans started bombing. 'We all lay under the wings of our planes . . . I've never been so scared in my life.' But even so they carried on, and in all No. 1 and No. 73 Squadrons shot down sixteen Germans that day and lost no pilots themselves. Charles concluded on the first day's fighting: 'The general situation seems to be on our side. The German attack has been held up all along the line – and held up on the one day when it should have gained most of its ground.' He later discovered this was not true, 'The French censor had been "faking the news" which should be a lesson to us.'

The following day – Saturday – at 5.30am he had his first experience of a bombing raid. 'The sirens fetched me leaping out of bed – and foolishly I went out into the street just as our anti-aircraft guns were opening up.' He saw a Junkers 88 'sailing serenely along, directly overhead at 10,000ft – just the height for precision bombing'. Then the 'crump crump' of the AA guns. 'This, I thought is no place for me so – so I went inside again,' he wrote.

A few minutes later a couple of Dorniers 'sprang from nowhere' and began circling the town with no fighter in sight. Down came the bombs and Charles wished he had made for the safety of a shelter rather than relying on the thin structure of the hotel. He watched from his window as the Dorniers circled at 500ft and so he went out again to watch and described the scene: 'The crump of the bombs reached my ears and I also heard a second Dornier flying at nought feet down the main street and letting off with his pop-gun. I went into the hotel again, as Cobb would say "like a dose of salts."' He discovered later that the Dorniers had dropped 2,000lb bombs but missed their target, 'which is bad bombing, especially from their low height and without interruption'.

Two days after the blitzkrieg, Gardner had news of a British bomber squadron attack which had saved a large force of French troops from being cut off in a difficult position in Holland. His report, which we have at home, is fascinating because it contains the actual pen-written amendments by the censor and a covering letter from him saying 'this is very good'. The amendments include substituting 'assisting' for 'saved' for a large force of French troops, replacing Holland with 'the Low Countries' and changing 'two flights of Fairey Battles' to 'two sections of bombers'.

However, the main story remained and Charles stated: 'Our pilots did their work so well that today the squadron has received telegrams of congratulations from the French High Command , from Air Chief Marshal Sir Cyril Newall in England and the Commanding Officer of the British Forces in France, Air Vice Marshal Barratt.'

He described how French forces were falling back to lines of defence (crossed out and changed to 'a prepared line of defence') and, he wrote, 'were engaged in a race with an advanced German motorised column which was rushing round to try and cut them off. It seemed possible that the Germans might manage it – and so the order went out –"hold up the German column."'

He continued, 'Maps were produced at our squadron headquarters and the road situation studied carefully. It became obvious that the enemy might be able to use either of two roads . . . so both were marked down as targets and the pilots told to bomb them until they were both blocked sufficiently to hold up the enemy.'

This they successfully did and two of the pilots, one from Australia and the other from Canada were interviewed by my father. They told how they did this at very low level taking care not to hit any civilians on the ground by flying up and down to warn them to take shelter. The only potential casualty was recalled by the Canadian pilot whose name was Crooks (but not used). He said, 'On the way in he heard noises which sounded like machine gun fire – but nothing hit the plane, although I believe a bullet did come up through the floor of the leader's machine – and just missed his legs.'

Back at Reims, Gardner reported that the raids continued nightly pinpointing the RAF airfields and the Chateau Thierry HQ, which had a near escape when its windows were blown out, 'so much for our closely guarded secrets,' he remarked. And every night he continued to broadcast, often while bombs were going off. The sound of these explosions he continued to capture by dangling the microphone outside the window. During one raid by two Heinkels who were machine-gunning the main street in Reims, he was trapped in the back of a car. 'I tried to get out, but the door was jammed. I yelled "Let me out of here" – and Noel Monks came running up and undid the damned thing.' He dashed into a shop and saw a Hurricane go after the Heinkel and shot it down. In his diary he reflected: 'I must say that I viewed this with great pleasure. Not long ago I would have been disturbed at the unpleasant end of these Germans, but now I am jingoistic and as bloodthirsty as anyone.'

The Germans were now reported to have got through the Sedan region of north-eastern France, but what about the impregnable Maginot Line which he had visited a few months ago? 'I always thought that although the Maginot Line proper ended a little south of there, (Sedan) that an equally strong line turned round Luxembourg and Belgium.' He was wrong and the Germans were through and advancing quickly.

The two Hurricane squadrons were now having to face odds of up to twenty to one on every encounter and had been fighting and flying since the blitzkrieg had begun. 'How any of our people get out alive beats me,' he wrote. But casualties mounted, especially with the bomber force which was now attacking German airfields, roads, bridges and other strategic targets. They took terrible punishment and lost nearly 60 per cent of their aircraft and crew. Flight Lieutenant Kerrigan, whom Charles had met many times and to whom his book was partly dedicated, was killed. He was last seen low down over Germany – and in flames. 'I suppose we shall get used to seeing people we like going west one way or another,' Charles wrote.

With the blitzkrieg tanks and troops moving towards them, my father 'slipped up to Versailles' to see how the family was. 'Poor Eve was worried stiff with uncertainty', and he decided he had to get them back to England as soon as possible. 'I think she is far safer in Fetcham, and I don't like the nearness of those big barracks at Versailles.'

Back at Reims he found the whole of the AASF were already 'on the run – though heaven knows where', and everyone had been put on one hour's notice to leave. So after a visit to HQ at the Chateau Thierry, where many colleagues had gathered, Charles drove first back to Paris where he found the Embassy 'in a flap' burning all its papers. 'Everyone was preparing to evacuate town. I've never felt so depressed. If only we'd got more aeroplanes,' he wrote. This was because there had been much debate about the deployment of the RAF's scarce resources and whether they should reinforce the AASF at the expense of depleting the home-based squadrons which would be required to defend the country against a likely attack by the Germans. It was decided to protect the homeland first.

My father then drove on to Versailles to rescue Eve and me. In Paris he had heard that there was a boat leaving for England from Le Havre. He loaded us and as much of our belongings as possible into 'Harold' and set out for the port only to find when he got there that the boat wasn't leaving for two days. Charles wrote: 'We managed to find a hotel after a long tour – and I spent two of the worst days in my life getting the family away. All the time I was scared stiff that Le Havre would be bombed.'

Finally, despite a false air raid alarm in the night while the boat was by the quay, it sailed at 4am. It was the last passenger vessel to cross the Channel until the end of the war. Having seen Eve and 'Umbrage' off, Charles turned round and drove for Paris having had no food or sleep only to be arrested by French soldiers on patrol looking for German parachutists. He was hauled off to a police station where he was eventually able to convince them of his observer status and was allowed to drive on. 'You were lucky you weren't shot,' he was told by a friend.

Back in Paris he discovered that the Press Officer system had broken down, and there was no communication with the AASF. Most of the correspondents were now there, having left Reims, while the BBC office was 'down in the mouth' and talking about evacuating the place. No one knew where the AASF were and he could get no military information except what he read in the newspapers. He confided in his diary: 'Everybody's been hanging around this town getting depressed-er and depressed-er but we have found out where the remains of the AASF have beaten it to. As I write this the place is so secret that I can't even put it down here.' It was Troynes.

Troynes was about the same distance away from Paris as Reims, so everyone wanted to go down there despite there being no telephone or any other way of getting news out. Nevertheless they set up a rota system whereby two of them went down in the morning and returned in the afternoon, 'to give the other boys the dope'. Nobody knew how long the AASF were going to stay there. 'Everyone is under six hours notice to get out. The aerodromes are established but only just – and anyway we've got precious few aircraft to put on them,' Charles wrote.

Eventually permission was given for Charles and his colleagues to move down to Troynes but now there was no one who would censor their stories so they returned to Paris. 'Our job was now virtually washed up,' Gardner wrote, although he tried again to get news from Troynes by driving down 'once or twice to see what I could pick up'. But this proved hazardous because of numerous armed anti-parachute patrols which often waved them to stop. 'These men may quite easily not be French troops at all – but parachute spies themselves.' So when he was driving alone he always carried an automatic pistol 'prepared to take at least one German with me'.[3]

And on one occasion he nearly had to use it, as he described in his diary:

At one particularly fishy-looking control I was within an ace of trusting to luck and using it. One of the unshaven dirty-looking French soldiers, who had sprung out of a ditch at the car, walked behind it when I stopped and covered the back of my head with a gun. I watched him through the mirror – and just as I was going to my pocket for my pistol, he let the barrel of his gun drop while he talked to a companion.

Gardner then produced his papers and the moment he was given them back he, 'trod on the gas – ducked and beat it'.

At the time nobody knew where the Germans were, and at Troynes he found 'no one seemed very coherent about the doings of our own squadrons'. The only concrete story Gardner got was the raid on a secret target. This was a chateau in the Ardennes where members of the German High Command were believed to be gathering. A squadron of Fairey Battles found the target and scored direct hits. 'The chateau was certainly blown out but whether there was anyone inside it at the time isn't known,' Charles reported.

Although RAF squadrons were involved in some of the fiercest fighting against overwhelming odds trying to contain the ever advancing Germans, my father found that 'any attempt at reporting was more or less abandoned' and other journalists were now being called home.

But one piece of news he was not pleased to report – 'Cobber' Kain had been killed. The irony was this was not in mortal combat but was on his very last day in France before being transferred back to England. As a celebratory gesture, Kain decided to 'beat up the airfield' and put on a display of aerobatics, something he had enjoyed doing since he first joined the RAF and particularly over enemy search-lights. As a last manoeuvre he performed a low-level loop but failed to pull up in time and crashed fatally into the ground. It had only been a few days since Charles last met up with 'Cobber', which turned out to be the last time. 'How that lad does keep alive! He'd been in about ten scraps, but, like all his squadron was losing count of how many Germans he had shot down,' he wrote. His last words were, 'See you in England.' Three days later he was killed.

Looking back at the blitzkrieg campaign which began at 5am on 10 May and lasted for one month and six days, Gardner wrote: 'Great deeds were done particularly (as the fighter pilots will tell you) by the bomber crews. Sometimes escorted – but many times not – those Battles and Blenheim pilots fought their way to glory, in their attempts to succeed where the French army failed.' He added, 'No praise is high enough – and no courage in our history has the better of theirs.'

Of the fighters, he declared, 'Outnumbered but never subdued – leapt off the ground day after day to attempt the impossible. They knew they had little chance of holding up the sky-filling waves of escorted German bombers; but they still entered the fight with their tails up – and often left the Germans with theirs either well down or shot off!'

With communications gone, and with no chance of doing any live broadcasts, it was now time to go. With some luck and some aviation knowledge, my father managed to get a passage on an Air France flight via Cherbourg and Poole to London returning to Heston on 2 June. The day after, Paris was bombed for the first time. As for his BBC colleagues, he had already managed to get his two engineers and radio gear back to England in a Bristol Bombay aircraft 'we found at Le Bourget'. He wrote, 'The pilot was only too pleased to take it to Hendon – provided he was absolved of all responsibility.'

He enquired after the other correspondents and friends and how they had got on. He discovered later that some were able to get out by air and others had to take their chance on a ship at Bordeaux and other Atlantic ports. Noel Monks had driven south and managed to collect his wife 'somewhere'. But 'Groucho' Roland and his family were missing for some time but were eventually located still at Le Tremblay and safe.

Chapter Nine

Sedan and the Last Days of France

Before leaving France, my father put together a series of consecutive despatches from 17 May to 1 June covering the last days of France before the final capitulation. They detailed the RAF response to the Battle of Sedan and subsequent engagements which the French papers described as 'the biggest the world has known'. The town of Sedan, located on the east bank of the River Meuse, close to the Belgian border, was captured 'without a struggle' by advancing German forces on 10 May. It allowed German armament to cross the river on the undestroyed bridges and move towards the English Channel, cutting off the main French forces.

It was a decisive move, and Winston Churchill described in his history of the Second World War how he learned of the disaster.

He wrote:

> About half-past seven on the morning of the 15th I was woken up with the news that M. Reynaud (French Prime Minister) was on the telephone at my bedside. He spoke in English, and evidently under stress. 'We have been defeated.' As I didn't immediately respond he said again, 'We are beaten, we have lost the battle.' I said 'Surely it can't happen so soon?' But he replied: 'The front is broken near Sedan; they are pouring through in great numbers with tanks and armoured cars' – or words to that effect.

Shortly afterwards the Germans entered France and on 22 June the French were forced to sign an Armistice leading to the German occupation.

As an introduction to his despatches, describing those terrible days, Charles wrote:

> The messages which follow were the last I managed to get out of France. The first ones were put out from the Paris studios in

Rue de Grenelle, but one night, just as I was beginning to start there was a loud 'plop' in my phones and that was the end of the Paris – London line. It had been blown up to prevent it falling into German hands and, since there was no alternative route, that was that.

Charles continued, 'For a day or two both Edward Ward [his BBC war correspondent colleague] and I put some talks across in French broadcasting time in the hope they would be picked up and recorded in London. But there were many flaws in this system and, in the end we had to give up.' He concluded, 'These despatches are often reproduced just as they were passed by the censors save that, in several places, I have again added names or short notes in brackets.'

The following despatches began on 17 May, two days after the French premier's call to Mr Churchill. They are written in an over optimistic way, for at the time he would not have had much to go on except his belief in the prowess of the RAF over the Luftwaffe. Even if he had known of the full extent of the tragedy on the ground, he would almost certainly have been prevented from reporting it by the censors.

Because the reports cover a period of great importance in the losing fight for France and are less well-known – particularly the Sedan operation – I have devoted this chapter to them.

May 17. In the last five days the Royal Air Force has written into its history pages which, I'm certain, can never be forgotten. We here, who are permitted to know and to see some of their work can at least pay tribute to a bravery which has always gone far beyond the needs of duty. And although the pilots themselves would be the last to want it, I feel that in this – the first despatch from here for three fierce days – one can do no less than express a sincere and, to us who have met the men, personal admiration.

The main task of these pilots and crews has been concerned with the Battle of Sedan, a battle which is, at this moment still raging. The action of the Advanced Air Striking Force in the earlier phase was to bomb and to bomb again – without cessation and in the face of enormous odds. Those columns of German armoured cars, their lines of supply, and the bridges over which they came had to be stopped or destroyed, and the Royal Air Force, flying literally side-by-side with the French Armée de L'Air took it on. Backing up the French ground troops they played a decisive part in slowing up that first rush, and gigantic air battles had covered the skies over the contested ground.

And now the Germans are pushing against the French defence again – but today they have another problem as well as that of the actual battle. It is one of supplies, and particularly supplies of petrol to the armoured columns. So, once again our air forces are taking what may prove to be decisive action to help the defenders. They are going full out for those lines of supply, and they have already had great success. In addition the RAF has gone even deeper – it has bombed the fuel stores at Bremen and other places, knowing that petrol is the life-blood of this blitzkrieg.

The Germans are aware of that and are defending those supplies with vast hordes of fighters. The result is that the air war is now in its most confusing but vital stage. The size and fierceness of the dog fights one has to leave to the imagination, but what is a concrete fact is that we have always come out best of the fighter to fighter encounters and our bombers have practically always reached their objectives. Some times they have gone down to tree level to do it and they have even flown round trees with machine guns blazing away at them from the ground with our rear gunners fighting successions of chasing Messerschmitts.

And in all this, our losses have been less than one might have thought. And one of the most amazing things has been the way in which our pilots who have been given up as lost keep on rolling in. It is sometimes days after they have been put down as missing, they have turned up at squadron headquarters in borrowed motor cars, on foot and by all sorts of transport. The important result is that our losses in crews *is* considerably less than our losses in aircraft.

Now, a final word about the work of the fighter squadrons. I think a fair summary of the situation was given to me by a young Hurricane pilot [Ginger Paul] who was taking a couple of hours off after two days of dawn to dusk flying and fighting. He said, 'We had a wizard scrap this morning – five of us and only eight of them. We got five and lost nothing and the other three ran away.' The phrase which impressed me was 'five of us and only eight of them.'

May 18. Today's news is that our bombers have continued their vital attacks on the now struggling German lines of communication. They have done their work with great success and the fighters which escorted them have shot down another large number of Messerschmitts. One large formation of medium bombers has concentrated on targets in the Rethel area. The formation came down the road at almost no height at all, skimming over the tree tops and dropping shower upon shower of bombs upon enemy convoys and supply columns. They destroyed one pom-pom battery and two machine gun nests and subsequently blocked the road in several places. We only lost one machine in this raid.

You may remember that I said last night that one of the features of this air war has been the reappearance of our pilots and crews who had provisionally been reported missing. To-day I heard a couple more stories of this happening, one a particularly gallant adventure. One of our bombers had been shot down and all three of the crew were wounded but managed to get out of the machine but in enemy country. Two of the men were so badly wounded that they could not avoid capture. But the pilot, although he was hit in two places, managed to hobble away from the Germans. Wounded as he was, he then swam the River Meuse at a point where it was under German control, and managed to crawl to French lines where he was treated and taken to hospital.

The second adventure was that of a sergeant, who bailed out with his parachute after his machine was shot down. He fell into No Man's Land and, being unarmed, made for the shelter of a wood. As soon as he got there he heard someone moving about and realised capture was inevitable. The noise of the movement got nearer and nearer and then around a tree came another man – he was a French pilot who had also been shot down. The two shook hands and together they escaped to our lines.

May 22. For the last two days the extension of the German advance has been throwing more and more work on the bombers of the Royal Air Force and both the machines from home and from the AASF have been flying and attacking incessantly. A squadron leader in one of the units has told us of his impressions of bombing German supply columns and tanks. He said, 'The first time I saw them on the move I thought – what a wonderful target they make. And when I came to bomb them I found I was right.' He said that time and time again when attacking lorries he saw them crash into the roadside and into each other, and the men inside scuttle out for shelter. Bombing them was far from easy as they were defended by strings of mobile light machine guns and by heavier, but still mobile A.A. guns.

One of the latest big raids by the AASF was with forty or fifty aircraft bombing targets in German-occupied Belgium. These included Dinant, Givet, and Fermoy, where fires were started and direct hits were seen. In woods, which might be hiding German ammunition and supply dumps, were also bombed and gunned. In all these attacks only one of our planes is missing. Another night raid located a group of twenty-three German searchlights north west of Sedan, and these were put out of action.

A pilot from a squadron which is now famous throughout the whole of the Air Force in France, and which – if we could have revealed its number – has not long ago been given his DFC, the second in its unit [this was Orton of 73 Squadron]. He has just reappeared having been shot down. He bailed out at 500ft – and he was lucky because his parachute opened in time, although he did drop heavily he got away with an injured shoulder [actually he was badly burned too].

A good many of the pilots in this squadron – including this one I have just mentioned – have got victories which run well into the twenties. And now they've started a sweepstake among themselves as to who is going to reach fifty first.

May 23. A number of estimates – both official and unofficial – have been made lately as to the number of planes which the German Air Force has lost since the beginning of the war and, especially, since the beginning of the invasion of Belgium, Holland and Luxembourg. The latest of this series of estimates is said to come from Germany itself and this puts the Lufwaffe's losses at 2,237 machines since September and 1,522 pilots killed, wounded or missing.

I think we would be deceiving ourselves if we said that the morale of the German air force is bad. There is, so far, little sign of that. But what I think is true – is that their pilots aren't very good and must get worse. Incidents that I have seen out here, in air fights and in enemy bombing raids, lead me to the conclusion myself – without reference to figures – or even to admissions by prisoners – about the small number of flying hours they had got in before being sent over the lines. [At the end of this despatch my father wrote: 'The above message was sent to London by air, but it was not allowed to be published at the time. An almost similar article, compiled from the same figures, did, however, appear in the Times and, in fact, Narracott, the Times man with the AASF and I wrote our pieces together and swopped notes.']

May 24. The work of the Royal Air Force, both at home and here in France with the AASF is still to disorganise the German communications and columns. This work has now reached an intensity which only the German Command can appreciate. We here only get news of isolated raids – of bombing carried out by this particular squadron or by that. But these raids, dovetailed as they are with raids from home and with attacks from the bombers working in the army zone, fit together with the efforts of the French to make an almost non-stop shower of bombs on the whole of the German occupied area. This goes on, thanks to the moon and the brilliant navigating of our observers by night as well as day.

The confusion behind the spearhead of the German attack must, by now, have reached grave proportions. One of the biggest difficulties in a total air war of this sort is knowing just what damage has been done. Naturally, the Germans themselves won't give anything away. The night raids from here have been particularly successful, all the more so because interception by fighters at night especially by those German fighters now operating from temporary bases, is very difficult, in fact without searchlights almost impossible. We have managed to inflict a lot of destruction among these searchlights, which the Germans have rushed up to help them out of this night raid menace, with the result that our black-out attacks have been very fruitful indeed.

Last night, for instance, a force of our medium bombers found a line of German lorries and other transports all drawn up for night alongside the roadside. Down they went and scored direct hits – all along the line – and then they spared some bombs for an AA battery which opened up on them. Later they bombed tanks and troops, and also a convoy which was trying to move up under cover of darkness. Apparently it didn't move very far.

Still flying on, looking for targets, our bombers made what they themselves called a 'furious machine gun attack' on another convoy, on which every machine gun on every plane was blazing away. And then, before coming home they found a long column of German armed fighting vehicles, by which they mean light tanks and motorcycles. This convoy was struggling through a village, and stuck out – as it were – at both ends of it. Several direct hits were seen on this line and a lot of havoc caused. And this is last night's diary of only one raiding force.

Going even farther behind the immediate line, there has been an attack on a Rhine town [Bingen], where a convoy was caught, and other bombing raids were on re-victualling yards, blast furnaces, railway junctions and factories.

On 30 May and 1 June (his last despatch), my father recorded similar bombing raids, and of further tales of individual bravery. Clearly, the RAF did inflict much damage on the Germans from the air, but on the ground it was a very different story as German forces were now thundering towards the French border.

The German advance, of course, caused a huge number of casualties, both French and Allied soldiers and thousands of fleeing refugees. In one of his last and most moving reports my father witnessed their distress, and said:

> All this weekend on the roads leading west there have been streams of refugees. They have come from Luxenbourg, from towns on the French–Belgium frontier and all are being evacuated. These people are using anything on wheels that they can get hold of to move their families and to salvage a few of their most treasured belongings.
>
> In five minutes today I passed a couple of farm carts drawn by tired-looking horses. They must have started out last Friday morning. Then came a motor car of unbelievable age piled high on top with bedding and a couple of perambulators.
>
> This morning I spoke to some of them, tired, unshaven men, silent women clutching pathetic little parcels of food, children bewildered and frightened. And yet all of them so touchingly grateful for the least kindness one could do. I asked them where they were going, they didn't know – Paris perhaps – they used to have some relations there years ago – perhaps they were still there, they weren't sure. And if the relations had gone – a shrug of the shoulders, that was a trouble for tomorrow. Until then there remained the problem of the moment which was getting the car to start again.

The memory of those poor people, who in increasing numbers wandered the roads of France, dodging the many air attacks and frightened they would be over-run by German patrols or tanks at any moment, never left him.

To conclude his reports on his last few days in France and later in retrospect with the gift of hindsight, he was able to give a truer overall picture of what went on during those first few desperate days of the real war and, in particular, the response by the RAF which took very heavy losses, while its 'secret aerodromes' were heavily bombed forcing them to withdraw and eventually return to England.

By introduction, he stated that looking back on the active life of the AASF in France fell into four sections thus:

Phase One (May 10 to May 16). The AASF had particularly heavy and dangerous work to do. German troop concentrations and columns had to be bombed and every effort made to prevent the enemy from reaching the line of the Dyle before the British and French forces had taken up their positions in Belgium.[1] In addition the Dutch had failed to blow the important bridges at Maastricht and French Fifth Columnists had deliberately omitted to do the same thing with their Meuse bridges.

This period was one of heavy losses to the Battle squadrons because their attacks had to be daylight ones against small and heavily defended targets. These raids were difficult in other ways as well, and many times machines had to fly around in danger areas, looking for enemy troops, who had either moved, or dispersed since our last Intelligence reports of their whereabouts.

Also, right from the start, the AASF was troubled by the heavy German air attacks on its bases, attacks which coupled with the land force threat via the Sedan, forced the move to Troynes on May 16.

On May 10 and May 11 the Battles had to bomb German troops advancing through Luxembourg and on May 12 the canal bridges on roads leading west from Maastricht had to be destroyed.[2] On the same day and the following day more raids were made on German troop columns advancing – particularly those advancing on Antwerp.

On May 14 the French had to admit the seriousness of the advance over the Meuse at Sedan, and at once the Battles were ordered off to bomb the remaining Meuse bridges. They pressed home low-level attacks in the face of very heavy defences – and caused great damage but their losses were heavy, but the bridges remained intact.

On the night of May 15 the enemy advanced at Sedan and made the position of Reims insecure, and at dawn on May 16 the AASF was ordered to the new aerodrome at Troynes. One thing had become very apparent during the first phase and that was the high percentage of losses resulting from daylight attacks on heavily defended targets. Unfortunately, the Battle squadrons were not too well trained in night flying, having concentrated mainly on the practice of low-flying day attacks in conjunction with land forces.

There was, therefore, a swing round in opinion and as a result of general readiness to go over to night flying as the best way to maintain attacks and, at the same time, reduce casualties. Night operations were accordingly begun on the night of May 20 and the losses enormously reduced. For example, between May 20 and June 15, the Battles flew on 996 raids – 528 by day and 468 by night. The day casualties were 100 or 19 per cent, and the night casualties were 5 or 1.07 per cent. In that time the AASF dropped 317 tons of bombs on the enemy.

Phase Two. During the period when the AASF were based at Troynes, the fighters were used mainly for cover for the Battles, and there were far fewer combats than there had been at Reims.

German air attacks on new aerodromes near Troynes were also less intense probably because of the more natural camouflage of the fields in Southern Champagne and Operational HQ continued to remain at Troynes until June 10. On that date Air Marshal Barratt's HQ moved from Coulomniers (where it had remained all the time until then) to Orleans and AASF HQ moved with it to Muides near Blois on the Loire. The Troynes aerodromes were still used for re-fuelling, but the squadrons were based on the Blois basin.

Phase Three. In this, the Battles were used right to the end, in attacks against Germans crossing the Seine. The enemy was very well defended, both by AA and by Messerschmitts. The AASF with much pin-point work to do, had many more losses. They were then, obviously, fighting a forlorn hope, and it is very doubtful if their gallant raids had any appreciable effect on the enemy advance. The French Amy had cracked and our bombing was not backed up by any ground defence against the invaders.

Although the weary pilots and crews still went for their objectives with a zeal and courage, the inevitable end of the campaign was becoming depressingly clear. On June 15, therefore, the Battles instead of retreating, as once planned to a new aerodrome round Rennes and Nantes, were flown straight home.

Phase Four. This was purely a fighter phase. Up to June 15 the Hurricanes had both been covering the Battle raids and the evacuation of British troops at Le Havre. They had many successful flights, but, as usual were always outnumbered.

When the Battles went home, three fighter squadrons Nos 1, 73 and 501 remained at Nantes to cover the retreat, while Nos 17 and 242 went to Dinard. They too came to England when the evacuation was complete.

In conclusion Gardner stated:

> The main lesson learnt from the unhappy experience of the AASF was that accurate attack against small and well defended targets is bound to be costly, particularly so when aircraft are called upon – as the Battles were – to do the work which infantry and artillery failed to do. Night operations greatly reduced losses, and though the AASF was only at the beginning of its experience as a night-flying force, there was great improvement in the casualty figures after May 20.
>
> It is no good speculating on the difference better or earlier night-flying would have made, because many of the targets, such as bridges, were so small and so important that day attacks were essential for their greater accuracy.

And so ended AASF's campaign in France and so began a completely new phase of the Second World War as Britain defended its home base, and the Battle of Britain began.

Chapter Ten

Blitzkrieg to Dunkirk

An entry stamp in my father's 1937 passport confirmed his safe arrival at Heston airfield on 2 June 1940. He would have had a reasonably comfortable flight, even though there were two stops on the way. My mother wasn't so lucky. Her voyage back to Plymouth and the subsequent events have become a family legend.

Having spent three miserable days in Le Havre waiting for the ferry, she had eventually boarded the boat in the middle of the night for a 4am departure. She now found herself allocated a very small cabin which she was to share with another lady who also had a toddler in tow. Eve was lucky to find a cabin at all. Apparently she only did so because I ('Umbrage'), now on restraining reins, rushed ahead of the queue kicking the ankles of everybody in front and making a path through to the boat.

The problem for both mothers now was that after those days on shore waiting the delayed departure they had run out of nappies. Furthermore there were only the most rudimentary washing facilities in the ladies' lavatory. The cabin frankly stank. So when at last they arrived safely at Plymouth, having spent extra hours at sea dodging possible German air attack, my mother made her way to the comfort of the hotel which she knew and where she and Charles had spent a holiday the year before in Torquay.

But her hopes of a friendly welcome, having a wash and a comfortable bed after many sleepless nights were to be thwarted. Arriving on the steps of the hotel – one harassed mother with smelly child and battered baggage – she tried to enter the lobby. 'You can't come in' the doorman told her, 'I don't let vagrants in.'

My mother tried to explain the circumstances and the terrifying escape from France, the cause of their poor condition. She asked to speak to the manager, but this was refused. The doorman was having none of it.

So my mother, plus foul-smelling me, trudged off and eventually, after a long, crowded and uncomfortable train journey – unpleasant no doubt for fellow passengers – made her way home to Fetcham.

My father, on arrival at Heston, telephoned home and was relieved to find his wife and child safe and well. He was told what had happened at the hotel. Instead of going straight home, as would be expected after three gruelling weeks apart from his family, he went directly to Paddington and caught a train to Torquay. There, at the hotel – he was allowed in – he confronted the manager. I don't think the poor man knew what had hit him, but his offer of a free week's holiday at the hotel's expense was accepted. We do not know if it was ever taken up, nor what happened to the officious doorman.

Charles Gardner, as we know, was a compulsive writer. Apart from his work, he wrote everything from short stories, poems and essays of his personal observations and experiences. It is not surprising that he had it in mind to write the book about the AASF when he returned to England. He could draw upon all his original scripts for broadcasting and his frequent despatches, together with his daily diary for its content, as we have seen. The diary was, in fact, of some concern to him after the blitzkrieg in case it fell into German hands.[1] So he took the precaution of writing it on separate pieces of paper which he concealed in different places in his room until he safely brought them back to England.

He must have worked very hard, very quickly, for his book was published just before Christmas 1940 by the well-known London company Hutchinsons. It was probably the first authoritative account in book form of the RAF in action in France. But most particularly, it contained an informed analysis of the fighting strengths of the two opposing air forces together with future predictions on the likely outcome of the continued air battle over England, something that was on the minds of everyone at home.

He wrote:

> If Hitler ever counts on getting the RAF into a tails-down position, he is mistaking his men badly. All the time I was with AASF, in good days and bad, there was never the slightest doubt in the minds of our pilots that they were the better men. . . .
>
> Given anything like equality in performance of their aircraft, this glorious morale will carry us through weight of numbers. At the moment we have that precious thing – technical superiority. We must hold on to it, because in that and our men, is the certainty of victory.

This optimistic outlook was backed by a revised and complete summary of the achievements of the two Hurricane fighter squadrons, Nos 73 and 1, from 10 May (blitzkrieg) to 1 June, when they were re-deployed to safer positions in the south-west of France. During this period, when the fighting really started, 73 Squadron 'had bagged' fory-five certainties and thirty-one probables, while No. 1 Squadron had a similar record.

Charles also gave an indepth analysis of the likely threat to Britain of persistent bombing attacks by the Germans. In a broadcast in November, after taking his first spell of leave at home, he said the question he was most asked was what chance England would have against German bombing raids when the war in the air started. To answer this, while still in France, he sought the opinions of three of the most distinguished aviation journalists: the aforementioned H.F. King and Peter Masefield, together with Oliver Stewart, a former First World War pilot who had won a Military Cross and was now Editor of *Aeronautics Magazine*. They sat down with him in a Paris cafe to consider the situation and, he said, 'after a lot of discussion and drawing a lot of diagrams on the tablecloth came to certain conclusions'.

These conclusions, based on their analysis, were informed and thorough, taking into account all likely German bombing strategy and tactics, including long-range mass assaults, night bombing and short-range attacks. These were set against their chances of survival against the speed and manoeuvrability of RAF Spitfires and Hurricanes. The crucial effect of radar in identifying incoming raids is not recorded, either because they didn't know about it, which I think is unlikely, or because it was still secret and could not be reported. My belief is that it was covertly taken into consideration.

The team's reasoning and their conclusions filled three pages in the book. But in brief summary they concluded that 'slow and heavy long-range bombers which would require them to fly 1,600 miles (800 miles there and 800 miles back) carrying at least 1,000 lbs of bombs could not escape RAF fighters in good weather'. At night and in bad weather they stated that 'the odds swung slightly towards the bomber assuming the navigator can fly blind within say five miles of his target which is putting his navigation skills rather high'.

They decided that in, 'ignoring one of two unknown factors such as luck, surprise, or the failure of the defence in some unexpected way', long-range bombing over time couldn't pay economically, 'as it means the loss of a large number of aircraft and trained crews'.

As far as the prospects for the short-range bomber, Gardner said the team analysed the essential requirements for such a machine. This would require a range of around 300 miles, bomb load of about 500lb, armament of four forward fighting guns and two at the rear with a speed of around 320mph. This would give it 'almost a fifty-fifty chance in a fight', but the British had the geographic advantage of range to make short-range attacks against the Germans. However, after the collapse of France and the Germans now being able to use French airfields, Gardner stated that, 'The short range advantage was now with the Germans and they are trying to use it to the full. Unfortunately for them, however, our fighter defence is still better than their attack, and the results have been very heavy losses for the Luftwaffe.'

These predictions and their overall accuracy during the duration of the war is arguable. What they did was to cheer people up at home at a time when everyone feared the worst.

My father was also able to express again his deep appreciation for the RAF and in particular its men from his experiences in France which were to be contained in his AASF book. In an article for *London Calling*, the overseas journal of the BBC, in August, he wrote: 'It is the deeds of these men which I want to put on record, because, though they may be comparatively unimportant against the enormous and horrible backcloth of war, they do, together, form the glorious pattern of victory.'

In praising personal achievement he, perhaps controversially, challenged the traditional RAF position as expressed by Sir Kingsley Wood, Secretary of State for Air, when he summed up the RAF policy to a group of journalists in France. 'Remember, in the Royal Air Force it is never the individual man who does anything – it is always the RAF which does it.' He recalled also that the RAF had, 'high on its list of unforgivable sins the major crime of what it called "shooting a line." That was talking in an heroic sort of way about a job done, or a fight, or, in fact, about any of those adventures which are just things that you or I, as outsiders, like to hear or read about.'

Gardner responded:

> Being an ordinary individual, who so far hasn't had that Service ideal put into me, I haven't been able to look at these things in quite the same light. Whenever I think back on the many glorious things done by the Royal Air Force, particularly that part of the RAF which was in France, I obstinately find myself thinking, not of the Service as a whole but of the individual pilot. In writing, therefore, it is the deeds of these men which I want to put on record.

In compiling his book and its contents, my father was, as we have seen, conscious that the heroics of the 'glamour boy' fighter pilots often took pride of place in his reporting. But there was also the collective effort of equal heroic value. So he decided to devote a whole chapter to the attack by Fairey Battles on the strategically important bombing of the Maastricht Bridges in Holland two days after blitzkrieg. He wrote: 'The most famous raid ever undertaken by any of the machines of the AASF was the bombing of bridges over the Albert Canal near Maastricht on May 12.'

He told how, as soon it was known that two of these bridges were still open, the RAF realised it was essential to destroy them to stop the German advance.[2] The Commanding Officer, Air Marshal Barratt, knew that the bridges were so heavily guarded by fighters and anti-aircraft guns that an attack would be 'virtually a suicide one'. He therefore called upon volunteers from No. 12 Squadron and found that every crew member put their hands up to go. The selection, therefore, had to be done by drawing names from a hat.

Six aircraft took off in two flights, attacking from 6,000ft, diving to 2,000ft to deliver their bombs, while being assaulted by a flight of Messerschmitt 109s and AA fire. Despite this, enough aircraft got through and both bridges were destroyed. But at a terrible cost, as predicted, and all the RAF aircraft were lost. Only two crew members – who bailed out – returned. The two flight leaders, who were both killed, were awarded posthumous VCs, the first air VCs of the war.

Gardner wrote: 'We can only wonder at the bravery of those flying crews and pay humble tribute to every man who took off to almost certain death on the morning of May 12.'

At the time of Charles Gardner's return home from France on 2 June, there had began in Belgium the historic evacuation of the British Expeditionary Force from the sand dunes of Dunkirk (26 May–4 June). Although he did not witness it, Charles included a chapter in his book in which he could reflect on its impact and the mood in England at the time.

He described how everyone had been 'gloomily' looking at maps and reckoning nothing could save the army who were stranded in Belgium in the face of the advancing German troops. 'Despair was written on nearly all faces in the street. The country was facing the most disastrous loss in its history,' he declared.

Gardner then recalled how suddenly news began filtering through from the south coast of soldiers coming home and shortly afterwards reports of boat-loads of troops arriving at Dover. Details began to emerge of how an armada of small boats and Royal Navy vessels had rescued the soldiers and people wondered how many of the BEF could be saved. 'Then came the Prime Minister's famous statement – not only half of the BEF – but four fifths of it – had been rescued. The most desperate combined effort ever undertaken had been a success.'

But it was the vital battle in the air over Dunkirk that interested him the most. The Luftwaffe, he said, had been presented with 'a compact, congested and almost sitting target'. The only defence for the troops on the beach came from RAF fighters stationed on the south coast and within range of Dunkirk. 'The time had come, if ever it was to come, for the German Air Force to prove that it was the most formidable weapon in the war. It tried and it failed,' he wrote. 'German air losses were considerable, and RAF fighters, although heavily outnumbered, took an average toll of four to one.' Gardner added, 'They did this because they are by far the better fighters, and have the better machines.'

Evidence of this superiority came later when my father reported the estimates of German losses, both official and unofficial, since the beginning of the invasion of Belgium, Holland and Luxembourg. This included data from Germany which put their losses at a staggering 2,237 machines and 1,522 pilots killed, wounded or missing. No figure was given for British casualties, no doubt the hand of the censor intervened, but the ratio of 4 to 1 would be an intelligent guess.

It was not until after my father returned from France that he became aware of the impact of his broadcasts and despatches had had at home. Two press cuttings are preserved. The first from the 'leader' newspaper states: 'Recorded despatches from the front by BBC reporters are listened to eagerly by millions of people in all parts of the world. Edward Ward, Bernard Stubbs.[3] Richard Dimbleby and Charles Gardner have done amazingly good work, particularly Gardner whose picture is at the top of the page.'

In the *Star* of 28 May 1940 a feature about the four BBC 'Men of War' appeared. Of Charles Gardner it was said, 'His voice is familiar to all. His is the task of describing the superb feats of the Royal Air Force. He too does a dangerous job with coolness and efficiency.' It added, 'In March Mr. Hugh Dalton MP (Minister in the Air Ministry) paid tribute to Gardner's work in the House of Commons.' This accolade from Dalton was already known to Charles when his BBC friend Michael Balkwill told him on a visit to France in April.

In view of such interest it is not surprising that the AASF book was very well received, and clearly the publishers thought so too. My father had many letters of appreciation, none more moving than from the sister of Flight Lieutenant Brian Kerridge, who had been killed on operations and to whom the book was partly dedicated, the other being 'Cobber' Kain. He also received a nice letter from the Revd John Haswell, who had been the first person to broadcast from his newly opened studio in Reims, and a request from the Librarian at the Imperial War Museum for an autographed copy of the book for their library.

But probably the most meaningful and treasured letter came from his friend Hugh de Sellincourt who, as a distinguished author, evaluated the book on its own merits. He wrote: It's a damned good book Charles, amusing, vivid, intimate at times, harrowing, never pompous or written up. What I think makes the book of great value – quite special value – is that without effort you made the reader feel in his bones the quality of those amazing boys, what they achieved and how they achieved it.' He added, 'They remain so utterly human that their heroism just shines out in a way that any poet must envy.'

However, de Sellincourt was a little displeased by my father's reference to propaganda following the tragedy of the sinking of the battleship *Royal Oak* with the loss of 800 lives on 15 October.

Gardner wrote:

> The Navy will get their own back for that. The British Navy propaganda is put over really well when you come to think of it. From the age of about four I have been taught about the invincible sailors; now at twenty-eight I am prepared to argue with anyone that our sailors are invincible, though I know nothing about it.

Edward Stourton picked up the propaganda point as it applied to the BBC. He believed many listeners 'did not expect the BBC to tell the truth'. There was evidence of this in some reactions to Charles Gardner's Battle of Britain broadcast. 'People were much more inclined to believe that the BBC would lie to keep the nation's spirits up and would always do what it was told by the government. The idea that "truth was the first casualty of war" was common currency by the 1930s.'

However, Stourton refuted this and stated that the BBC was allowed to go on telling 'what Dimbleby called "the exact truth every detail of it"'. This was indeed the deeply felt principles on which he and Charles Gardner worked from their first days at the BBC. Edward Stourton concluded that telling the truth worked, 'and helped Britain win. Far from being the first casualty of war the habit of truth-telling grew into a strapping lad, and Auntie deserves credit for the way she nurtured him.'

Looking back at the AASF and its short history, Winston Churchill probably had the last word. In a speech in the Houses of Parliament on 4 June, he said:

> I will pay my tribute to these young airmen. The great French army was very largely, for the time being, cast back and disturbed by the onrush of a few thousand armoured vehicles. May it not also be that the course of civilization itself will be defended by the skill and vision of the few thousand airmen. The knights of the Round Table and the Crusaders now fall back into a past not only distant but prosaic.

My father commented: 'He put into words something which those of us who had seen the fighter squadrons at work had felt and perhaps in a less coherent way had tried to express.'

But for now it was back to the day job with the BBC and back to a familiar scene as German bombers mounted one of the earliest attacks – but not in France but in England. For my father was standing for the first time 'somewhere near the south coast' surrounded by searchlights and AA guns, microphone in hand, in the middle of the night describing the scene. 'We have just heard in the distance a heavy bomb drop. The searchlights beams north of us are all very busy and we are looking up in the sky to see if they can pick out the enemy machine,' he reported.

But the men on the ground were not just worried about bombs dropping. Gardner continued, 'just a little time ago we heard a whistle blown too, and that was for the mobile squad in case any of the machines that are over tonight are thinking of dropping parachute troops'.

Several more German aircraft were heard but not seen. 'I think it is a single engine machine coming in from the sea. I can hear its engines – again like all the others we have heard they are running a little out of synchronisation producing a sort of wham wham. I am putting the microphone up and you probably can hear the noise yourselves.'

In fact, no further bombs were dropped and the German aircraft were heard but not seen and as their engine noise became fainter they 'banked hard and turned back towards the sea'. This broadcast, which lacked combat action and an eyewitness account, was, however, a prelude to his most famous eyewitness report of a dogfight over the English Channel that has already been described, but the reaction to it was, as we shall see, overwhelming and controversial.

Chapter Eleven

A Controversy that Gripped the Nation

Within hours of my father's eyewitness account of the dogfight over the English Channel on Sunday, 14 July, he became aware that it had stirred the nation. The impact was such that the BBC took the unusual step of repeating it the following day and the newspapers were full of it for days. According to later surveys, 'everybody was talking about it'. Most were uplifted by it – a small victory at a time of peril. Others were 'revolted' for treating the air battle like a football match when men's lives were at stake. It was a controversy that was to last for weeks and the broadcast itself was to be played and played again seemingly forever.

The immediate and extensive press coverage from all over the country can be seen in a complete press cuttings book we have at home.[1] The *Daily Mirror* headlined 'Channel Air Fight Broadcast – Crash by Crash' and followed up with 'And they call it Bad Taste!' The *Sketch*'s famous columnist 'Candidus' wrote:

> For my part, although I did not deem it a masterpiece of description, I could find nothing in it to quarrel with on the grounds of good taste. . . . the best judges of whether or not the broadcast should have been allowed are surely the men of our fighting forces . . . So far as I have been able to sound their reactions they have few criticisms to offer.

The *London Illustrated News* commissioned an artist to depict the scene and wrote to my father for his help in describing it. It was later to feature in a centre-page spread. One publication, *Cavalcade*, printed a flattering cartoon of him over the heading 'Radio Scoop'. While the influential *Manchester Guardian*'s radio critic stated that it was 'a brilliant, exciting broadcast. It sounded, of course, like a sporting event, punctuated by the thud of bombs, the rattle of machine gun fire and the cheers. The effect was far from being alarming but positively stimulating.'

The cuttings book also contains numerous letters reacting to the broadcast and other matters from strangers and friends. One letter with a difference came from a Mrs Mary Butler, addressed from Spofforth Rectory, Harrogate (presumably the Rector's wife). She wrote: 'It illustrated the terror Nazi rule had brought to France. I do hope the BBC will let you do some more recordings, it put more heart into me than I'd had for ages.' She was 'speaking' from experience when she also asked my father if he could help locate her missing daughter, Bridget, who he had met earlier in Paris. This request concealed the real terror families under particular threat from the Nazis were now facing, and I will refer to this later in the chapter.

A less friendly letter came from an officer who 'went through 1914–18'. He wrote: 'I can only describe your ideas of an air fight which involved the loss of brave men's lives as disgusting.' But a letter addressed to 'Charlie' from an old colleague would have cheered him up. 'My wife and I were thrilled at your account of the air raid . . . perhaps you will remember me, I was in the composing room of the Leicester Mercury'.

Inevitably the matter was raised in the House of Commons. A Labour MP asked the Minister for Information to give 'an undertaking that steps would be taken to secure in future that public taste should not be offended by broadcasts of war operations in the manner of a sporting commentary'. The Minister, Duff Cooper, replied that official permission had been given. 'Although he was aware that there was considerable division of opinion about the taste of the broadcast in question, he was not prepared to give the suggested undertaking.'

But the most serious criticism came from a letter in the *Daily Telegraph* by Major General Guy Dawnay. He wrote, 'The BBC standard of taste, feeling, understanding and imagination is surely revolting to all decent citizens.' This provoked a lengthy response from the Director General himself, F.W. Ogilvie, which was reproduced in most papers.

Ogilvie stated: 'These are grave words which Major General Dawnay, no doubt, weighed very carefully, before he felt justified in using them. May I, for the BBC, which, subject to the necessary government sanctions, was responsible for this broadcast, explain that it, too, was earnestly considered before it was included in the news.'

He continued, 'This broadcast gave an eyewitness account of an air action – successful without loss of British aircraft – against enemy attack on a convoy. The business of news broadcasting is to bring home to the whole public what is happening in the world and at a grim time like this to play some part in maintaining civilian morale.'

He added, 'people in all walks of life have assured us since the broadcast that they found it heartening and a tonic. One group of 15 listeners voted it the finest thing the BBC had ever done.'

In fact the BBC had carried out a Listeners' Research Report involving some 220 'local correspondents' and 30 industrial welfare workers. Its positive results in favour of the broadcast threw up two major points, as Edward Stourton in his book *Auntie's War*, pointed out: 'The results illustrate the BBC's remarkable reach and influence. Over 90% of the correspondents and all but one of the welfare workers had heard Gardner's report.' He added, 'A number of correspondents especially those in factories, say that it was the only topic of conversation that Monday morning and that it was exhilarating to have something to talk about instead of rumours.'

The other interesting aspect of the BBC research was its credibility at a time of heavy censorship.

Stourton wrote:

> Charles Gardner's vivid reporting style was, of course, the most obvious quality that attracted listeners (some admitted being ashamed that they had found it so exciting), but another hugely important factor comes through the Listeners Research Report. There was a widespread feeling that telling a story as it happened made it much more difficult to put a propaganda gloss on the truth.... the evidence is overwhelming that the appetite for first-hand accounts that are known not to have been doctored is enormous.

In conclusion the Listeners 'Research stated: 'A number of replies say that the realism of the account did much to restore faith in the standard news reports of one British plane being equal of a great number of German planes.'

But of all the reports and correspondence probably the most pleasing to my father was a letter to the *Daily Telegraph* and a cutting from his old newspaper the *Nuneaton Tribune*. The *Tribune* ran a headline 'Charles Gardner's Triumph' and reminded readers that he was a former member of their reportorial staff. Among those who would have read it would have been his father and mother who still lived in Nuneaton. The letter to the *Daily Telegraph* was from a Mr H.T. Edmunds, copied to Charles and summed it all up. He wrote: 'In our excitement and enthusiasm in witnessing such a spectacle, we are not praising the horrors of modern warfare, which all normal people detest, but are feeling thrilled to see at long last the beginning of the destruction of the Nazi horror.'

In the extensive article in the magazine *Britain at War* Martin Mace wrote:

> Throughout the country, everyone was talking about the broadcast. One veteran pilot of the First World War was highly indignant at the manner in which Gardner had delivered his report and he wrote to the Times: 'Where men's lives are concerned must we be treated to a running commentary on a level with an account of the Grand National or a cup-tie final?' By contrast another reader was uplifted by the broadcast: 'To me it was inspiring for I almost felt that I was sharing in it, and I rejoiced unfeignedly that so many of the enemy were shot down and the rest were put to ignominious flight.'

The broadcast and the extensive press coverage had brought my father into some prominence. There were photographs and cartoons of him and every time his name was mentioned his Dover commentary was recalled. One headline stated 'Charles oh boy oh boy Gardner'. In *London Calling* his indepth feature on the AASF was reproduced with a photograph and reminder of his air battle broadcast.

There was international interest too. His good friend the journalist Mary Welsh filed a story for *Time Magazine* in New York.[2] She described how his account had 'set a new record in war reporting'. She told of the reaction in England and wrote:

> It thrilled Britons, and sounded like an American baseball broadcast. Final score, Britain nine shot down, Germans one. . . . Since last September, as first newsman with the RAF in France, Gardner has tried to synchronize air battles and only once got a near-chance when 30 Junkers 88s bombed Reims H.Q. Then he ducked into a champagne cellar saying it was a pure question of self-preservation.

Mary Welsh, who was shortly to marry Ernest Hemingway, also gave an enlightening personal description of my father. She wrote:

> Gardner is 28, wiry nervous gentlemannered, started work as a provincial reporter at 18 and has been at the BBC for three years

specializing in flying news. He holds a flying certificate and at his Surrey cottage home builds a flying collection of model planes including front line strength of 15 with reserves in the nursery. . . . Since exodus from France he claims a special stake in the war having left three sets of golf clubs, one in Reims, one in Versailles and one in Paris. At Reims he was bowling champ of 20 correspondents and here (England) he works Sundays so he can play cricket Saturdays with village team (Leatherhead CC). He is contentedly married to ex-newsgirl and has a son called Umbrage but named Robert Antony Charles.

I don't think I ever recall my father's prowess as a model aeroplane builder, not really in his character, although my brother Patrick disagrees claiming he remembers seeing him do it. And the story of losing three sets of golf clubs is a little far-fetched and probably a private joke among friends.

The last word on his broadcast is that of Simon Elmes in his book *Hello Again*, published in 2013, in which he records nine decades of radio broadcasts. He reproduces in full my father's 14 July commentary, and after listing the pros and cons concluded: 'There can be no doubt that this broadcast was enormously appreciated, that it gave a great fillip to morale, and that most Correspondents believe that the public would welcome more such items if broadcast.'

Returning to the letter from Mrs Mary Butler, who asked if my father could help locate her missing daughter in France, she revealed another frightening purpose to her request. She wrote, 'I understand you had met my daughter Mrs Charles Ahrenfeldt in Paris but I have heard nothing from her for a month. We are desperately anxious, have you any idea whether she stayed in Paris or whether they tried to get to America? I do hope they did but am afraid that they might have been taken to prison.'

It transpires that the Ahrenfeldt family were well-known and their name was associated with porcelain plate with connections in France, the United States and many other countries. It would appear that the name had aroused suspicion from the Nazi regime and, judging by previous atrocities, they were now under real threat. My father replied, although we do not have a copy, but obviously he remembered Mrs Ahrenfeldt (Bridget) judging by Mrs Butler's 'thank you' reply. 'I am sure Bridget was kind to you, she is very good to everyone, and so capable,' she wrote. Alas there was still no news, although her husband had written to the Red Cross for help.

Mrs Butler wrote again on 31 July to say she had heard via New York that the family were still in Paris and they were hoping to make their way to the United States. Unfortunately we have no further information but hope the family survived.

As the Battle of Britain now gathered pace, my father decided it was time to move on. Having served alongside the RAF in France for nine months and having reported subsequent actions back home including the famous one, it is not surprising that as the holder of a pilot's licence, he should decide to join up, leave the BBC and apply for a pilot's job in the RAF.

It was to be four years before he was to return again to the BBC.

Chapter Twelve

Joining Up

Charles Gardner 'joined up' with the RAF on 20 September 1940. Having attended a selection board at Adastral House in the Kingsway, London, and a medical board later, he received a letter of appointment from the Air Ministry on 6 September. It offered him a commission in the General Duties (Flying) Branch of the RAF Volunteer Reserve as an 'Acting Pilot on probation'. A further letter of the same date required him to report to RAF Loughborough, Leicestershire, for basic training a fortnight later.[1]

With his background as a reporter, his pilot's licence and his pride in Britain, this would seem a logical step. But it was none of these things. What drove him to the recruiting centre was simply 'boredom'. In a detailed and sometimes amusing account of his recruitment, my father tells the whole story from his ennui at the BBC, through to the process of selection and his eventual arrival at Loughborough.

In his typewritten fourteen-page document, which happily has survived, Charles explained what happened:

> Having followed the RAF progress as best I could at the BBC, I became bored; bored not because nothing was happening, but because so much was going on and I was reporting so little of it. News stories were to be had at the time but which, for reasons of censorship and security could not be published. One saw the necessity of the greater part of this secrecy, but none the less it was galling at the time.

So Charles, one sunny evening (in early August), sat down with my mother to take stock.

He wrote:

> There was a chance that I could go to the Near East to share the war coverage with Richard Dimbleby, but this did not

appeal to me overmuch and we decided against it. That left two alternatives – staying at the BBC until I was eventually combed out and put in the army, or joining the RAF right away. . . . there seemed to me to be no real future in war reporting in this country. As an air correspondent I could not hope to get anything other than official releases, and even if I was exempted, I did not fancy the idea of staying on to become a kind of stooge, going out twice a week on official sorties, however interesting. Eve agreed with me, and so, next morning, I called at the Air Ministry recruiting depot at Adastral House, Kingsway.

It should be noted that my mother's apparent compliance with my father putting his life on the line in the RAF would not have been easy for her. Indeed she would have understood from the beginning that that was what he was going to do and the only course of action was to support him, something she did unselfishly throughout his life.

My father then goes on, in his inimitable fashion, describing what happened, and giving a fascinating insight into how the system worked in those days.

He wrote:

I was unsure as to which branch of the service I should go for. My age was 28, I was married with one child and had a current 'A' licence. My flying hours, however, were not very high. My own piloting time was little more than 50 hours, although I had hundreds of hours passenger flying in my log book a lot of it with the RAF.[2] On the other hand I had been a war correspondent in France since the start of the war and had been accredited to the RAF there. That together with my experience as an air correspondent in London for four years had given me some knowledge at least of our own Air Force and of the air forces of Europe. I put all this down on the application form and in the space for what branch of the service I wanted, I entered two choices – general flying and intelligence.

When he arrived at Adastral House he found an enormous queue composed mainly of young men. Quite a number of these had already been turned down 'because they were in reserved occupations who were seeking to get out of their jobs'. When his turn came he filled in his form, collected a few pamphlets and left hoping 'the wheels would not be too long in turning'.

He did not have to wait long, and ten days later he received a letter telling him to attend a selection board which was picking out candidates for commission in the special duties branch of the Volunteer Reserves. 'This surprised me because I was still of flying duties age and special duties could only mean that the second string of intelligence was the one under consideration.'

So he returned to Adastral House with his birth certificate and a glowing reference from the BBC which stated: 'Mr. C.J. Gardner has been on the staff of this corporation as a member of the news department since 20 July 1936. His work and conduct have at all times been most satisfactory and, we can, with every confidence recommend him for a commission in the Royal Air Force.'[3]

On arrival he found the anteroom full. 'We sat round, self-consciously, some pretending to read but the majority, myself included, were trying to appraise the others and judge our own chances of success.' Eventually after a wait 'which seemed like ages' he was called before the Board. The President was a Group Captain supported by a Squadron Leader, a Flight Lieutenant and a civilian clerk.

Charles recalled the interview and wrote down the dialogue as follows:

The President: How many hours solo have you?

C.G.: About 50.

President: Have you flown in Service machines?

C.G.: Many times, mostly on combined exercises.

President: I see your age is 28. Would you like to go on to flying duties?

C.G.: Yes, I put this on my application (a remark that might have been construed as insolent).

President: Do you think you can pass the flying medical?

C.G.: I hope so.

Squadron Leader: Have you held a commission before?

C.G.: No. I was an honorary captain when I was a war correspondent with the AASF in France, but that was purely a courtesy and meant nothing.

Squadron Leader (looking at my application form): You are the BBC Charles Gardner aren't you?

C.G.: Yes.

Squadron Leader: Your Dover broadcast caused a bit of an uproar didn't it?'

C.G.: I'm afraid so.

The President: Well, your age is below that for SD duties, but if you agree I will pass you onto the general duties branch for flying, that is if you pass your medical. If you don't would you like to be a Link Trainer instructor?

C.G.: Flying is what I wanted sir, and I hope I can pass the doctors. If not, I suppose Link Instructor is as good as anything.

President: All right, off you go and have your medical.

The thought of my father becoming a Link Instructor is inconceivable. It would not last a week. Patience was not one of his virtues nor was his quick temper. So everything hung on the medical.

Unsurprisingly, Charles Gardner was 'nervous' as he walked to the Central Medical Board building on the other side of Kingsway. 'I knew how tough the examination was going to be – and failure meant a doomed life instructing on a Link trainer – a prospect which appalled me,' he wrote.

The system of medical examinations he found to be simple and efficient. 'It ran on the cafeteria principle. You take your body round to various cubicles labeled – Ears, Eyes, General, and so on – and get a chit of inspection at each one. Eventually, when you have been through the lot, all your chits are collected into a folder and taken to the President who has the final say.'

So Charles started the rounds beginning with Ear, Nose and Throat, and then on to General where he was examined in the same excruciating way we all know. Eventually, he came to the crucial eye test which 'was the most searching of all' and which is still the most common cause of failure for pilot duties.

And he nearly failed. He wrote: 'I had to focus on a stick which was moved towards me and the doctor measured the distance from my eyes to where I could no longer hold the stick in clear vision. The moment of losing focus is clearly shown because your eyes shoot uncontrollably outwards. You can feel them go and the examiner can see them go as well.'

Unfortunately in Charles's case he lost focus too far out. 'The doctor was very patient, he tried and tried again and although I reduced my first figure, I was still not reducing enough.' So they took him to another doctor and then introduced him to a machine which measured his odd convergence in a more exact way.

Following a little conference by the doctors, by which time my father 'had resigned myself to a life in the Link Trainer room', the senior doctor told him that the rest of his eye report was so very good that he would overlook the convergence. 'He then asked me if I had been doing anything to strain my eyes lately. I told him that I'd been sitting up late at night typing out my book on the RAF in France to which he replied – then that's the reason.'

But there was one last hurdle, the interview with the President. Charles wrote:

> He sat at a large desk with my reports in front of him. He read them through and through without saying a word. Then he pressed a bell and sent for the ear, nose and throat doctor. Together they whispered over my chits, while I sat trembling in my chair. Eventually the President said, 'You've got catarrh. You will have to get that cleared up. Otherwise you are alright. Go to your own doctor and get treated for it, and when he says you're better just send us his certificate. We shan't want to see you again, good morning.'

It was a feeling of both relief and exhilaration as he rode (in a bus) back to the office. He wrote, 'I happened to read an article on the RAF which said only the fittest of our young men are accepted for flying duties – and for the first time in weeks, I began to feel really well.'

A few weeks later, he received his official confirmation of a commission and was ordered to go to Loughborough for basic training.

Chapter Thirteen

Life in the RAF

Two weeks after receiving his letters of instruction from the Air Ministry, Charles Gardner arrived at Loughborough to begin his RAF training. During those two weeks he had to get fitted out with his uniform and clothing, and say farewell to the BBC. He also learned of Air Ministry bureaucracy and meanness.

Enclosed with his joining letter was a railway warrant and an instruction that plain clothes should be worn for the journey but on arrival he should change into his uniform, thus avoiding a first class fare (the entitlement of all commissioned officers). He had also received a £40 allowance for his uniform which stretched him to the limits.

'I found it just enough and no more,' he wrote. 'I managed to get two uniforms, a great coat, a raincoat, four shirts, one pair of black shoes, ties and socks, a side cap, and a peaked ceremonial cap for £38. Luckily I had a pair of black shoes that were practically regulation and also some Air Force blue shirts.' He ignored 'a lot of the gubbins' such as camping gear, cooking utensils and reckoned the Air Ministry knew it could not be done on £40.

He then found he was expected to pay the £38 out of his own pocket in the trust that the Air Ministry would repay him as soon as he joined. Having discovered this would take weeks – months – he came to an arrangement with his own tailor who was prepared to wait for the Ministry to re-fund him. Apparently many London tailors had received such requests and were complaining bitterly about it.

My father had other financial worries too. He wrote:

My own pay as an Acting Pilot Officer was 10s/6d a day with an allowance of 3s/6d a day for my wife and 1s/6d a day for my infant. This was not particularly handsome – but I was lucky in that the BBC had generously agreed to make my pay up to the equivalent of my normal salary. Without that help I doubt if

I could have paid my way for the first six months when my rank was only Acting.

His recruitment had not gone unnoticed by some newspapers. Under a large headline – 'BBC Air Fight Reporter as Pilot' – the *Sunday Graphic* stated, 'Charles Gardner, famous BBC reporter of air battles hopes soon to be looking for more battles as a pilot. He has passed his medical and now awaits his call up. He is 28 – and that's a bit old for a fighter pilot.' In an interview Charles said: 'Of all the things I saw during the war among all our forces the one which impressed me most was the marvellous show put up by our fighter and bomber pilots. It staggered me. I have wanted to be one since.'

His old newspaper, the *Nuneaton Tribune*, reported simply, under a youthful photograph of my father: 'Nuneatonians will be surprised to learn that Charles Gardner, formerly BBC air expert and member of the reportorial staff of the Tribune, has left the BBC to join the RAF.'[1]

My father was glad to be posted to Loughborough. It was a town he knew well and near to where he once lived. He had friends there and he found a place 'quite handy' where Eve and 'Umbrage' could stay at the same time. He had little idea of what lay ahead. But he soon had a taste of it, when he looked out of the window while unpacking. Out in the grounds of the college, which had been commandeered as a training base, he heard the tramp of marching feet, accompanied by the drill sergeant's voice yelling orders to a bunch of new recruits.

So his hopes of early instruction on flying, lectures on tactics and strategy, went literally out of the window. For the next few weeks it was going to be mainly 'square bashing' – RAF style. 'My immediate reaction on hearing this din going on was to laugh, but after I had been doing it myself for a time it became so much part of the daily life, that I hardly noticed it,' he wrote.

Charles later recorded the objectives of the three-week course. 'First and foremost, it was designed to teach drill and discipline, together with RAF customs and a general outline of duties of an officer. In addition there were high speed lectures on King's Regulations, Air Force law, powers of arrest, the composition of the Service, administration and so on.'

On his first day he found that there was only one other General Duties man on the course, a PO John Kennedy who had come over from Kenya, where he had done a fair amount of flying in his own aeroplane. The rest were mostly fresh from university or training college and were all either equipment, technical or administration people.

Having lodged his family nearby, my father, 'contrary to general instructions', absented himself to join them for the weeknd.

He wrote:

> It was fairly easy to do this sort of thing at Loughborough provided you kept all your lectures and parades. One of the officers, who had installed his wife about three miles away, proceeded to live out, cycling backwards and forwards to the College. He was never found out, but if he had been I think he would have been treated leniently. He had only just been married and his course would normally have been his honeymoon.

After ten days both he and Kennedy were notified that they were to be posted away from the College for flying training and would not be required to take an examination which normally came after three weeks. They were warned that they might have to do a drill test for the Wing Commander, but no test was forthcoming, other than satisfying the Warrant Officer that they knew how to get a squad on the move and halt it again.

So Charles and Kennedy left Loughborough and were posted to an Elementary Flying Training School (EFTS) where, at last, they would start flying in RAF Tiger Moths or Miles Magisters.

'Since we both could fly already we were looking forward to this part of our training with relish,' he wrote, adding, 'and I must say my days at EFTS were the happiest I have ever spent in the service.'

Unfortunately we do not have any notes or description of these happy days. But we do have his RAF flying logbook which is in itself revealing, logging, as it should do, his complete RAF career with hours, dates, places, names and some comment.

It shows that 2 EFTS was based at RAF Staverton, Devon, where Charles made his first RAF flight in a Tiger Moth on 7 October 1940 under the instruction of Flight Lieutenant Giffiths. He made eighteen more flights in the same type during which he had to demonstrate turning, take-offs, gliding, stalling, spinning, gliding approaches and landings, all with an instructor in the rear seat. Nine days later on 16 October he made his first solo flight. It is underlined in red and noted 'three landings'.

On the opposite page he certified that he had been 'instructed in airscrew swinging' (for propeller start) and that he 'understood the petrol, oil ignition system'. It was signed C.J.T. Gardner Acting Pilot Officer. So, unfortunately for him, as an APO he still was not receiving full pay.

By 13 November, with 50 hours under his belt, including instruction on night flying and Link Trainer experience, he was passed as 'average' by the chief instructor and posted to the RAF's prestigious officer training establishment at Cranwell in Lincolnshire. There he resumed the next stage in his service career.

Again, we have no personal recollections of his time at Cranwell except class photographs which show him as the senior student – by age – sitting in the centre with the rank of Pilot Officer, so I assume he was now on full pay.[2] This was especially important as soon after enrolling at the College he moved my mother and myself onto a farm at nearby Sleaford. My mother at the time was heavily pregnant with my brother Patrick, who was born on 13 February 1941.

I remember the farm, playing with the chickens in the yard, and then being faced with eating one – I have never been able to eat chicken since.

My father's logbook shows that from 19 November he began training on the twin-engine Airspeed Oxford advanced trainer, which was used particularly for bomber and coastal command appointments, thus indicating where his future RAF flying duties lay. By this time he realised anyway that any early ambition to become a fighter or front-line pilot was extremely unlikely, and in any event his age would have counted against him.

The Oxford had accommodation for two pilots sitting side-by-side with a place for a wireless operator in the rear fuselage. He later described the aircraft as 'a nice aeroplane to fly, although there is sufficient bite in it near the stall to dissuade the pupil from getting careless'. This comment was made in *The Gen Book*, written by my father and which became his second published work. It gave details of all current British and American military aircraft together with an explanatory foreword by the author. It was published a year later again by Hutchinson, who advertised it as being by the same author as *AASF*. Alongside an illustration of an RAF pilot in flying kit on the front cover, the blurb read: 'An indispensable profusely illustrated book which brings together all available details of machines used by the RAF.'

Whether it was the publishers or my father who wanted to do the book, we do not know, but it must have meant working long late hours again researching and writing it. *The Gen Book* was published in 1942 under the name of Flight Lieutenant Charles Gardner, so by now he had been promoted. In his foreword he wrote: 'There is a fascination about collections whether they be of old china, ancient masters, stamps, or cigarette cards. In this book I set out to collect aircraft, and, with the traditional unscrupulousness of the collector I have filched my specimens from all the reference books and publication I could find' (So he hadn't lost his way with words.)

On the practical side, his book gives an excellent insight into the 'state of play' in the war at the time of writing. He was able to note, for instance, that the total number of types of machine which could be linked to the RAF and Fleet Air Arm 'now approaches the hundred mark', a far cry from the desperate days of the Battle of Britain only two years before. And of particular interest was the American contribution. He stated that it was only when he started to collect material that he 'fully realised the enormous supplies that are coming to us from the other side of the Atlantic'. He estimated there to be forty-two different types of American aircraft 'and nearly all have been delivered to the RAF already, or have been ordered with a view to delivery in the near future'.

Gardner concluded his foreword by making comparisons with Germany. He wrote, 'In 1941 the RAF reached air parity with Germany, thanks to the magnificent effort of the Russian defences. Soon we hope to have numerical superiority, and this, coupled with great technical advantage, which our newest and most secret types will give, encourages this observer at least, to end his introduction on a note of optimism.'

On the lighter side he could not resist a glossary of slang terms used in the RAF. 'It would be idle to delve into origins, though some of course are self-evident,' he wrote. 'Others, though are so obscure to be almost untraceable and I for one have never met anyone who could tell me why the RAF order to give a concentrated pull or heave is "Two Six".' Among other example given were: 'To Trang' – to crash; 'Brown Type and Pongo' – soldier; 'Glamour Boy'– Fighter pilot; 'Stuffed Cloud' – a cloud containing land; and 'Nautic' – a sailor.

So, returning to his RAF career in 1941, he had now completed more than 130 hours on the Oxford and was assessed as 'good average' as a pilot and above average as a pilot-navigator. This is not a surprise, as he had always been fascinated by the science and mathematics of navigation, an interest he retained for the rest of his life. But, from personal experience of his sailing boat on the Solent in later years, his practical knowledge was excellent, his execution less so.

As a result of his assessment, my father passed out successfully from Cranwell on 8 March 1941 as a Pilot Officer and was posted to Squires Gate, Blackpool, to begin his operational training. Here he was introduced to the Blackburn Botha which was used largely for navigation exercises. From 26 March he completed 23 hours flying mostly in the Botha as second pilot and later in the Blenheim fighter-bomber and Anson reconnaissance aircraft. He completed the course in early June. A one-day visit to RAF Ford in Sussex followed for an air firing test in a Blenheim. The target, according to the logbook, was Selsey Bill. Since the family had an uncle living in Selsey, I can attest that either he missed the village or his target was out to sea!

It would have been at this time that he learned that he was to be attached as a pilot to RAF Coastal Command which was equipped with flying boats, mostly stationed in Scotland and Northern Ireland. Their main job then was to fly sorties far out into the North Atlantic to try to protect the vital convoys from German warships and submarines. The convoys from the United States were carrying life-saving supplies and equipment to a beleaguered Britain and were under constant attack. Their importance to the country's survival cannot be underestimated, as the Germans knew well.

And so in early July 1941, he packed his bags and initially joined the 4th Operational Training Unit at Invergordon, which lay within the sheltered waters of the Cromarty Firth on the east coast of Scotland. Here he was first introduced to the flying boat, initially the twin-engine Saunders Roe London. His first flight instructor and Commanding Officer was Squadron Leader John Barraclough, who no doubt wanted to assess his new recruit personally. A handwritten note in my father's logbook dated June 1942 states that Barraclough 'was now a Wing Commander with a DFC and AFC'.

In fact, Sir John Barraclough, as he became, was a legendary figure in the RAF and he rose to the rank of Air Chief Marshal after the war.[3] In 2004 as Chairman of a Coastal Command appeal committee, he was responsible for raising funds for a plaque in Westminster Abbey as a tribute to the men of Coastal Command. It was unveiled by the Queen in March that year.

As a member of that Committee, I spent some time with Sir John from 2003. He remembered my father well. He recalled an early night navigation training exercise when Charles was flying with a hood over his head to replicate night-flying conditions. He was concentrating hard on the instruments, when Barraclough tried to give him further instructions. Pilot Officer Gardner replied – 'Do you want me to listen to you or to fly this bloody aircraft!' Later, Barraclough assessed his overall performance as just 'average!'.

For the rest of that month he had to learn the art of take-off and landing on water, how to judge the sea state for safe operating and how to fly at very low level on patrol for many hours at a time. By 31 July he piloted his first flight in command and two days later was introduced to the Catalina, the aircraft in which he was to serve throughout his operational career and for which he had great affection.

In fact, the American Consolidated Catalina flying boat was the backbone of RAF Coastal Command throughout the war. With its huge duration of over 20 hours and range of 4,000 miles, it was ideal for long-range patrol, search and rescue and attack duties and particularly suited to protecting the North Atlantic convoys.

Designed and built in the United States, the Catalina had twin propeller engines, a high wing, a fat and roomy hull and characteristic blisters for observation and gunnery mounted behind the wings – an RAF derivation. It was able to defend itself with machine guns and could attack with depth charges. For such long sorties it needed a crew of up to ten, including two and sometimes three pilots so that they could have rest periods, for which it was equipped with primitive cooking and toilet facilities.

Charles Gardner, in *The Gen Book*, wrote:

The Cat is a grand flying boat, perfect for its job and of inestimable value to us in the Battle of the Atlantic. It is impossible to say how many U boats have been sunk by Catalinas, but it is certain that the last thing that many a German has seen has been the head-on view of a Cat rushing at him low over the waves.

One of the great things about the Cat as an aeroplane is that she will maintain height with load on one engine, and will even climb on it. Her cruising speed is on the low side, but in deep sea patrol work, speed is of no great importance.

This characteristic gave much comfort to all the flying crew, as Pilot Officer Gardner was soon to learn.

Charles's first flight in the Catalina was on 4 August and his first flight in command was seven days later. It was on this flight that he encountered his first emergency with an engine problem requiring him to put down on one engine on the nearest stretch of water, an inland loch in Scotland.

And thereby hangs a tale, which my father repeated often many years later. According to him, as soon as they had landed on the loch they rowed ashore in the aircraft's dinghy seeking habitation and particularly a telephone to report back to base. They found a solitary house near the shore and were invited in by a kindly couple who said they were only too pleased to help. And, yes, they did have a telephone, the only one for miles around.

While telephoning in to base, my father noticed a photograph in the hall which he recognised as a familiar cottage by the watercress beds in Fetcham, less than a mile from home. Astonished at such a coincidence, he asked about the picture, and was told by his hosts that they had lived there for more than twenty years and had only recently moved up to Scotland to avoid any bombing raids.

Training continued at Invergordon but by October my father learned he was to be posted to 240 Squadron at Loch Erne, in Northern Ireland and thus be closer to the Atlantic approaches. No. 240 squadron, whose motto was 'guardian of the sea', had a long tradition of operating flying boats and sea planes from the First World War. In 1919 it was disbanded but reformed in 1937 and now was equipped with the new Mk1 Catalinas. Since Loch Erne, a few miles north of Belfast, was to become a semi-permanent base, Charles decided to move his family nearby.

Loch Erne itself, formerly RAF Castle Archdale, comprised two connecting lakes, the second largest lake system in Northern Ireland. But it was its location that was so important as it was as close as the RAF could safely get to the Atlantic approaches to fly protection missions for the incoming convoys from the United States. However, the shortest route to the sea took them over Irish territory which was neutral during the war and officially 'out of bounds'. Happily a secret agreement with the Irish government had already been reached allowing them to over-fly their territory.

I can just recall those days in Northern Ireland. We lived in a fairly primitive cottage near a bog and my mother was assisted by two local Irish girls who were not too much help and she was always having to 'chase them up'. A highlight for us was the occasional visit to a local hotel where there was more comfort and good food. My only other recollection was in the woods with my father and RAF colleagues who were shooting rabbits. I managed to run away but was quickly rescued by him as I was in danger of being a target.

For the next three months my father was away, flying long-range, dangerous and tiring missions miles out into the Atlantic escorting the convoys. He was soon to experience his first operational sorties and attacks on enemy submarines. What was to come later was totally unpredictable.

Chapter Fourteen

Flying in the Battle of the Atlantic

Pilot Officer Charles Gardner's first taste of operational flying began from Loch Erne on 2 October 1941. His 240 Squadron were engaged in the desperate battle to protect the supply convoys from North America against German submarines and shipping in what has been called the 'Battle of the Atlantic'. Without these supplies, Britain would not have been able to survive. He described their daily routine protection missions as 'nothing marvellous or wonderful about it,' adding, 'yet until the last day of the war it will continue to go on, day or night come rain or shine'.

And the Battle of the Atlantic, which had already been raging for two-and-a-half years, did go on – on until 1945. It was to be the longest continual military campaign of the war and cost thousands of lives, 3,500 merchant vessels and 175 warships. The Germans were to lose 783 U-boats. Throughout, the Catalinas remained on patrol and Winston Churchill in his speech after signing the Atlantic Charter with American President Franklin D. Roosevelt in August 1941 referred thankfully to the presence 'of those far-reaching Catalinas'.[1]

For his first 'ops' flight, Gardner flew as one of the two second pilots (the usual complement was three including the captain) on a typical mission looking for German submarines. They flew way out into the Atlantic, for it had a range of over 4,000 miles. His logbook only states 'search patrol' during which he flew the aircraft as second pilot for over 13 hours of which 5 were at night. No U-boats were found this time, nor were they sighted two days later on another patrol. If they had been, the Catalina would have approached the submarine at ultra-low level for best sighting of the target, and released its depth charges, for which the aircraft had been designed. It had also been designed to accommodate a flight crew of up to ten so that on these 20-hour plus missions they could be rested during the sortie. 'Conditions aboard were very primitive,' he wrote. 'We had an electric kettle for brewing up and a loo.' They were also very cramped for space and, 'it was very difficult to rest and sleep which we rarely did'.

Eight days later, after a short spell of training – 'local flying and practice bombing' – Gardner did experienced his first attack on a German U-boat. His logbook for 16 October simply states '11 track sweep. Sub attacked.' Five days later on convoy patrol another 'Sub attacked.' Whether these strikes were successful or not is unknown.

From the end of October 1941 to February 1942 Gardner logged over 200 operational flying hours at the controls as second pilot on Atlantic anti-submarine and convoy protection missions. Of these 85 hours were at night with one flight of over 14 hours in the dark. All were in Catalinas.

Unfortunately, we have no personal record of these sorties which were all flown from Loch Erne. We do have a fascinating personal document giving instruction on the procedure for the dangerous task of meeting up with a convoy. This illustrates the rigorous and strict attention to detail that had to be observed to avoid any enemy intrusion or misunderstanding with the ships. I have included a sample to illustrate this.

The instruction states that the approach to the convoy should first be made '20 miles ahead before forming a creeping line ahead of patrol to 15 miles each side of the convoy track to within minimum distance of four miles. The approach should be by level flight bows on. Never down sun. Do not close to less than 3,000yds until recognised – and then keep minimum of 1,500yds.'

It then gives details of how to ensure convoy recognition. These include, 'Flash letter (with a signal gun), if not effective – fire cartridges and or turn so as to give SNO (Signals Naval Observer) a silhouette of aircraft.' It warns against radio communication from aircraft to ship: 'Open RT (radio) watch but Not RT communication. Onus for this always with SNO except in emergency. If recco (recognition) is by cartridge – ship reply is by flag.'

Much to remember and act upon, especially after many long hours in the air, often in poor visibility, darkness, bad weather and experiencing enemy intrusion.

To help paint a picture of those days, how operations were planned and executed, we do have a preserved script for a BBC broadcast by Charles Gardner at the end of 1941 in which he describes the routine and dangers facing Catalina patrols.[2] Clearly he had not lost touch with the BBC and, indeed, for the rest of the war as a serving RAF officer, he remained a regular broadcaster. The following are extracts from that broadcast.

Charles Gardner:

Painted over the whole of one wall of our operations room is a map. It traces part of the western coastline of the British Isles and a bit of Iceland. All the rest is Atlantic Ocean stretching out halfway to America. Dotted about it, here and there, are numbered red arrows, which are convoys, outward and homeward bound. Also dotted about, perhaps singly but more often in packs of three, four or more are black pieces of cardboard – U boats.

And there, moving over the grids of Latitude and Longitude on our wall you can watch, day after day, as though it were a huge chess game, the progress of the Battle of the Atlantic – the battle which has been fought every minute of the last two and a half years – the battle which we dare not lose.

For us that map with pin holes in the painted wood marked our adventures and our successes – other pinholes show where we conducted unavailing searches for survivors, one of the bitterest and most nerve-racking jobs a flying captain can have.

He then describes a routine mission:

Early this morning, before day was hardly born, the crew of a flying boat was here, being briefed, working out courses and times, studying the map and wondering about the weather. They walked down the rickety stairs to go aboard and take off in the pitch dark on their way to find a convoy which is no more than a pin-head in the middle of our ops room wall.

A glance at the aircraft's position on the map shows they did find the convoy for the chalked word MET, followed by a time tells us they reached the pin head two hours ago. So right now they're out there, a lonely dot in the Atlantic sky, circling in the bumping greyness, keeping in touch with three neat rows of ships which are playing a long game of hide and seek in the rain, fog and spray.

To the men in those ships the Catalina is the advance guard of Britain welcoming them home. They trust her to keep a U-boat periscope from peering into the patrol area and to fend off the long range air raider whose job is to act as the eyes for the whole submarine pack. Skimming along, two or three hundred feet above the spuming white horses of breaking seas, the Catalina captain knows all that his boat means to the men below. He knows

121

too that now in the afternoon is the danger period when the U boats will try and get into position ahead of the convoy ready for a night attack. But the captain has another worry – that of his own boat and crew. He has to decide how long he can maintain his protection and yet be able to bring his men back before the bad weather hits our Atlantic coast.

In our ops room and in the vaster ops room at Group headquarters, flying controllers are wondering the same thing too. Measurements are being made from that mid-ocean pin-head; weather reports are called for from all possible landing places and a decision taken to re-route the Catalina to another base, two hundred miles or more from the one it left this morning.

This will mean a night landing after 18 or 19 hours in the air, but the landing will be clear of fog and low cloud and, with reasonable luck, the last column on the position board – a column headed WATERBORNE – will be filled about 21,00 hours and another routine A.S. patrol will be over.

Charles also recalled other missions, other acts of bravery and endeavour which were recorded in the Ops Room logbook.

He continued:

Before you leave the Ops Room you might spend a minute or two turning through the pages of the log book on the controller's desk. If we go back a bit we'll find an entry for the day Bismarck [Germany's most powerful battleship] was sighted. That was the day one of our boats went out and shadowed the German ship for five hours, dodging flak, and keeping up with her till our navy took over. When the Catalina got back she had been flying for over 25 hours.

Another entry tells of the search to find survivors of the ship *Empire Endurance*: 'He found 'em and brought a corvette along to save dozens of seamen out of a little dinghy. And here's the time when he got a sub and fought a Condor in the same trip.[3] For that and the rescue in the same trip and for other work he's now got the DFC and Bar.'

He concluded: 'Our squadron is but a small part of the picture. Yet until the last day of the war it will continue to go on day or night come rain or shine until that fat log book has been filled and until no pieces of black cardboard are plotted around our convoys on the wall of our ops room.'

It was during this time my father wrote a short story describing a typical Atlantic sortie. It is, in fact, a thinly disguised account of one of his first operational missions and his nerve-racking experience as second pilot being put in temporary command for the first time during a night-time return to base. It also expresses how vulnerable the convoys were, despite every effort to protect them. I have therefore included edited extracts conveying something of what life was like aboard a Catalina patrol.

The extract begins:

Catalina 'L' for Leather, pulsing homeward after a 17 hour sortie was riding easily, a small oasis of life between the heaving ocean swell and the faintly friendly stars. Two hundred and 20 miles ahead of her lay the Irish coast; two hundred miles astern was the inward bound convoy she had been escorting since dawn, tossing relentlessly at the start of another night of danger and probably death.

Sitting in the first pilot's seat, her captain thought of these things, he knew, as indeed did all of his crew, that the convoy was 'for it' before dawn. The night before, two ships had been lost. One a precious tanker carrying heaven knows what sort of supplies from the Americas. Tonight, unless the convoy was lucky, one or two would go – for the U boats were ganging up in their packs, and were even now creeping round to lie in the path of the ships.

The captain shook his head and then switched his mind to the business in hand and turned his torch on the instrument panel. The pencil shaft of light held still at the Air Speed Indicator while he absorbed its reading, then prodded his second pilot. 'I told you to keep her at 100 indicated – now look at the bloody thing – 96 – and what the hell are you climbing for?'

With hasty hands the pilot officer adjusted the elevator control knob of the automatic pilot brought the climb and dive indicator hand to zero and nursed the airspeed indicator back to 100. The captain watched for a time and then with a kindlier 'Ok keep her at that' hopped down into the gangway and made his way through the bulkhead door into the navigation department.

Up in front the second pilot, not long out of the O.T.U. [Operational Training Unit] to have not got used to being in sole charge of a big flying boat at night, bent himself towards the controls with a quick stab of unease. He peered around in the unyielding darkness before his windscreen, and then glanced along the faintly illuminated instruments. He sought reassurance in the steadiness of the engine needles; revs synchronised at 1850; boost at 27 inches and gazed at the dials fearful of any flutter that might be the herald of trouble.

In his mind he ran through the immediate action drill should one of the motors fail and gropingly he practised finding in the dark the lever behind his head which disconnected the automatic pilot. With a sudden start, born from his night fancyings, he noticed that the Cat was climbing at 100ft per minute and his hand shot out to the elevator knob. Gently he wound it in, and then more quickly as the rate of climb needle rose higher on the dial. Still the Cat climbed and a clutch of panic seized his heart as he saw the airspeed falling off from 90 knots towards 85. Out came the auto pilot and with hands sticky with sweat he pressed the Cat's nose downward with the control column. The needles dropped back into line, and feeling suddenly cold as the little crisis passed, realigned the indicators of the automatic unit, and reengaged it.

Back in the chart room the Captain smiled. He knew even better than his second pilot what had been going on up forward. The moment he saw the airspeed fall back on the navigator's clock, he had been ready to jump up into control, but long experience told him that it was far better for his second to fight the tussle himself unless things looked like getting dangerous. He had over 3,000 hours in his log book but he had never forgotten that feeling of loneliness and quick surging of fear which came with the first few night flights.

My father's Atlantic convoy protection duties were to continue well into December. And then everything changed, although he did not know it at the time.

For, on 8 December 1941, Japanese dive-bombers attacked the US fleet in Pearl Harbor. 'A day of infamy' was how President Roosevelt described it as war against Japan was declared. Shortly after Nazi Germany declared war on the United States and immediately the conflict became global. Three days later, the British battleship *Prince of Wales* and the cruiser *Repulse* were sunk also by Japanese dive-bombers off the Malaysian coast. The complexion of the war had completely altered. Now Britain faced the impending threat of the Japanese to her Far East colonies, to Singapore, Malaysia, Burma, India and Ceylon.

And suddenly mission priorities for 240 Squadron and Pilot Officer Gardner were irrevocably re-directed. Within weeks it was to take him nearly halfway round the world – to the island of Ceylon, there to await and defend the anticipated onslaught of the Japanese war fleet. It was described by the Prime Minister, Winston Churchill, as 'the most dangerous moment'.

Chapter Fifteen

'The Most Dangerous Moment'

Eight days after the fall of Singapore, Pilot Officer Charles Gardner of 240 Squadron, strapped himself into the co-pilot's seat of a Catalina bound for Ceylon. It was 23 February 1942, and just over a month from what was to be his last Atlantic patrol when they had successfully met an incoming convoy and escorted them to safety. He had been at the controls for nearly 15 hours. Now came the news that his aircraft and three others from the squadron had been selected to fly to Ceylon and exchange the grim winter of the Atlantic for the tropical climate of that friendly island, which was now under threat from the Japanese navy heading towards them and the Bay of Bengal.

The news of the change would have come as a shock to my father. Not just because he was to be posted so far away to the Far East – a region he didn't know – that was bad enough – but because, for the first time, he would be totally separated from his family. Furthermore, he would need to make swift plans to move them back home. This was worrying in itself, especially as Eve now had to cope not only with the mischievous 'Umbrage' – me, but also my 1-year-old brother Patrick. She was now on her own and faced the likelihood that she might never see her husband for a long time, if ever. Sometimes we do not acknowledge the bravery and fortitude of military wives. In my mother's case, she never showed us children the continual anxiety she must have felt, for which she deserves much credit and our gratitude.

Her journey home, not for the first time, was not without incident, as we shall see.

Although members of 240 Squadron would have been surprised they had been chosen, further swift reinforcements in the Far East were expected, for we were at war with Japan. On the very day the Japanese had attacked Pearl Harbor on 8 December 1941, they had invaded the British colony of Hong Kong and two days later, as we have already noted, their bombers had sunk the battleship *Prince of Wales* and the cruiser *Repulse* off the east coast of Malaya, which they had already occupied. Then came what Churchill called 'the worst disaster in British history' – the fall of Singapore which surrendered on 15 February. By then the Malaysia peninsula had been taken and Japan had also added Indo China to their list of conquests, having been allowed to walk in unopposed, thanks to the agreement of the French Vichy government.

The threatening Japanese fleet was essentially the same that had attacked Pearl Harbor. Still under the command of Vice Admiral Nagumo, it was estimated to comprise 5 aircraft carriers with over 300 aircraft on board, 4 battleships, 9 cruisers, 9 destroyers and up to 9 submarines. They now had set their sights on Ceylon in a naval advance from the Indian Ocean to the Bay of Bengal. Beyond was the land mass of India and to the south, off the east coast of Africa, the island of Madagascar, a strategic point for the Royal Navy in protecting the convoys coming up from the Cape bringing supplies to British troops in the Middle East.

Reinforcements on Ceylon were thus desperately needed, particularly air power and long-range air reconnaissance, for which the Catalina was designed, to find and locate the Japanese fleet and report its position to the defending forces and the Royal Navy's Eastern Fleet. Churchill now described the worsening situation as 'the most dangerous moment' and the one which, he said later, was to give most alarm in the Second World War.

This was the frightening prospect facing my father and his Catalina colleagues as they headed East. His response was typical of him. He recorded in detail his own experience in a preserved sixteen-page despatch, probably meant for future broadcast or publication. Although we have no record of its publication, we know he had already 'broadcast once or twice', according to his former BBC boss R.T. Clark, in the 1942 Handbook. In any case it is a treasured document which gives a graphic personal account of his experiences in those dark and dangerous days.

He wrote:

In the middle of February, just about the time of the fall of Singapore, Coastal Command sent an urgent signal to 240 squadron at Loch Erne asking for four boats (including 'L' for Lionel captained by Flight Lieutenant Bradshaw and Pilot Officer Gardner as second pilot) to be chosen although the squadron were left with only three aircraft themselves.

And so, on that February morning in Northern Ireland, Bradshaw and Gardner and a crew of seven took off from Loch Erne heading first to the Coastal Command Mount Batten base in Plymouth for supplies. He described the base as 'an old hunting ground' after a visit in BBC days where he experienced his first long-duration flight in a Sunderland flying boat. After two days at Mountbatten stocking up and no doubt being issued with tropical kit, they began their journey proper heading first for Gibraltar. By some fortuitous reason their allocated aircraft, 'L for Lionel' (more often called 'L for Leather') number W 8405, was the most celebrated aircraft in the fleet and known as the 'Bismarck Cat'. For this was the very aircraft which had found and shadowed for many hours the German battleship *Bismarck* until it was engaged and sunk by the Royal Navy. There was still a hole mark in the fuselage where it had been hit by the battleship's guns, although it was now securely patched up.

His logbook gives their precise route out and was described in his report thus:

> We flew out via Gibraltar [1 March], Abuquir [5 March], Basra [7 March], Karachi [9 March]. The trip was uneventful although somewhat hampered by bad weather, which slowed us down a little. The other [three] boats managed to keep company as far as Karachi, but various minor inspections and snags held three of them up for a day or so leaving L to make the last stage alone to Koggala [an inland lagoon on the south westerly tip of the island].

They duly arrived on the morning of 9 March. Gardner wrote with some surprise, 'news of our impending arrival only having preceded us by a few hours'.

My father knew little about Ceylon when he arrived, except that it was a tropical island with a monsoon which began in May and lasted up to six months – which would have a large bearing on operations, and its capital was Colombo, its major port. Although he didn't know it at the time, he was to spend over three years there and despite the fear and anxiety of impending invasion in the early days, he quickly admired the beauty of the place, so much so that later he wrote a commentary for a BBC film lecture on Ceylon and recorded a travel talk for schools. 'Ceylon the "lovely Lanka,"' he wrote. 'There must be very few of our garrison who, even if nostalgic for the English countryside – or the tulip fields of Holland – or the Lakes of Canada – have not paused at some time to say of Ceylon –"This is very beautiful."' He told the schools in his broadcast while back in London in 1945, 'When flying over the country the thing I noticed was the glorious colour of it all – white concrete buildings dazzling in the sun and the deep green of the fields. Ceylon is an island of colour – the flowers, the birds, the countryside and the beaches.'

Koggala was also very beautiful. A sheltered lake near the coast and close to the old Dutch fort of Galle, it had already been used for flying boats. Now it was of great strategic value as a calm water base for the reconnaissance flying boats which were to search for the incoming Japanese fleet.

The crew of 'L' had just two days to settle in, before the arrival of the three remaining Catalinas of 240 Squadron reached them from Karachi. These aircraft soon became, in Gardner's words, 'The vanguard of the whole flood of new strength at Koggala as more aircraft joined them from other RAF squadrons together with three Dutch Catalinas which had escaped from Java.'

My father described the defensive preparations that had already been rushed in, although these were still inadequate against the threat, particularly the need to strengthen air force capability. Two RAF fighter squadrons equipped with Hurricanes had arrived together with a squadron of Fairey Fulmer fighter/bombers.[1] They were joined by an odd assortment of outdated machines already in Ceylon. A new runway had been constructed on the racecourse at Colombo and the civil aerodrome at Ratmalana, 7 miles south of Colombo, had been taken over by the RAF and the runway extended.

Soon all the ships in the major ports of Tricomalee and Colombo, which would be key targets for Japanese attack, were ordered to sail so as to leave no shipping at the mercy of the enemy.

Charles Gardner then described how the Koggala base defences were being prepared:

> Accommodation and flying control facilities around the lake had been established. This required the demolition of many houses and closing down of several temples near the lake. The Buddhist priests left their holy places on the understanding that the temples would not be demolished, that they would be wired in and that they would be camouflaged. Compensation was paid to the priests. The station at the time of arrival consisted only of an officers' mess block with six bedrooms, an old two-room bungalow, which served as an operations room, a couple of houses which had been made into a sergeants' and airmen's' quarters and various tents.
>
> The arrival of more and more airmen from a fair cross section of the Empire, from Singapore and other places put a serious strain

on resources and the local school, Richmond College, was take
over and used for billeting. More blocks of officers and sergeants
sleeping quarters, and a complete set of station offices (including
a fully equipped squadron headquarters) were already being
built, and a new slipway was then nearly finished.

The transition from a lazy and pleasant advanced landing area
to a secondary base had been steady but gradual. Its promotion
to the first rank of Far Eastern importance came upon it suddenly
with the collapse of Singapore.

The most-wanted arrivals on the island were the Catalinas, and my
father was only too conscious that it was they whose task it was to try
and locate the Japanese fleet and thus be reported back to base. He and
the rest of the Catalina crews were under no illusion that to fly these
long-range search missions was extremely dangerous, particularly as
the Japanese carrier-borne aircraft would present a real threat to them
of being shot down.

So, regular standing patrols were quickly organised. Gardner wrote:

> These patrols known generally as the Bread Run was a crossover
> about 400 miles due East of the southern tip of Ceylon. Its
> objective was to cover the likely approach to the island by
> the Japanese naval forces which were now known to be in the
> Andamans (in the Bay of Bengal). The Bread Run was flown daily
> and during that time the weather was brilliant with unlimited
> visibility.

Charles's logbook shows his first patrol from Lake Koggala was on
17 March to '90 degrees E' during which he flew for 14 hours 30 minutes.
Further patrols were recorded on 20, 22, 24, 27 and 30 March, all searching
for the Japanese fleet but with no success. In those six days he flew nearly
97 hours of which 7 hours were at night. His only consolation for these
long flights was the cramped but accommodating interior of the Catalina
and the provision, as we have already noted, of a few comforts including
bunks, a primitive electric stove and a toilet.

Unsurprisingly by now he and the other crew members must have
become very weary, although Charles does not mention this. He does
relate other duties, which included 'flap patrols to investigate alarming
(but unsubstantiated) reports of enemy aircraft formations'. All the same,
a Japanese attack of some sort on Ceylon was obviously in the wind and
the 'Bread Run' became the island's first line of defence.

My father continued, 'The air of tension on the island was growing steadily. Practice air raid warnings caused locals to rush headlong through the streets.' At the beginning of April the first of the Catalinas of 413 (Canadian) Squadron arrived captained by Squadron Leader Burchall from St John's, New Brunswick. They were immediately re-fuelled and brought up to availability. Zero hour was approaching.

Charles wrote:

> On April 4 came the first news of the approach of the long awaited Japanese formation. Sqd Ldr Burchall, out on his first patrol, sent back a first sighting report of an enemy force about 350 miles south east of Galle. Confirmation was awaited (regulations required it to be repeated three times) – but none ever came and we can only presume that the Catalina was shot down almost immediately after signalling the invaluable first warning to Ceylon.

In fact, Burchall's aircraft was shot down by Japanese carrier-based aircraft and crash-landed in the sea killing several crew members. Burchall and several others got out alive, were captured and had to endure horrific torture and punishment. Burchall survived the war and later gave evidence to an international tribunal on Japanese atrocities.

Gardner continued:

> Immediately the sighting report was received in Colombo Jock Graham (who had escaped from Singapore) was ordered off to assist in the shadowing of the Japanese force. He took off just after tea-time and before turning out to sea did a low beat-up of the mess. The red glow of his painted hull as he pulled up over the lake was the last Koggala saw of Jock. He reached the patrol area at last light, and soon afterwards sent a signal saying that he had sighted three enemy destroyers.
>
> Back in the Ops Room everyone waited for a further signal saying he had picked up the main fleet. Another signal did come – reporting six more destroyers – after which there was silence. Messages sent to Jock produced no acknowledgement and it soon became clear that Graham was lost. All that can be presumed is that he flew over the top of the Japanese fleet at night without seeing them and that they shot him down before he had time to get a message out. The loss of Jock a few hours after the loss of Burchall cast a gloom over Koggala [Graham's aircraft was never discovered].

At this point, according to the book *The Most Dangerous Moment*, by fellow RAF pilot Michael Tomlinson, my father's aircraft 'L' was ordered into action to find and track the Japanese.

Tomlinson wrote:

> When Graham's Catalina had failed to return, assumed like Burchall's shot down, the essential need remained of keeping watch on the Japanese warships. The chances of a third flying boat doing so without being destroyed seemed poor indeed, but the men who were detailed to regain contact did not shirk from the unenviable task. They were Flt Lt Bradshaw DFC (with P/O Gardner as second pilot) and his crew in the Bismarck Catalina from 240 Squadron.

However, according to my father two Catalinas took off at first light on 5 April to patrol two lines – one east, the other to the west. The two captains tossed up for which one and his aircraft took the westward run.

Charles described what happened next:

> We reached the area at first light and were on the first leg of our patrol when we sighted a formation of aircraft which appeared to be Fulmars. Since Fulmars were known to be in the area we recorded the fact and continued the search. Almost immediately afterwards we saw on the horizon a naval force steaming west. Flt Lt Bradshaw ran in towards the ships with the objective of identifying them as Japanese (our own naval forces were quite probably in the area) when the leading battleship opened fire with her secondary armament.[2] At this time we were only 20ft above the sea and a good six miles from the battleship. Despite this the first salvo was only 100 yards short and other salvos came even nearer.
>
> We turned into the sun and for the rest of the day the Catalina shadowed the Japanese without experiencing any further opposition. The force sighted consisted of three battleships, four cruisers, an aircraft carrier and destroyers; and this was the strength we estimated which was received in Colombo about the time the first shots were being fired from the warship.

Although neither Gardner nor the crew knew it at the time, they were extremely lucky. The aircraft they had sighted earlier were not Fulmars but Japanese Zeros on their way to bomb Ceylon. They were not interested in a lone Catalina and, unlike the fate endured by Burchall, there were no available aircraft on the carriers to shoot them down. In any case the Japanese realised their position had been plotted by now and this sighting could be treated with indifference.

It was 7.50am on Easter Sunday, 5 April when the first enemy formations appeared over Ratmalana. Through a breakdown in communications on the ground, nobody was prepared for the suddenness of the attack, including the Hurricanes which were caught on the ground or just climbing into the air.

The attack lasted little more than 20 minutes during which twenty-seven aircraft were lost including particularly a squadron of Fleet Air Arm Swordfishes who had been ordered to attack the Japanese with torpedoes. There was damage throughout the island particularly at the port of Colombo and eighty-five civilians were killed. But, to the disappointment of the Japanese, they did not find the British fleet in harbour, their main objective. The most serious effect of the raid was to civil morale and large numbers of the Ceylonese fled the city.

In the book *The Most Dangerous Moment* a full account of the air raid on Ceylon is given, together with a detailed description of the tactics employed by Catalina 'L' in shadowing the Japanese fleet. For this Tomlinson quoted my father who related how this was done. He wrote: 'God was with us because the carrier force aircraft were all away; otherwise, in the clear blue sky, we could not possibly have got away with it.'

After being shot at, his Catalina had first flown on to above Dondra Head at the southern tip of Ceylon from which they sent off a full amplifying report, before resuming their patrol duties.

Gardner continued:

> We then shadowed this fleet for the rest of the day. We invented on the spur of the moment an obvious tactic for survival. We flew at wave-slapping height and then, with all the crew placed at vantage points for look out, pulled briefly up to 100 feet. If no Japanese masts broke the horizon we went down to nought feet again and flew on to where the distant horizon had been. Here we repeated the exercise. In this way we successfully shadowed the Japanese, never, after the initial identification, seeing the tops of their masts and never being identified as a radar blip to them. (We did not know then that their ships were not equipped with radar.) We did not see the Japanese aircraft return, nor, mercifully, any Japanese aircraft at all.

Michael Tomlinson noted, 'Bradshaw and his crew in their Catalina, using the most skilled tactics, had been doing a splendid job keeping an eye on the warships for most of the day, and the fact that they managed this and returned safely to Koggala was one of the major triumphs of the day.'

It should be recognised that to fly at 'nought feet' on a hazardous patrol of over 10 hours took not only courage but great airmanship from both pilots. Flying so low over the sea is dangerous in any circumstances because there are no reference points and altitude at that level is impossible to measure accurately. That such tactics were designed mainly to avoid radar, it was no consolation to them to learn later that the Japanese had none. Years afterwards my father still agonised over this.

Following the Easter Sunday attacks there was a short period of 'lull' on the island. Search missions for the missing aircraft were carried out but no traces were found. Two more RAF Catalinas arrived to bring the total number to squadron strength. My father flew two more patrols and on 15 April they 'located and shadowed Jap warships – one was battleship Nagato'.

Referring to the two newly arrived Catalinas which had now joined the force, Gardner noted:

> The new arrivals were at Koggala just in time for the second phase of the Japanese raid, which began on April 9. It was reported that the force which had been sighted by us was off the east coast of Ceylon and making its way towards Trincomalee. We were ordered off on a night patrol which embraced the last hours of darkness. But because our ASV [Anti-Surface Vessel Radar] was unserviceable, Flt/Lt Thomas was sent instead. Thomas took off by flare path and, just after dawn, sent through an emergency signal reporting a large Japanese force. His message was interrupted before its end and it was obvious from his continued silence that he too had been shot down.

It is quite probable that if my father's aircraft had flown this mission he too would have been lost. He was always quite frank about his luck in later years, and in my room at home sits a miniature teddy bear, now in a glass case, which was his lucky charm which he carried throughout his RAF career.

As it happens there was no further major attack on Ceylon, although my father's aircraft continued to fly patrols. He recalled being on the old

'Bread Run' when they came across the Japanese battleship *Nagato*, again escorted by a cruiser. 'We shadowed all day using the techniques which had been successful before, and when last seen just at last light, the two Jap ships were heading west.' It was the last encounter he was to have with them.

But suddenly everything changed and Ceylon was no longer the object of Japanese attack. Winston Churchill, in his history of the Second World War, described what happened. In a letter to President Roosevelt on 17 April he asked for help and suggested that the US Pacific Fleet divert towards the Japanese 'which might be of such a nature as to compel Japanese naval forces in the Indian Ocean to return to the Pacific'.

But by the next day, 18 April, this was no longer necessary, even if the Americans had agreed to such action, for 'the grievous anxieties' were removed when the Japanese retreated.

Churchill wrote:

> We were in at the end of the Japanese advance towards the West. Their naval incursion was outside the main orbit of Japanese expansionist policy, They were making a raid and a demonstration. They had no serious plan for overseas invasion of Southern India and Ceylon. If, of course, they had found Colombo unprepared and devoid of air defence they might have converted their reconnaissance in force into a major operation.

However credible the Japanese excuse for withdrawal might seem, with the US Pacific Fleet steaming down towards them, it was withdrawn, much to the relief of my father, and all those on Ceylon. They might have wondered, 'If only we knew of Japan's true intentions in the first place!'

Thus the Japanese turned round and returned to the Pacific now under threat from the Americans. They had singularly failed to find and destroy the outnumbered and out-gunned British Eastern Fleet which had been a priority and had no idea where they were. In fact the bulk of the fleet, under orders, had withdrawn to Addu Atoll, a ring of coral islands off the Maldive islands, some 600 miles to the south-west of Ceylon. As Churchill put it, 'They might have encountered the British Fleet and inflicted, as was not impossible a severe defeat upon us . . . such a trial of strength was avoided by good fortune and prompt action'.

My father, in his sixteen-page report, concluded:

> At the end of this period of excitement it was obvious that Koggala had done very well indeed. Although three valuable

machines and their crews had been lost, the warnings which had been sent as their last act had certainly saved both Colombo and Trimcomalee from far heavier batterings than they actually received. In addition the defences were enabled at the alert, with the result that the Japanese lost far more aircraft than the raids were worth.

As a postscript, I have little knowledge or memory of this period or my father's departure from Loch Erne. In view of the emergency in the Far East this was, as we have seen, rather sudden and would have left my mother, with two small children, and one on the way – my sister Helen who was born in November 1942 – with the unenviable task of packing up and returning home. At the time we owned a small open-topped Morris 8 which had been left for her to use. Having not driven before, she was very nervous. I do recall travelling in the car with mother driving and father 'instructing'. One of his remarks does come to mind, 'stick in the bloody clutch!' This, of course, did little for her confidence.

Unsurprisingly, after he left for Ceylon, we had an accident. I remember sitting in the passenger seat when we suddenly rolled off the road and landed in a field. I can just recall scrambling out and being rescued by some Americans who happened to be passing. Happily, neither my mother nor baby brother were badly hurt and the car was abandoned.

We eventually reached home safely. Almost the first thing my father did when he returned after the war was to set about retrieving the car from Northern Ireland, which, after some time, he successfully did and we ran it for a few years.

Chapter Sixteen

End of 'Ops' – Broadcasting Begins

On 2 May 1942, my father made his first flight as captain of the 'Bismarck' Catalina. It was a patrol described by him as 'a special job'. There is no indication what that job was, although he had on board two Canadians, Wing Commander Plant, who later rose to become Air Vice Marshal in Canada, and Pilot Officer Bayley, who was to be promoted to Squadron Leader. This might have had some bearing on it. Unfortunately when returning to base at night, he suffered a total failure in one engine and had to limp home. Not the most auspicious start as 'skipper'.

During June, Gardner carried out seven routine patrols and test flights accumulating over 70 hours in the air before he flew the aircraft to Bangalore in India for a major overhaul. This gave him a break from 'Ops' but by early July he was flying again, this time as co-pilot in a DH 86, a four-engined light transport aircraft on a patrol over Cochin harbour. Later, in September, he was back in a Tiger Moth, flying himself 'on circuits and bumps' from Bombay. The purpose of the Tiger flight is unknown, although it might have something to do with his new job, as we shall find out.

By now, 20 September, his Catalina was ready and after an acceptance flight he returned for duty in Koggala shortly to find himself in the middle of a large air-sea rescue lasting eight days and involving eight Catalinas.

This occurred after a Japanese submarine had torpedoed the merchant ship SS *Martaban* in the Indian Ocean. We have details of this operation from his logbook and an official summary of events. It was on 13 October 1942 that messages were received that the *Martaban* had been attacked. My father was despatched to investigate and sighted the submarine, but it dived before he could retaliate. Shortly afterwards he found the stricken vessel on fire with lifeboats in the water signalling SOS.

Gardner radioed the position of the ship and lifeboats, and returned to base where a full-scale rescue operation was mounted using all available aircraft and deploying naval vessels to the area. Unfortunately no further sightings were made and after three days Headquarters in Colombo suggested they were unlikely to be successful and suggested abandoning the effort. Happily this view did not prevail, for the next day the wreck of the ship and the first of four lifeboats were located and navy ships raced to pick up the survivors.

By 19 October all four lifeboats had been found and a total of sixty crew members rescued. In all over 200 hours had been flown, of which my father's aircraft, which made the first sighting, spent 39 hours in the air.

More routine patrols and ferry flights for senior officers followed, including flying to Addu Atoll when he made his first crossing of the equator. What was not routine, however, was escorting the famous liner *Mauretania*, on which he had sailed on her maiden voyage to New York in 1939, from the port of Cochin on troop transport duties. She was escorted by HMS *Devonshire*, which was now attached to the Eastern Fleet.

By the turn of the year on 10 January 1943 my father made his last flight in his Catalina 'L for Lionel', having been posted as temporary Controller at RAF Ratmalana. With it came promotion to Flight Lieutenant. This change to shore duty must have been met with mixed feelings – relief that he had probably come safely to the end of his operational flying career, and some sadness at leaving his squadron and aircraft after a worthy contribution.

In a broadcast some time later my father again recounted the feelings and fears of a Catalina 'driver'. This time it was not for a short story. In a highly descriptive piece, he spoke of 'the loneliness of dusk 500 miles from the nearest land', and 'the anxious peering at the cloud formations ahead just as the light goes – wondering what storms lie between you and base'. But the worst fear of all was 'the almost certain knowledge that, if you do go down, no one will ever find you. The sudden jerk of worry when no land appears at the right time, and you wonder if you've missed your little island, and are now flying into nothingness.'

He added:

There are, of course, ways of coping with these situations – and all pilots out there know them – use them every day – but I have never spoken to an overseas pilot yet who hadn't been weather scared at some time, or who hadn't had the sudden panic of 'I'm lost.' . . . If you do panic, of course, then you have had it, but every time you take the correct steps – a star fix – a navigation check – a bearing – if you can get one – there's still that specter in your mind of being another Catalina that just flew on to vanish for ever in the night.

This is the only direct description we have of his experience of the reality of wartime flying, and like most veterans of both world wars he spoke little of it afterwards. What we do know is that of the original Catalina squadron that left Loch Erne for Ceylon in February 1942 his 'Bismarck Cat' was the only one to survive the war.

In later life, my father did tell of how he might have been awarded a DFC, particularly for the dangerous and unflagging shadowing of the Japanese fleet while under fire. Unfortunately, it appears he robbed himself of this gallantry award. For, unknown to him, while his squadron boss was making out the recommendation, Charles was playing 'silly buggers' with other colleagues. He was trying to steer paper darts on the draught of a fan into the CO's office. The CO, seeing Gardner as the main culprit, threw the application into the waste-paper basket.

Charles's new temporary appointment as controller at Ratmalana turned out to be short-lived and he was ordered to assist with a secret mission code-named 'Operation Pamphlet' in February 1943. This was devised to provide anti-submarine escort and protective air patrols for an important convoy during passage across the Indian Ocean, for which he was returned to flying duties.

We have a copy of the Operational Order signed by Group Captain R.L. Mills, Commanding Officer at RAF Koggala, marked 'Most Secret'. The Order is comprehensive detailing everything from the required navigational positions of three escorting Catalinas, to secret communications requirements, rescue procedures and crew accommodation arrangements.

So what was this convoy that required such attention and why did my father keep a copy of the operational order? On research I found this was probably the convoy he referred to in a BBC newsreel broadcast in July 1945. In it he stated that:

I can well remember in 1943 taking off in the dark from the Island of Diego Garcia (a Coral Island in the Indian Ocean used as an RAF base) to meet and escort a troop convoy consisting of such ships as the Queen Elizabeth, the New Amsterdam, Monarch of Bermuda and the Isle de France on their way to Australia.

With ships of that size and fame, full of many thousands of soldiers, no wonder a special operation had been mounted to protect them. It must have been one of the more important convoys of the war, and no wonder he retained the secret operations order. In fact, the ships were carrying the Australian 9th Division from Egypt, where it had been active in the Western Desert Campaign, back to Australia to be available for proposed offensive operations against New Guinea.

Later that month Flight Lieutenant Gardner was posted again to 222 Group HQ Air Staff (Training). It is not quite clear what his job was but his logbook gives a clue as he was now flying himself around the region in a Tiger Moth (as mentioned) and later a Lysander, the aircraft made famous for dropping SOE officers and partisans behind the lines in Nazi Germany.[1] These local flights across Ceylon and India in what he described as 'almost his personal aircraft' would have been a precursor to a change of direction which returned him from RAF pilot to information officer and campaign broadcaster.

This came about in September 1943, when my father wrote a memo to his AOC (Air Officer Commanding). He asked permission to carry out a weekly series of local broadcasts which were more or less a counterblast to Japanese propaganda directed at this country. He had been asked to do this by a Mr Aubrey Herbert (probably of the British information services). The programme was to be called 'Listening Post' and a draft script scheduled for transmission was attached.

The AOC 'washed his hands' with an ambiguous reply the same day – 'No Comment' he wrote, signed ARL (Air Vice-Marshal Alan Lees). My father took that as a 'yes' – after all he didn't say no – and began a series of broadcasts countering some absurd Japanese victory claims as the Americans moved ever closer to their shores. We still have several of these scripts in a folder marked 'Listening Post'.

These broadcasts were far removed from Charles's news reports for the BBC and were, as stated, unashamedly counter propaganda. For this he was given access to local monitoring reports of news and propaganda put out by enemy radio stations, and which he systematically exposed and de-bunked. This would explain why he was given the use of his own aircraft for news gathering and information around the area.

If the saying 'The first thing to be abandoned in war is the truth' was accurate, the following extracts from his frequent 'anti-propaganda' reports gives an interesting historical perceptive of how things were in 1943.

In his first broadcast in September 1943, he observed a serious change in Japanese propaganda, which up to that point had stated their belief that they had special spiritual guidance which would overcome anything the Allies threw at them. Gardner commented, 'In the last few weeks the Japanese have made one of the biggest changes to their propaganda since the beginning of the war. They have had to admit that Japanese so-called spiritual superiority is not going to win them the war – and that Allied production is now a vital and very chastising factor.'

Having summarised Japan's increased (and desperate) production efforts to support her armed forces, Gardner concluded: 'And so there in a nutshell we have it – a frightened Japan – face to face with the material quality of our enormous production. They cannot equal it and they cannot destroy it.'

Later in the month in his 'Listening Post' broadcast, he looked 'dispassionately' at the propaganda fronts. (The BBC and Richard Dimbleby would have approved of this.) He said, 'Amid all the noise of claims and counter claims in the explanations and interpretations of events which go to form the day to day propaganda fronts, we can see that the publicists on either side are working to a pattern, a pattern of policy which is woven for them by the fluctuating fortunes of the military position.'

As an example, which he probably expressed with a slightly triumphant voice, he declared:

> At the beginning we had the Germans working on the theme of splitting France and Britain. From there they moved to a peace offensive, which ended in failure. The next main pattern round on which the German propaganda was built, was tempered by the attack on Russia, and again they attempted to split the Allies by appealing to Anti-Bolchevist sentiments. This failed, and the cessation of German victories and the beginning of their long line of defeats caused Goebbels to turn with anxiety to his home propaganda. With a sudden and unexpected devotion to realism he began to tell the German people that they were fighting a defensive war and they had better win it, because there was no mercy to be had from the United Nations.

As for 'the pattern of Japanese propaganda', he said:

> We will see this too has reached the frank admission of difficulties stage. The Japanese, just like the Germans, are taking the line taken by Mr. Churchill in 1940, a year when our military fortunes were at their lowest ebb. In other words, at their own admission, the enemy are in the unenviable position in which we found ourselves three years ago. The tables have been turned.

143

His point was reinforced in early October when he stated, 'The fact that Japan is now spending something like 60% of her propaganda time shouting to everyone how happy her local enslaved population are, is one of the most direct admissions we could have that they are, in fact, very unhappy. In other words, Japan is very frightened indeed.'

Then on 20 October he referred to Japanese reports that at Trincomalee there had been a 'pounding' of harbour and harbour installations and the 'setting on fire' of a large transport aircraft. He countered: 'We who live on the island know that all that happened was that a Japanese aircraft approached our eastern coast and was, to use the words of the official communiqué, "destroyed."'

By December, the Japanese were clearly becoming desperate for some success – be it factual, which it wasn't, or imaginary, which it was. Two broadcasts for 'Listening Post' tell the story.

First, on 1 December, Charles reported:

> The Japanese propaganda machine has been thrown sadly out of gear this week by the American successes in the Gilbert islands. The Japanese have hardly known what to make of this and their attitude had swung right round the compass several times before settling down to claim that the whole thing was a Japanese naval victory.
>
> How the occupation by the Americans of several important strategic islands in the Pacific can be passed off as a Japanese victory is beyond me, but then so are most of the Japanese propaganda themes these days.

But the most outrageous Japanese claim came later that month, described by my father as:

> The most amazing propaganda feat of the war. It was nothing less than the sinking of nearly all the American Pacific fleet. Not only, of course, are these claims not true, but no major air or sea engagements have taken place at all lately. In Washington, even Navy Secretary Knox couldn't begin to explain it. 'The whole thing,' he said, 'is ridiculous, fantastic and incredible.' He concluded, 'Whatever the real reason is as to "why" it must be obvious that such desperate device could only have been occasioned by an equally desperate situation.'

Although 'Listening Post' was the first continuous step for returning my father from operational flying to broadcasting, the earliest indications of a change came previously in late May. He was asked to produce a radio version of the famous War Office film *Desert Victory* which recorded the triumph of Montgomery's Eighth Army over Rommel in North Africa in October/November 1942. For this he was sent the script of the film from which he was asked to produce/re-write an adaptation for the wireless.

We have copies of both the original film script and the adapted one. The original has my father's comments written on the back. It must have taken him some time single-handed to do this, although he was aided by an Ian Houston in Delhi who made the new recordings.

And so in June 1943, 'Desert Victory' was broadcast in Ceylon. It was clearly designed to give a morale uplift while still under threat from the Japanese. His re-worked script began in rousing words:

> For the Desert Rats . . . the men of the Eighth Army, who, on 23rd of October 1942 left the holes they had scratched for themselves in the rock and sand of the desert and moved forward to destroy the myth of Rommel's invincibility and to complete the liberation of the Second Roman Empire overseas.

It concluded in similar rousing fashion:

> In England when the news of the Eighth Army's triumph was broadcast, the people cheered and turned to their work with even greater determination than before. The Africa Corps, utterly broken, and possessed with no thought of flight, was hotly pursued. But the Eighth Army was not only the thunder behind, but the lighting ahead, as they chased them out of Africa.

We still have a copy of the station announcer's introduction in which he proclaimed: 'Desert Victory is the story of the Eighth Army from El Alamein to Tunis. It is a radio documentary based on the famous war film. Most of the sound effects including the El Alamein barrage were recorded in the field of battle or taken from captured German newsreels. The programme is produced by Charles Gardner.' (No indication that he was a serving RAF officer.)

How all this came about, especially 'Listening Post', we do not know, except several high-ranking RAF officers and British information officials knew of Charles Gardner, the BBC broadcaster. They would have known particularly his reporting of the AASF in France and the subsequent book and, of course, his Battle of Britain broadcast. It is also possible that Lord Louis Mountbatten, who was appointed Supreme Commander for South

East Asia in early 1943, had a hand in it. This was especially so as he was very much aware of the need to promote the successes of his command and to rebut Japanese efforts to undermine it. And later he was to recruit my father onto his own staff, as we shall see.

But for now, Flight Lieutenant Charles Gardner was acting as both reporter/broadcaster for 'Listening Post' and RAF officer. He continued his local flying, both in Ceylon and India, adding the Avro Anson and the DH Dragonfly to his list of aircraft flown as first pilot. There were more patrols, ferry flights for senior officers and air firing exercises, so apparently it was still possible that he could return to operational flying.

But in December 1943 matters came to a head when he attended a series of meetings at Mountbatten's South East Asia Command (SEAC) HQ in New Delhi. He met a Wing Commander Russell who told him he was to be offered the appointment of Squadron Leader Broadcasting for the region and later the possibility of taking charge of the RAF News Room. However, he was also informed that he was to meet Air Marshal Joubert, the newly appointed Director General of Information and Civil Affairs for SEAC who reported to Mountbatten.

But Joubert had other plans for him. This he outlined in a subsequent meeting. He described a new overall PR organisation to co-ordinate and direct the PR work of all three services. My father was to be appointed to Joubert's staff and his duties summarised in a seven-point plan. These included organising and 'bringing into effect' a radio news reporting set-up on the South East Asia fronts and 'to write and speak certain war commentaries'. He was also to act as secretary of a small committee governing policy of wireless entertainment for the troops and in addition organise visits to the front by famous people such as J.B. Priestley.

My father was not advised of the rank for the new job but he was assured 'it may possibly be a squadron leader appointment'. Before he left, Joubert told him to pack his kit and await posting orders to Delhi but to leave his 'heavy kit' in Ceylon, 'as you will be back there in April'.

And so from January 1944 Charles Gardner was to abandon his RAF flying career for a new job for which he was uniquely qualified. It was not quite the one described by Joubert.

Chapter Seventeen

The Forgotten Army

It was not until late in the war that the impact of the Japanese invasion of Burma in early 1942, and the subsequent heroic and brilliant counter-campaigns by British and Empire troops of the 14th Army – the 'Forgotten Army'– became fully apparent to those at home. And nobody could have done more to record their astonishing story, and those of its commander, General William Slim, than my father.

From early 1944 until the capitulation of Japan in September 1945, Charles Gardner's RAF job – and his passion – was to write and relay the news from South East Asia Command – particularly the fighting in Burma and the vital support role played by the air force. He made hundreds of broadcasts, commentaries and wrote many feature stories and communiqués. Together with other notable contributors, there was hardly a family in Britain who did not eventually become aware of the 14th Army, its suffering, endurance and eventually its great victory.

It all began, as we have seen, with his appointment to Mountbatten's South East Asian Command (SEAC) staff in January 1944. But it was not to be working directly for Joubert as the Air Marshal suggested, but to take up the position offered by Wing Commander Russell as Squadron Leader in the HQ RAF Public Relations Department in Delhi and later to be moved to Kandy, Ceylon. His promotion came through in February 1944 with the title DADPR (Deputy Assistant Director of Public Relations) with direct and particular responsibility for broadcasting.[1]

Initially, however, he was deeply involved in setting up the RAF section of the large new PR organisation for South East Asia Command at the instigation of Lord Mountbatten. The objective was to bring to the attention of those so far away at home the outstanding contribution his command was making to the war and the fight against the Japanese.

His appointment to Russell's staff and promotion was not without some persuasion. It is clear from the minutes of the Joubert meeting in December that he had made no direct job offer. My father wrote: 'It was difficult to sort out fact from rumour – I was not told, nor did I ask for the exact title of this appointment, nor the rank carried by this appointment.' He added, 'There is no doubt that a large public relations organisation is being formed on the orders of the Supreme Commander, the pattern of it is as yet obscure to junior personnel.'

In a later minute of a routine organisational meeting sent for approval to Air Marshal Sir Richard Peirse, Commander of the Allied Air Forces South East Asia, he got right to the point. In a paragraph at the end marked for 'Action' Gardner identified the urgent requirement to bring Russell's establishment up to strength by appointing a squadron leader and a flight lieutenant (Broadcasting). Pushing his luck to near insubordination (not for the first time), he wrote back, 'The vacancies exist – it is merely a question of choosing the bodies.'

This seems to have done the trick, for – of course – this was the job and the rank originally offered by Russell before Joubert's intervention. It should not have been too difficult for the Air Marshal to endorse the requirement and three days later we have proof of his promotion when he signed a minute on 'Air Communiques' as C. Gardner, S/Ldr PR (RAF).

Reading between the lines, it is clear that future intentions from Joubert, however appealing, did not match up to an established job with rank promotion, and particularly the extra pay. This would have been important to him whose flight lieutenant's salary would have been barely enough to support the family at home with now three growing children.

Not only was the increased pay welcome but my father had already formed a good working relationship with Russell. He had probably also received more than a nod and a wink that the new job would be his. This was particularly so because during the first two weeks of February 1944 he was allocated an American Argus light aircraft so he and Russell could make a number of fact-finding flights in India, including to Jodhpur, Bombay and Ahmedabad. In his logbook he described these flights as 'The Russell Gardner Series'. This turned out to be a mutual approach to the new PR set-up after the move to Kandy scheduled for April.

My father's introduction to RAF PR coincided with a notable success for SEAC in Burma. On 28 February 1944 a series of press releases proclaimed the first major British victory of the 14th Army over the Japanese in the western coastal province of Arakan, where there had been constant fighting since 1942. The press statement described how the British defended a Japanese advance and had been encircled and heavily outnumbered. But, in a three-week campaign, 'in the heat and dust of the jungle', they had fought off the attack and in doing so largely destroyed the enemy forces.

Gardner's contribution was to write a supporting press release which stressed the importance of air superiority which allowed fleets of Dakotas to drop the supplies which had made the victory possible. 'Flying in daylight with escorts of Spitfires and Hurricanes, the supply-dropping Dakotas defied the reinforced Japanese fighter strength over the battle zone. During the 21 days of the main action over 1,500 tons of vital supplies were dropped to our troops for the loss of one Dakota,' he wrote.

But to understand the significance of the Arakan victory and my father's subsequent reports of a mounting and astonishing engagement, it is worth taking a short look back at what went before. In his files there is a fiteen-page typewritten short history of the campaign dated March 1946, from which I have reproduced extracts, beginning with the Japanese invasion of Burma. But first in an earlier despatch, Charles Gardner gave an excellent description of the geographical situation of Burma and its surrounding countries which gave reason for the Japanese attack, as follows:

> The map will show you Burma as a wedge separating us from a landlink with China to the East and with Malaya to the South. It is geographically, a cone-shaped wedge – wide at the top, and narrow at the bottom, but for the purposes of strategy we will regard it as a cylinder.
>
> The Eastern wall of the cylinder is the River Salween, the boundary between Burma and China and held by General Chiang Kai-Shek's troops. Some of his divisions had crossed the Salween to put an inward bulge into the cylinder wall.
>
> The Western wall runs 700 miles along the Chindwin river, a front manned entirely by British Imperial troops – by our county regiments, by Indians and Gurkhas and by West and East African Divisions.
>
> At the North, on top of the cylinder, is the British and Chinese force of the American General Stilwell. And in the South, the base of the Burma cylinder is the firmest in the world, the sea. with the all important port of Rangoon at the centre of the base.

With this in mind I now refer to Charles's short history of the Burma war up to February 1944 and the British victory in Arakan.

He wrote:

> The Burma tale opens two days after Pearl Harbour. The Japanese mobilised and ready, sprang at Burma along a route opened to

them by the defection of the neighbouring French Indo China (on the eastern border) and the surrender of Siam. Burma was vital to the Japanese as its possession would isolate China from its Western allies. It would also force Britain into a hurried defence of India in the border jungles of Assam, a battlefront which the Japanese regarded at that stage as 'just their cup of tea.'

Opposing them were General Alexander's slender forces, mainly the Ist Burma Corps under the command of General Sir William Slim. But the Japanese were too strong and the fate of Burma was sealed when the key port of Rangoon fell after a 'bewildering' few weeks of fierce fighting. The British, together with Chinese forces under General Stilwell, Chief of Staff to Chiang Kai-Shek, and over 100,000 refugees, were compelled to retreat and, for those in the south, foot slog towards the Indian border over 700 miles away, where supply lines could be re-established. This they did, overcoming constant Japanese incursions and most of all the severe jungle conditions, as there were no roads. The withdrawal was historic, and was later described as 'one of the most gallant and skillfully conducted actions of the war.'

As they moved north, General Slim's forces fought what has been described as 'one of the great battles of the war.' This was on the East bank of the River Chindwin at Shwegyin a barrier which they had to cross. There were no bridges across the river and no ferries capable of taking the heavy equipment – the tanks, field guns and transports, so Slim ordered their destruction to prevent the Japanese getting them. By now they found themselves under fierce attack from the Japanese who had thrust up the Chindwin to get ahead of the retreating forces and had now moved down the river in assault boats and were trying to land. They were successfully held off and at night made their escape in native ferry boats to 'march' the next 200 miles to the Indian border. The question why the Japanese didn't follow up with an immediate invasion of India, which could well have been successful, is still a mystery.

The monsoon (May to October) forced a lull on both sides. By this time the British had re-grouped along the Indian border and in the fine weather of December a British-Indian force launched the first offensive along Burma's West Coast to the coastal strip of Arakan, with the valuable supply base, the port of Akyab, the main target. A three pronged attack made good progress at first but was eventually beaten back by heavy Japanese resistance.

PART TWO

To speed up broadcasts to London a new studio was established by Charles (seen at the microphone) in a vacated room at the AASF HQ in Rheims. This allowed for direct transmissions. To mark the opening, all the war correspondents in Rheims were invited to a champagne reception in the new studio to hear the first broadcast, but had to keep very quiet while it was on the air.

After the blitzkrieg in May 1940, everyone had to leave France and return home. Charles continued war coverage from London. In July he made his famous broadcast describing an air battle over the Channel when the Germans tried to bomb a convoy at sea. Here he can be seen in his tin hat preparing for that broadcast with the recording car heavily camouflaged against German attack.

"AH, HERE ARE THE HURRICANES — SQUARE FOUR"

With Grimsey's love.

Charles's air battle broadcast was headline news for days. In current terms 'it went viral' and even interested the cartoonists – as can be seen here. The broadcast is still played today and even a commercial record was made with proceeds given to RAF charities.

Charles Gardner recording a piece at Dover during the Battle of Britain. It is believed that this image was taken on 14 July 1940, the day that he recorded his famous account of an air battle over the Channel. Note the mattress on the recording car's roof.

The record and cardboard sleeve for the original BBC vinyl recording of Charles's live broadcast of a combat over the Channel during the Battle of Britain. Recorded on the cliff top at Dover during the day on 14 July 1940, the report was played that same evening on the Home Service's *Nine O'clock News*. The recording lasted 7 minutes and 27 seconds. This record remains in the possession of the Gardner family.

In the autumn of 1940, being 'bored' at the BBC because the censors prevented any proper news reporting, Charles 'joined up' and entered the prestigious RAF officer training establishment at Cranwell where he is seen sitting at the centre of his group.

A contemporary portrait of Pilot Officer Gardner after successfully passing out from RAF Cranwell in early 1941. After various training missions he was eventually posted to Loch Erne in Northern Ireland where he joined 240 Squadron flying Catalina flying boats. He completed several escort duties in the North Atlantic, protecting vital convoys, before being posted to Ceylon when it became threatened by Japan.

This painting, by the well-known aviation artist Mal Grosse, shows Charles's Catalina taking off from its base on Lake Koggola on the south western tip of Ceylon. 'His' Catalina was well-known in the RAF as the 'Bismarck Cat', for this was the very aircraft which sighted and followed the German battleship before it was destroyed by the Royal Navy. A bullet hole, caused by German fire, was still visible in the hull, although it had been patched over.

Pilot Officer Gardner, with fashionable moustache, in the captain's seat of what is probably a Catalina.

The interior of a Catalina looking towards the cockpit. The Catalina, designed and built in the United States, was a favourite aircraft in Coastal Command. With a duration of over 20 hour's flying time and a crew of up to ten, it carried torpedoes, depth charges and machine guns for attacking German submarines and warships. Gardner wrote, 'The Cat is a grand flying boat perfect for the job.'

The now Flight Lieutenant Charles Gardner pictured in tropical kit in Ceylon, where he was to spend over three years of his RAF career. He truly loved the island – 'the lovely Lanka' – for its beauty and people.

In the autumn of 1943 Lord Mountbatten was appointed Supreme Commander South East Asia Command (SEAC) – he is seen here, third from the left, in conference with other senior officers. By now Charles had been recruited onto his staff as a senior press officer. He was tasked with promoting the 14th Army, the 'Forgotten Army', whose astonishing achievements of defeating the Japanese in Burma was perceived to be little recognised at home.

Air Marshal Joubert, who was at the time this picture was taken Squadron Leader Gardner's commanding officer. He had been appointed by Mountbatten as Director General of Information and Civil Affairs for SEAC. Charles's relationship with Joubert was not as harmonious as it was with the Supreme Commander.

Lord Mountbatten spent much time 'meeting the men' who were fighting in the Far East – here he is inspecting naval personnel on an airfield in Ceylon. Mountbatten was always very publicity conscious and later he asked Charles to help with a 'Royal Secret' concerning his nephew, Prince Philip, and Princess Elizabeth about press rumours of a royal romance.

In March 1945 Gardner made a final tour of Burma. He interviewed both General Sir Oliver Lees, C-in-C of Allied Land Forces, seen here pointing out to Charles the current situation on a map of Burma, and the C-in-C of Allied Land Forces, the fabled General Sir William Slim. During his time in SEAC Charles contributed a multitude of radio scripts and articles describing and celebrating the Burma Campaign. It was his passion to make sure the 'Forgotten Army' was, indeed, not forgotten.

Photographs from the Gardner family.

The islanders in what is now Sri Lanka have not forgotten the Catalina and its crews and the role they played from 1942 in protecting them from the Japanese. In memory there is now a Catalina Drive and, as seen in this recent photograph taken by Charles's grandson, Alexander Gardner, a Catalina Grill, located by the Koggala air base.

Charles was back in London to celebrate VE Day and was included in a team of broadcasters who described the events that day. He was also invited to be a guest on the popular radio show *In Town Tonight* – he is seen here with Flight Lieutenant Maurice Scott DFC, who told listeners about his flying experiences in the Italian campaign.

Meanwhile, in Central Burma there was better news, where the first of the fabled Chindit airborne raids, led by General Wingate, was taking place and successfully causing havoc behind enemy lines – destroying, fighting and obstructing them in every way. In doing so they also proved the British were able to fight in the jungle. It was said the confusion caused by this small expedition of 3,000 men prevented the enemy from launching a big India-bound expedition in 1943.

Into this scene in the Autumn of 1943 stepped Lord Mountbatten, the recently appointed Supreme Allied Commander of the new South East Asia Command (SEAC). With his appointment he formed the 14th Army under the leadership of General Sir William Slim who would be responsible for all operations against the Japanese in Burma.

Mountbatten quickly issued a three point directive which were:

1. Re-open a land route to China. [General Stilwell had already begun this by building a new road to Ledo]
2. Retake Burma.
3. Prepare to re-take Singapore.

The new 'Supremo' soon had plans for all these things:

Firstly, Stilwell was to push on with his Ledo road project aided by a Wingate expedition dropped behind the Japanese divisions facing him.

Secondly, Burma would be taken by what was described as 'the impossible directive' by advancing through the jungle, over the mountains, down the rivers to Rangoon. Mountbatten insisted it could be done by moving in fine weather, and particularly by living on air supply for the whole advance, for which many Dakota aircraft, on which all depended were painstakingly collected.

Thirdly, the re-take of Singapore was put on hold, awaiting the outcome of the Burma advance and the necessary equipment, particularly amphibious vehicles which had been denied him in favour of requirements in Europe and also prevented an intended amphibious invasion of Rangoon.

The Japanese, sensing danger, struck and struck hard first in the Arakan (as we have seen). Following the earlier incursion, they had encircled the 7th and 5th Indian Divisions expecting them to withdraw, and in doing so would decimate them by

151

enfilading fire. So certain were they of this victory that Tokyo radio announced that they were now on their way to Calcutta.

In actual fact neither of the two divisions moved, but went into an all-round defence relying upon air supply to keep them going. For twenty days the battle raged, the first big 'try-out' of Wingate's theory that in the Burma campaign supplies for the fighting troops should be taken 'down the chimney.'

'Meanwhile the 26th Indian Division and the British 36th Division were sent down from the North to raise the siege. The enemy were caught between the 'hammer and the anvil,' and was forced to retire leaving 7,000 dead on the field.

This big defensive victory was the first defeat inflicted on the Japanese by the 14th Army.

And so, with this background, it was no great surprise that this was hailed as a great success and it is no surprise that my father reflected joyously in his chatty style in what we think was his first broadcast in his new role six days later. He said, 'Looking back on February I think we can say that it has been the most interesting month we have ever had on the Burma front. And a very encouraging one too – for, from it, emerges the shape of things to come – a cheerful shape for us – a depressing one for the Japanese.'

'In that battle can be seen a very pretty pattern of army-air force co-operation,' he continued. 'It has been impossible to write about it from an army point of view without mentioning the air force in every other line – nor has it been possible to talk about the air force without paying tribute to the army.' Looking particularly at the air force role he wrote:

> We can take great heart from what we shall find. In the first place the whole battle depended upon air supply to the encircled 7th Division and to our other ground forces. This air supply was the key to the whole business because without it the troops, great hearted as they were, could not have carried on for more than a few days.

Gardner, as an RAF officer, also took an indepth look at the part played by them, not just in air supply, but in strike actions against the enemy on the ground and long-rage sorties against distant Japanese bases.

He continued:

> But the air power which ensured our forces would stay put was not enough. More offensive things had to be done as well

152

in order to wipe out as much of the Japanese as possible and get the rest of it back behind its own lines. So, direct offensive action from the air was also needed. The relieving columns driving down from the North to squeeze out the Japanese needed help to do this. The ground troops looked to our dive bombers and fighter bombers and they didn't look in vain. The static positions on the ground were kept supplied by Dakotas, the relieving forces had the way blasted for them by the dive bombers.

My father noted that it was essential that the Japanese force should feel the 'pinch of hunger' and the need for ammunition and supplies be denied them. He continued:

The carts and sampans which they used to try and get material up towards the battle line were blasted by bombs, by machine gun fire and by 40mm 'Tank Busting' Hurricanes.

And into this general picture of disrupted communications the heavy and medium American and British bombers of the Strategic Air Force fitted like the missing piece of a jigsaw. Way south the Japanese base areas beyond the reach of our fighters were strafed and bombed. Stores that the enemy had accumulated to send forward to Arakan were set on fire and the railways by which they had proposed to send them were disrupted and the engines and rolling stock blown up.

All this, of course was achieved by air superiority. If our air was strongly challenged our position would have been difficult. It was here that the Spitfires came in. In the early stages of the battle the Japanese, who had scrimped and saved to produce enough fighter planes for the job, found that their best was not good enough. After a few days their precious fighters, already seriously depleted by the Spitfires, decided not to throw good money after bad and their bombers remained on the ground with no sortie flown.

So there we have the full pattern of our victory. The threads and cross threads of the Army and the Air Force. We do not need to be told in operations such as these lies our real strength, nor do the Japanese need to be told it. That is the lesson to be drawn from the last month's operation out here. We should look at it without complacency, but, at the same time, recognise that it is the security of our hopes.

A few days later in a broadcast to All India Radio, Charles was to continue the optimistic theme by describing more success. This time it was by the Chindits again. He referred particularly to their recent seizing of a Japanese base in Northern Burma, 200 miles behind enemy lines, which was a feat 'which makes military history'.

He stated:

> A large number of gliders were towed over the Chin Hills on a moonlit night and at previously chosen spots – places marked as likely landing grounds by the expedition a year ago – the gliders were cast off and landed. Out of them came American airfield construction engineers and British Chindits who helped and protected them as they worked. In 12 hours a useable landing strip had been made and by the evening troop-carrying Dakotas and C.47s were using it.[2] The Japs made no attempt to interfere – the surprise was complete.

Some four months later my father followed this up with an indepth feature article on the Chindits and their methods. The original script is marked 'Secret', and in an advisory note at the top of the page from SEAC Chief News Editor to the Air Ministry stated: 'Feature article by Gardner on glider led landings not released to correspondents. Suggest it might be illustrated with drawings of Illustrated News type.' Below was stamped 'Passed by Censor', so why the script was marked secret we do not know.

Because of the fascination which has been aroused by the Chindits and their leader General Wingate, both then and now, I have reproduced salient parts of the article below.

It reads:

> The principle of landing large forces behind enemy lines through the medium of aircraft is one which has been experimented with some time before the war, and has been put into practice, especially by the Germans and the Russians on several occasions. Crete was perhaps the outstanding example of co-ordinated glider and parachute troop landings. But these were all made on existing aerodromes. It was not until the Wingate expedition of Spring 1944 that airborne troops were used to seize land for the purpose of constructing an aerodrome on it.
>
> In the Wingate plan the first troops to come to earth on the chosen area of enemy held territory were not parachutists, as has

several times been mistakenly represented. They were glider-borne troops, flown in as passengers. In other words they were ordinary troops who required no special training for their method of arrival – a big point which means that any good troops well versed in jungle tactics can be made into the spearhead of such invasion.

In theory it does not seem to be a practical proposition to put down gliders at night into rough jungle country surrounded by the enemy and expect to fly men in troop carriers onto a serviceable aerodrome on the same spot the very next night. Yet this is exactly what was done in Burma with the Chindits – and the operation has since be repeated and with success.

General Wingate himself laid down the basic law for success of a glider-led expedition. 'We must go where the enemy temporarily is not,' he said. The sites chosen were ones which fell in with Wingate's axiom and everything was done to ensure there was no strong force of Japanese in the area.

The surveying and choosing of sites is not an easy task. Too close an inspection of the ground from the air might well tip our hand with the enemy. And there is always the danger that photographs taken by high-flying reconnaissance machines might fail to show some serious obstruction or fail to show the exact nature of the terrain. In Burma, however, Wingate had the experience of his last year's expedition to fall back on. He himself had marched through the country concerned and had, at the time, marked several places as likely glider-landing grounds.

The essentials of a glider site are that it should have a 600 yard landing run with reasonably clear approaches and the 600 yards should be capable of extension to 1,500 yards. The whole position, if possible should be defendable militarily if attacked.

When the first 'area-holding' troops are landed from the gliders, they are, of course, only lightly equipped. The next stage in the plan is to drop heavier arms, ammunition etc. which should be timed to start as soon as the last glider is down.

Thus, as we have seen, in a glider invasion which runs to schedule the site is rough-cleared, the holding troops and the combat engineers are down, mules, jeeps and bulldozers have been glider-landed and work has started on the extension of the area. And, all achieved within the first hour or so on the first night. At dusk, the first carriers will arrive with petrol, troops, food and supplies and an aerodrome stronghold will have been established in enemy territory.

This form of tactic – or modifications of it – has already proved a success in Burma. There everything is in its favour. The enemy cannot garrison every possible clearing, nor can it rush reinforcements about the country. In the Burma skies we have strong air superiority which is essential to such an enterprise. We are aided too by the Japanese seeming not to do much effective night flying or fighting.

In conclusion my father wrote: 'Anything in the nature of glider led invasions would be difficult in Western Europe, but modifications of the plans worked out by Wingate and his American associates might well be suitable to areas such as the Balkans.'

Three days later a successful British-led glider attack on the German-held Pegasus Bridge in France became the first engagement of the D-Day invasion.

Chapter Eighteen

Air Power and the Imphal Campaign

It was at this time, with the victories at Arakan and by Wingate's Chindits, depending on air support, that my father became involved in a serious dispute between the RAF and the United States Air Force, on which the British depended heavily both for men and aircraft. For, by now, the Eastern Air Command (EAC) had been formed combining the US 10th Air Force with the RAF 3rd Tactical Air Force under the command of US General George Stratemeyer.

Not for the first time, relationships between the RAF and USAF became strained, especially when the new Commander demanded control of all public relations and press information in his area to be issued through their headquarters in Calcutta. This was firmly opposed by SEAC commanders who wanted all communiqués from the front to go direct to one place, soon to be Kandy where Lord Mountbatten was now setting up his HQ.

In a widely distributed detailed memorandum of 2 April, Charles Gardner wrote that such orders had been issued by EAC suggesting they were to be put into immediate effect. 'It is this unilateral action which has brought matters to a head as SEAC has been put into a false position by a series of fait-accompli,' he wrote.

There followed a series of meetings, new proposals, re-proposals, more wrangling, much of which is detailed in further minutes written by my father before an uneasy truce was declared. Meanwhile he had taken delivery of a Percival Proctor, a three-seater communications aircraft widely used by the RAF, for the use of Russell and himself to travel the region easily and see for himself what was going on and, as it turned out, fierce action during the memorable siege at Imphal.

But first, some fun. As part of his 'familiarisation' of the type he flew from Delhi to Agra to see the great wonder that is the Taj Mahal, choosing to stay the night in Agra. I wonder if he found the view of the Taj more impressive from the air than from the ground?

It was now the last few days in Delhi before the great move of SEAC HQ to Kandy on 16 April 1944. Gardner (at the controls) and Russell set off in the Proctor on the long flight to Ceylon to RAF Ratmalana, the airfield that served Kandy. They arrived on 20 April coinciding with the official opening of Mountatten's HQ. My father was probably pleased to be back in Ceylon and no doubt recalled Joubert's instructions in December 'to leave heavy kit behind as you will be back there in April'.

The formal centralising of all SEAC activities in Kandy provoked more arguments with General Stratemeyer and his staff in Calcutta over PR control and other matters, including the use of the vital broadcasting transmitters. It was decided that Gardner and Russell would tour the EAC front on a fact-finding mission. They departed seven days later in the Proctor with my father 'driving', arriving at Calcutta on 28 April having made numerous stops on the way to meet local station commanders. At one stop-off he noted in his logbook: 'Landed on a pre-prepared strip with maintenance party only – 110 degrees in the shade – no ice!'[1]

After meetings in Calcutta with EAC staff, they flew on to the head-quarters of RAF 3rd Tactical Army in Comilla, near the south-western coast of India on the Burma front. A new airfield had been constructed by the RAF which was now heavily engaged in the crucial air supply to marooned British and Allied troops around Imphal on India's north-east border with Burma. Here heavy fighting had broken out as the Japanese attacked in an effort to drive into India. A siege situation developed around the defending British forces before eventually they were to force the enemy back, pursuing them even through the monsoon, inflicting heavy losses on the Japanese, who thought they were protected by the weather.

My father and Russell particularly wanted to witness the air operations around Imphal and on 4 May flew in an RAF supply Dakota which made several passes in the area to air drop jeeps and other supplies to the Chindit forces on the ground. He wrote in his logbook: 'Japanese attacking and surrounding Imphal. Flying in supplies. No Japanese fighter over Imphal Valley on any trip, lucky for us, [our] load included Jeeps for the Chindits.' No doubt my father 'filled his notebook' for later broadcasts and commentaries (which he did) describing these life-saving operations.

On return to Kandy, Squadron Leader Gardner filed his report. He made several suggestions including the linking of the three radio transmitters available (only one, that in Delhi, had the range to reach

Britain), the synchronising of all press releases and the placing of EAC/ American personnel at Kandy and vice versa in Comilla. He amplified this by proposing, 'An officer with enthusiasm should be posted to Comilla and naturally one who gets on with the Americans!' However, as he pointed out, 'It is time this matter was firmly settled on high level, and I understand it was probably being settled at this moment.'

In fact, as EAC and General Stratemeyer reported into SEAC High Command, Air Marshal Peirse, after discussion, and clearly with the support of Mountbatten, came down hard on EAC and decreed that all their PR and press matters must go through Kandy. Gardner's suggestions of interchanging staff were probably adopted to 'ease the pain'.

My father also highlighted problems with the press camp at Comilla which had been established to keep war correspondents close to the unravelling Imphal campaign. He described the atmosphere as 'bad,' adding, 'the mess is uncomfortable and ill equipped and the quarters are dark . . . there is no fly or mosquito proofing and no ice or Frigidaire'. He noted work had already begun on building a new press centre and with SEAC support other amenities should be provided including a PR aircraft so press could observe for themselves what was going on around Imphal. No doubt the unhappy war correspondents in Comilla would have appreciated these recommendations from a once 'fellow traveller'.

By this time it had become apparent in 'making themselves heard' in Britain, that a dedicated SEAC PR desk should be established in London at the Air Ministry.[2] It was, in fact, my father who pointed this out and after some research wrote a paper amplifying the proposal which he called the 'Rear Echelon'. He reckoned that a single officer might not be enough and that a full time PR officer should be sent to London to 'lay the foundations'.

He then sent a personal memo to Air Marshal Peirse asking for an interview concerning the 'Rear Echelon' with an unabashed proposal that it should be he who should be sent to visit the Air Ministry to 'see what goes on in the News Room and to get in touch'. Unafraid of putting himself forward, he concluded, 'I have not been in the U.K. for three and a half years of the four and a half of the war.'

In fact it is unlikely there could have been anyone better qualified to do this with his background as a reporter on two provincial newspapers, as well as being a well-known broadcaster with the BBC.

It was at this time that Charles became involved in what he considered to be an outrageous article written by a Mr Martin Moore in the *Calcutta*

Statesman. Moore had written that HQ staff in Kandy were 'living in exotic surroundings, leading a sybarite life'. He added that, 'there were three swimming pools, tennis and squash courts, three cinemas and, just around the corner – waiting for their master's pleasure, were troupes of Wrens and WAC's in strictly non issue evening gowns'.

Unable to contain himself, Gardner responded in an amusing letter to the Editor.

He wrote:

> With the warm glow which comes from knowing one is a sybarite, we thus all went out with swimming costumes and tennis and squash racquets. A little healthy exercise, will put us in good trim for the evening party. As a matter of form we asked the Camp Commandant where the nearest of the three swimming pools, the one measly squash court and the tennis courts were. He said he was busy and would we please go away.
>
> So we read the appropriate bit out of the Statesman and I regret to say, Mr. Editor, that the Camp Commandant said rude things and our morale fell. It appeared there were no swimming pools, nor tennis courts or squash courts. But we brightened up, after all we could go to one of three cinemas. But we couldn't. There were no cinemas but we are happy to say one is in fact being built – but the opening date is a little remote.

Unfortunately we have no knowledge of the Editor's response or if this letter was ever published – probably not.

Between 8 May and 28 July 1944 Squadron Leader Gardner made no further flights and the only entry in his logbook, written across the page, was 'D-Day' which soon was to change the whole course of the war and bring the Burma campaign into greater prominence. 'Very soon now, we hope, the spotlight of world attention is going to swing from the European war to the Far East,' he wrote later. 'General Slim's great 14th Army and the Allied Air Forces of Air Command South East Asia are winning a war which is imposing as greater strain on our soldiers and airmen as anything in which our troops have been engaged.

By now, after further discussion with the hierarchy, approval came through for my father's return home to start work on the new London PR organisation.

But before leaving, Charles was to make further broadcasts about the Imphal siege and its consequences, and write articles, including for the *RAF Journal*. His broadcasts were made in celebratory mood, beginning with his confirmation that at last a land victory had been achieved at Imphal.

He wrote:

> The clearing of the Kohima–Imphal road by our troops of the 14th Army brings an end to one of the most interesting combined land and air operations of the whole war. The supplying of the garrison at Imphal by air freighters of Troop Carrier Command for a period of nearly three months has been a colossal feat. In the present rush of excitement of the events in France, Italy and Russia, it has probably passed unnoticed by the majority of people – but, in years to come, I think that the text books of war will find several chapters to devote to the implications of the air maintenance of Imphal.
>
> At Imphal the lines of communication of a major force 'took to the air' – and the Divisions there were triumphantly maintained for 84 days. If necessary we could have gone on maintaining them – monsoon or no monsoon – for another 84 days.

He estimated that supplying the three divisions on the ground needed no less than 600 tons a day which were flown in by 200 Dakota trips per day 'wet or fine'.

Gardner concluded by pointing out, once again, that such operations could only be achieved by having air supremacy. 'The Japanese stood helplessly by and, from their hilltops and muddy tracks they watched overhead the procession of air freighters which was ruining their whole plan of campaign . . . such was the state of their air force – and such was the power of ours, that their fighters never took to the air.'

In a later broadcast, he reflected broadly on the Imphal campaign and its future consequences for the Japanese:

> In April last I wrote an article which was published in the RAF journal commenting on the Burma war up to the point where the operations in the Kohim–Imphal area had reached a critical stage. Both places were invested by strong Japanese forces and we were only kept going by air supply on a scale never before attempted in South East Asia. I expressed the view that before long the weakness inherent in the method adopted by the Japanese for the

conduct of their offensive, together with our strength in material, would lead to a Japanese defeat.

That defeat has come about. The broad outline of the campaign is probably well known to you. The enemy, unable to take either Kohim or Imphal, and therefore unable to re-provender their poorly maintained divisions gradually lost grip and initiative. Our forces defending stubbornly went over to the offensive at the opportune moment. The Japanese divisions to the North of Imphal were driven, a disorganised and unco-ordinated force into the unsympathetic jungle and the siege of the gateway to India was raised.

South of Imphal, the troops of General Slim's Imperial 14th Army have, through the drench of the monsoon, pushed the Japanese back to Tiddim, 150 miles to the south. What may well be the last Japanese attempt to invade India has been heavily defeated, at a cost of 50,000 counted dead and probably another 50,000 dead through starvation, disease and wounds.

On 13 July my father left Ceylon and took off in a Dakota for England by way of Bangalore, Bombay, Karachi, Bahrain, Cairo, Tripoli and Gibraltar, arriving at Hendon on 22 July.

Chapter Nineteen

The 'Rear Echelon' and
Victory in Sight

It must have been a happy homecoming for my father in July 1944, even though it was to be for only eight months. He had been away, as he had pointed out to Air Chief Marshal Peirse, for three-and-a-half years. He had never seen my 2-year-old sister Helen, who was born in November 1942, and my brother Patrick was only 4. As a 6-year-old I can just remember his return. He was, I can recall, in khaki shorts, was very brown-skinned and was wearing his RAF cap at the back of his head. My brother Patrick has more vivid memories particularly the effect on Helen. He recalled that when she first set eyes on this man she had never seen before kissing my mother, she had a screaming fit. My mother had to put her to bed to calm her down.

After a short holiday Charles was back to work which was in fact located at the Ministry of Information in Malet Street in London. His objective was to see that the 'Forgotten Army' was not forgotten. One of his first contributions was a broadcast, not as usual for home consumption, but directed back to those fighting in Burma to assure them that their exploits were no longer going unnoticed. He began by presenting his credentials: 'My name is Gardner – I'm an RAF type – with a basic trade as a driver of flying boats. I'm lucky. I've done my overseas tour – all of it in the SEAC area – and now I'm back in London.'

He continued:

I'm still with SEAC, though I run an office for Air Marshal Joubert over here, with a Chindit Major as half my section and we try to tell the people at home something of what you – the 14th, Air Command South East Asia, the Northern Combat Force and the East Indies Fleet are doing. Now in case you think people here aren't interested in the Burma war – let me tell you they are wrong. I suppose the newspapers and the wireless bulletins are a fair guide to public interest, but taking it to be so then SEAC is now an item of considerable public regard. You've been hitting the headlines – which is as it should be.

We have little information about his efforts in establishing and manning the London office – the 'Rear Echelon' – other than the presence of a Chindit Major. But we do know that for the next six months he continued to broadcast and write about the Burma campaign and the region at every opportunity. This even included a BBC travel broadcast to schools in which he described the island of Ceylon and the importance of Colombo as a shipping port.

In a broadcast for BBC News Review in February 1945, he gave a personal insight of how Admiral Lord Mountbatten conducted successful operations from his base in Kandy, together with news of the ever-increasing advancement of SEAC on all fronts. They were now driving the Japanese back and out of Burma, something that would have been inconceivable less than two years ago.

As far as Mountbatten was concerned, my father outlined his daily routine:

> Every afternoon Admiral Lord Mountbatten, Supreme Allied Commander South East Asia, leaves his single story red-bricked office in his Kandy headquarters and walks a hundred yards along a gravel path to his war room. This war room, the design of which the 'Supremo' had a large say, is arranged something like a typical village hall at home. There is a wide stage and in front of it are arranged rows of chairs. All around the walls are war maps and under them diagrams showing statistics that the Japanese would give an Emperor's ransom to possess.
>
> When Mountbatten walks in, dead on the second of three o'clock, his staff officers are there seated on rows of hard-bottomed, straight backed kitchen chairs. 'Supremo' walks straight to the front row and takes possession of the central chair – the only one fitted with arm rests. He looks quickly around the first three rows to see that all his most senior officers are there, and then he nods to a major who is standing in front of the stage, stiffly at attention, with a long wooden pointer held as though it were a rifle.
>
> The daily War Room conference has begun. The Major snaps his fingers to someone hidden in the wings of the stage and with a rattle of ropes and pulleys, a large map almost as big as

a cinema screen is trundled across as though it was a prop at a theatre. The map is showing the main area of SEAC operations and the Major runs through the whole of the last 24 hours developments. . . . Every now and then Mountbatten stops him, asks a pointed question and if the Major cannot supply an answer, he turns to his chief of staff with a request that the information be provided.

As far as the general situation was concerned, Gardner reported in some detail the continued success since Mountbatten had moved his headquarters to Kandy in April 1944. The most recent of which had been the landings and capture in early January 1945 of the strategic island port of Akyab, on the western shore of Burma. This denied the Japanese supplies from coastal shipping. Shortly after Ramree island, opposite Akyab, had been cleared.

My father continued:

Meanwhile the 14th Army had advanced and cast a semi-circle around the ancient city of Mandalay, 'Where the flying fishes play.' But when Kipling wrote 'On the road to Mandalay' he did SEAC a disservice, as many people still think Mandalay is on the coast near China. It is, in fact, 250 miles from the nearest 'flying fishes' and 250 miles from the China border. The city is being converged on from the North, West and South West by troops who have shaken themselves clear of the jungle and who are now in the Burma central plain, which is more free from monsoon rains.

The army was now also focusing on the last Japanese stronghold, the Burmese capital and port of Rangoon. Here the Japanese High Command was virtually cut off from the sea and the land and they could see a great trap closing. Charles concluded: 'Any day may bring some new Mountbatten move – by sea or by air. The Japanese never forgot the Mountbatten factor. They have seen what has already been done with the veterans of the "Old Guard" of the Burma war – what will happen when the reinforcements flow from the west is not likely to bring them comfort.'

My father then gave a graphic account of just what the troops on the ground had put up with during the long struggle in Burma, particularly during the monsoon. His report is truly eye-opening and explains why the Japanese didn't even consider fighting in these conditions. I have reproduced part of his report to illustrate further the impact of their magnificent achievements.

He stated:

> The men, British, Chinese, Indian, East and West African have had to endure conditions such as no major army has had to fight in before. They had to fight in and against the jungle. Our troops have been operating in swampy rice fields, on scrub reminiscent of the desert, over granite-like rocks rising sheer in one-on-one gradients. They have been pushing their way through flowering bamboo shoots which clawed at their faces, while underneath pot holes, three feet deep, are churned up in the monsoon rains into slimy mud pools worse than was experienced in Flanders in the last war. And during the day the persistent horse flies worry the men while at night the 'dive bombing' mosquito takes over.

Gardner then told of some of the dreadful personal discomforts they faced.

> It is discomfort on a large and lengthy scale which existed for months on end and is heightened by jungle sores. A tiny scratch in the tropics turns septic within an hour or two if not treated. Men fight and live for days with bodies covered in elastoplast. And during the day the salt from their bodies turns their jungle shirts to a whitish colour under their 60 lbs of equipment. By nightfall the temperature has dropped with a thud. They are cold, they don pullovers and go to sleep in wet clothes sharing a blanket or a waterproof sheet with their colleagues.

After describing other hardships such as, 'as much rain London gets in a month seems to fall personally in one day' and 'their blood was sucked by leeches in their boots', he concluded: 'Against all this human background, the Allied Forces made up of a hotch-potch of nationalities have done and are doing a superb job driving the Japanese out of Burma, while on the American Pacific front, they are now on the run, not yet in disorderly retreat, but on the run.'

My father was now due to return to Ceylon to carry out a tour of 14th Army operations. Just before leaving, in a broadcast, he gave another very up-beat assessment of the current situation.

He stated:

> Things are beginning to happen out in Burma. The Japanese are
> wondering what is going to go on in the fair weather between
> now and next June or July. This past fortnight they have faced
> our three land drives plodding steadily to Mandalay and making
> better and more dangerous progress as the tropical sun dries out
> the waterlogged roads and trenches of that appalling jungle.
>
> But the Japanese from Thailand to Bhamo and from Chindwin
> to Mandalay, know that the fine weather means something else.
> It means the unleashing of our air power, a power which since
> SEAC was formed has destroyed nearly 1,000 of their aircraft
> and directly and indirectly many thousands of their men. Does
> the Japanese soldier, fighting the relentless attacks of the British
> 36th Division in the North, the Chinese divisions pushing near
> Bhamo, or the 5th Indian Division round Kennedy Peak think
> things are going to be different this year – I doubt it.
>
> I think you can take it that the 3rd Tactical Air Force, which
> a few months ago played such a great part in smashing the last
> enemy hopes of an Indian invasion, will now be supporting our
> land forces in even grander style.

He continued:

> New air support of the army in and over the jungle is a tricky job.
> Objectives are hard to see – harder to hit. Fighting is often at close
> range and greater accuracy is probably needed in Burma than any
> other front – bomb lines just 50 yards in front of our own troops
> have, in the past, been given – and accepted – and the job has
> been done with no mistakes. General Slim's 14th Army knows its
> 3rd Air Force, and is happy with it. The Japanese otherwise – and
> will remain so – his bleak prospect.

Charles then turned to another major factor in having air superiority – the
unchallenged strategic bombing of communications. 'We know they have
the advantage of inner communications, but our bombers are offsetting
that and now, this last week or so, the Super Fortresses have come in
and pasted Rangoon with the biggest load of bombes ever dropped in
Burma.'[1]

Charles concluded, 'Our own lines of communication are, perhaps,
even more vulnerable than those of the Japanese, but we have the air

power to protect and reinforce them. They haven't and there in a nutshell you have it.'

In March 1945, my father, as planned, returned to Ceylon to carry out a tour of the 14th Army. He flew in an RAF York by way of Malta, Cairo, Karachi and Colombo, in a journey which took three days. Preceding him were letters of introduction written by Air Marshal Joubert from Ceylon to both Lieutenant General Sir Oliver Leese, Commander in Chief of Allied Land Forces, and Lieutenant General Sir William Slim, Commander in Chief of the 14th Army.

Joubert wrote:

> He [Sqadron Leader Gardner] has come out here to refresh his experience of the Burma front before returning to London to take up his duties again. I shall be very grateful if he can be given every opportunity to see the operations that are in progress so that on his return he will be able to speak with authority to correspondents who seek his guidance on general matters.

Such introduction was to bear fruit for my father in an exhaustive two-week tour of the front, beginning 'with more conferences' in Bombay and Calcutta at the end of March. Here he spent time with General Lees himself, General Stratemeyer, US Commander of the Easter Air Force, and with Air Marshal Coryton, Commander of the 3rd Tactical Air Force, who, 'on pain of death', lent him his own Harvard aircraft to make the tour.

We have details of his journey through entries in his logbook, and from many subsequent articles and broadcasts describing what he saw. By this time the 14th Army had now just broken through and captured the 'prize city' of Mandalay and, to the south, Meiktila. 'This was a great and significant victory and would soon lead to the expected final Japanese capitulation with only the key port of Rangoon left in their hands,' he reported later.

So it must have been with a sense of pride and achievement that he set out on 30 March heading for Comilla, which he had visited eleven months before. He landed on the RAF-built airstrip, one of some 200 constructed during the campaign. As the headquarters of the 3rd Tactical Air Force, Comilla was still at full stretch providing air support for troops on the ground as it had been for the relief of Imphal. Whether he inspected the press facilities which he had criticised on his earlier mission, we do not know, but he certainly spent time with the Base Commander, Air Commodore Hardman and stayed the night there.

The following day he flew on to Akyab and Ramre islands, the scene of the recent fighting and capture. He interviewed Sir Philip Christison, Commander of the XIV Corps which had made the assault on the islands, and met up with an old friend, Air Commodore the Earl of Bandon, who was commanding 224 Group and was affectionately known in the RAF as the 'abandoned Earl'.

After a short visit to Ramre island to see the naval coastal force which had done so much to hunt down Japanese submarines and keep the waters safe for Allied shipping, he returned to Akyab. Here his journey came close to ending when he 'nearly pranged' the precious Harvard – 'when avoiding log while taxying'. And then he had a fright flying 'blind' too close to high hills on his way to Monywa, 60 miles west of Mandalay. 'Co-er' he wrote in the log. Here he met General Slim himself who later wrote him an appreciative letter of his descriptive reports. At the time his army had entered and now occupied the ruined city of Monywa, although the Japanese had been holding out at Fort Dufferin to the north. My father flew over it, recording 'Eureka!' when he saw 36 Division encircling the fort.

He was now 'in the thick of it' and later observed: 'I flew in my little trainer over many parts of Burma – but there was never a time when I could look out of the cockpit without seeing at least half a dozen Dakotas within eyeshot.' He flew on to Nagpur where he interviewed Lieutenant General Sir Montagu Stopford, Commander of the newly formed 12th Army, and then over the Irrawaddy River to the captured town of Meiktila, 30 miles south of Mandalay, landing on the former Japanese airstrip which, he recorded, 'Had been much fought over but in good condition.'

His earlier meeting with General 'Monty' Stopford was both timely and productive because he was able to give some details of Burma's newest Army General and its newest Army, which, with Slim's 14th, would double the Allied strength in the field.

Gardner wrote later:

General Stopford is known to the Japanese, he has been commanding 33 Corps of the 14th Army. This was the Corps which crossed the Chindwin and paved the way for the great Burma victory. It was Stopford who forged the broad Irrawaddy river at four bridgeheads and it was his 33 Corps that captured

Mandalay. Since then he has led his Corps down through the Burma oil fields and along the Irrawaddy to join up with our troops coming up from Rangoon.

Further visits to RAF and Army bases were made, including to Major General T.W. Rees, Commander of the 19th Indian Division. A photograph of the two together, which appeared in the *Illustrated Magazine*, is in our possession, together with a nice personal letter of thanks signed Peter Rees. On 10 April he returned to Calcutta to hand back the Air Marshal's aeroplane. 'Harvard back unbroken, life saved,' he wrote. After more conferences he was, five days later, on his way back to London. But not before an engine failure to the RAF York in Karachi had forced them to return and transfer to a Dakota. This finally arrived at RAF Lyneham on 22 April after a seven-day journey.

With so much success going on in Burma, Charles Gardner was anxious to write and broadcast the good news as quickly as possible. Four days after returning he produced a special 'indepth' piece for the *Sunday Express*, and was able to reflect the very different conditions the army were now facing as they broke out speedily onto the plain in the monsoon-free weather.
He wrote:

The 14th Army is now on the eve of a great victory. Before long we will be writing the final chapter of the Burma campaign, and the shield which Tokyo had put up between the Allies and the Japanese conquests in South East Asia will have been knocked out of their hands.

Up to three months ago the fame of the British Imperial 14th Army rested, and rightly so, on its unsurpassable skill in jungle warfare. The story was of one long drawn out fight against the terrain, against the rains, against tropical diseases and against the Japanese – hindrances which were rated by General Slim's men in approximately that order. Since they re-crossed the River Chindwin on to the plain of Central Burma, the men of the 14th have had now to fight a new sort of war. From the close tactics, patrols, and ambushes of the undergrowth they had to switch to mobile desert warfare. Men who for 18 months had fought, hardly able to see two or three feet in front of them, were now able to see 20 miles of open rolling country at a glance. Their commanders began to deal in motorised thrusts of as many miles as they had been used to thinking in yards.

The Japanese, blinking in the unaccustomed sunlight of the plains were bewildered. Beaten out of their own chosen battle ground – the jungle – they went to ground in foxholes while Slim's men cut and thrust around and behind them in a series of sweeps and flanking attacks, which have brought them to within 300 miles of Rangoon.

My father was also able to give an eyewitness account of the country the army was now fighting in:

I have this week returned from the Burma front where I flew over much of the front line territory. It is flat and arid – dust desert-like brown, save for the green grass of the Irrawaddy basin. A few scrubby trees provide the only natural cover and a few isolated ridges of hills – easily by-passed – provide the only defensive features. It is in this country that our men have, for the first time, been able to go ahead in top gear.

The 700 mile journey which they began at the borders of India last August is nearly over. Rangoon – that once seemingly far and remote capital at the end of the Burma trail is now just down the road.

Paying tribute to their leader he stated:

Commanding them is the man every soldier, British, Indian and Gurkha on the front likes and trusts – Uncle Bill Slim. This short, tough, outspoken general, the man who was once a corporal in the last war – until he was busted back to private for drinking a mug of beer on a march – has a personality and brain which dominates the Burma battlefield.

Three years later, my father was able to pay further tribute to Slim, in a rather unusual but descriptive way, on his appointment as Chief of the Imperial General Staff, the highest rank in the British professional Army. In a broadcast he told the story:

I was walking down the street with a 14th Army man when we bought a newspaper with the headlines 'General Slim – CIGS'. Not being in 'informed circles' – we hadn't been expecting this – and we looked at the heading for a moment in absolute silence. Then we both said exactly the same three words – Jolly

Good Show, except that the first word wasn't Jolly. And I'll bet thousands – tens of thousands of soldiers, airmen and sailors who had served under Bill Slim of Burma said the same thing. It's a measure of Slim's character that this soldier I was with – he was a captain – had only seen Slim twice in his life and heard him speak to the men only once. And yet he had known – as all have known who have come in touch with him – that here was a great man. There is some instinct in us that is never wrong on things like that. The Slim legends are many, only when you chase them up as I did once, you find they are not legends but fact.

He recalled again the story of Corporal Slim being reduced to the ranks for drinking an offered glass of beer and added:

And then there was Slim parlying with the envoy of a certain friendly power in their only common language – schoolboy French. On being told that this power's forces could not be withdrawn in two hours ('Ce n'est pas possible mon General'), Slim replied, 'Mais oui, c'est jolly well possible' – only again the word was not jolly. And it jolly well was too!

And then again there was Slim, wounded in Eritrea by what is euphemistically known as the 'lower back' lying on his face in bed while the Italian airman who did it was wheeled in with an identical wound with a card pinned on him 'With the compliments of the RAF.'

Having recalled all the great campaigns of Slim's 14th Army, Charles concluded: 'And Uncle Bill – his long jaw stuck out – his mouth a tight line – being cheered by Londoners all the way to the Guildhall when he thought Londoners had never hear of him.'[2]

By 2 May my father was able to report: 'The fall of Rangoon is pretty imminent. Armoured columns were only a few miles away from the North and airborne and amphibious landings would cut off the port from the South.' The next day, 3 May 1945, the fall of Rangoon was confirmed. In a radio newsreel broadcast, which would be seen by the forces in Burma, he stated that the news of the capture of Rangoon had 'gone over big – as it deserves to. Last night the BBC home news announced it in a banner headline – a new departure for them. The first words of the 9 o'clock bulletin were – "Victory from Hamburg to Rangoon."'

The following day in a prepared article, my father was again able to draw particular attention to the part played by air power in the victory. He wrote: 'The fall of Rangoon brings to an end – for the moment at least – one of the most amazing sustained air campaigns of the war.' He stressed the uniqueness of the air support in a mountainous country where road and rail was virtually non-existent and where the monsoon made most routes virtually impassable. 'It was fitting then that when the first Allied troops entered Rangoon they were saluted from the air by their faithful Dakotas. The transports dropped a load of fluttering Allied flags over the Burmese capital.'

This theme was repeated by Lord Mountbatten in his Order of the Day relayed by my father. Mountbatten said: 'Our forces were supported and supplied from the air on a scale never before attempted in any theatre of war.'

To mark the victory in Burma, two SEAC souvenir newspapers were produced and edited by the well-known journalist Frank Owen, who had served as a colleague in SEAC for some time. Mountbatten refers to this in an undated personal letter to my father written in his own hand on HMS *Kelly* notepaper from his home at Broadlands, in Hampshire, addressed to Squadron Leader Gardner.[3] It shows just how much the Admiral liked to keep very close control on all publicity regarding his command.

He wrote: 'I would like you to telegraph to my secretary saying exactly what chapters have so far been received complete from Owen, and also the point at which MOI propose to make the split between volume I and volume II, also dates of publication (however approximate) for each volume.'

The Supreme Commander continued, 'Can you tell me what has been arranged for the montage of half a dozen photos of me talking to Navy, Army, Air Force, British, Indians, Americans, Africans etc to go with Frank Owen's extracts from my speeches. I think they could be small all on one page.'

He concluded by asking my father to follow up his contacts with Fleet Street's four major press barons. 'I told Lord Kemsley to get into direct touch with you if he wanted to accept my invitation to come out or wanted any information for publication. He has been most helpful. Tell him I could only reach Beaverbrook, Kemsley and Rothermere by telephone but I invited all three to come out and see things for themselves.'

At home we have copies of two SEAC 'Souvenir' newspapers. The first includes Mountbatten's address to the press, descriptions of the operations, photos of the Generals and maps of the area. The second headed 'From

Tiddim Road to Rangoon' does indeed have a full-page montage of all the Force leaders as requested by the Chief in his letter to Charles.

Shortly after the taking of Rangoon, VE Day was celebrated on 8 May 1945 across the country and especially in London with vast crowds surrounding the front of Buckingham Palace to catch a glimpse of the royal family and Winston Churchill, who appeared on the balcony. There had been a long-held belief in the family that my father not only enjoyed the celebrations himself but, in addition, broadcast back to Burma and contributed an eyewitness account for the BBC. This was, in fact, true and research later confirmed that he was on the Mall in London, with microphone in hand describing the victory parade and the fly-past of Spitfires over Buckingham Palace. He later appeared on the popular radio show 'In Town Tonight' and his photograph released for publication by the BBC as 'one of the personalities brought to the microphone to mark the special VE edition of the Home Service'. We now have a copy of the photograph at home.

One problem that Charles was conscious of at the time was the concern that had been expressed to him by SEAC colleagues that despite all the victories in Europe, the war was still very much alive in the Far East. So in his VE Day broadcast to them he was able to give reassurance that this was not the case. 'I spoke to a lot of people on V.E. Day itself and almost without exception they all said to the effect that "It seems a bit silly, doesn't it celebrating peace when we are still at war."'

There was also very good media coverage which had not forgotten this nor the Burma campaign. 'Practically every London newspaper introduced into their columns a tribute to SEAC,' he said. He quoted from the *Daily Mail* leader which stated that: 'Although the cease fire had sounded in the West, the gallant 14th Army had battled on to new victories. We owe it to them that after the brief period of relaxation we shall return with renewed energy to our task, determined to do all we can to end the fight in the Far East at the earliest moment.'

And then Charles added what SEAC most wanted to hear. 'With release of Forces from Europe the days of short shrift and scanty equipment in SEAC will be finally over. More men, more aeroplanes, will be coming to help them carry on the fight from Rangoon.'

A week later, my father contributed a special article for the *Daily Graphic*. He wrote:

A brief pause for thankfulness – and then the Japanese! – That is the King's message to this country – Mr. Churchill's also. After three years of fighting the 14th has liberated all Burma and holds the vital port of Rangoon. From Rangoon Mountbatten is free to strike towards Siam or Malaya. It is generally accepted that in the future role of SEAC, amphibious operations will play a large part. For a year he was without the necessary equipment, but now the story was likely to be different. Already he has mounted three successful amphibious operations – Akyab, Ramree Island and Rangoon. Bigger operations are likely to follow. We have complete control of the Indian Ocean and the Japanese have long coast lines to defend.

But it never happened.

Chapter Twenty

Build-up for Invasion of Japan

Following the German surrender on 8 May 1945, and the death of Adolf Hitler a week earlier, the full attention of the Allies was now directed to the invasion and the capitulation of Japan. 'This is the time of the build up against Japan. On a 4,000-mile front from Okinawa to Rangoon, Allied forces are pouring into the Far East for the next stage of the war,' wrote Squadron Leader Charles Gardner from his London HQ in Malet Street. It was the first of a series of his war commentaries beginning in June 1945.

He continued:

> In the last few weeks we have seen Admiral Mountbatten's victorious South East Asia Command geared up for its 1945–46 drive. Two British armies, the great 14th and the new 12th are getting ready. The re-aligned Burma Command of the Royal Air Force [the Americans had by now withdrawn from Eastern Air Command] is even now supporting our troops through the terrible rainstorms of the monsoon. They are giving the Japanese no rest, attacking and pressing them back, denying them the chance to re-group and recuperate. It was our insistence on similar fighting in the last monsoon which paved the way for the liberation of Burma. It is reasonable to expect that this year also, the monsoon fighting will be the prelude to a fair weather onslaught.

Gardner described the magnitude of the build-up:

> Men and ships which took part in Western European actions are already in theatre. More are on the way. In London announcements have been made of a gigantic scheme for air-trooping to India-Burma. Thousands of battle-tried troops are being flown to

the Japanese war by RAF Transport Command. Aircrews from Bomber and Coastal Command are now being re-allocated in whole squadrons to this job and to the reinforcement of the general air power in the East. All this is being speeded up so that, whenever Mountbatten strikes in force when the rains clear in October, it will be certain he will have the men and equipment for the task.

At sea the British East India fleet reigns. From Rangoon down towards the South Pole and round to Australia, its ships interpose a barrier between the Japanese and the Western World – ensuring the safety of our supplies and denying surface movement by the enemy. In the air the RAF has already moved its squadrons to replace those of the 10th USAF which were withdrawn after the capture of Rangoon. That great Burma port is now the western pivot of the allied plan of the strangulation of the Japanese Empire.

Comparing the relative sea power of the Japanese and the Allies he wrote: 'The Japanese still have a fleet, but it is doubtful if that fleet can do more than make a dramatic big scale suicide defence of its own home shores.' Gardner estimated the current size of their fleet and said:

According to a careful check I have kept of known enemy naval losses, the total Japanese naval strength is now down to six or seven battleships, two or three fleet carriers, up to half a dozen smaller carriers and about 18 cruisers. Any of the American Pacific fleet could take on their navy now. Admiral Bruce Fraser's British Pacific Fleet could itself cope with the job. So could the SEAC East Indies fleet.

For the next eight weeks my father continued to write and broadcast news of the advance towards Japan. But for SEAC, their immediate objective was to drive out the remaining Japanese troops, over 40,000 of them, from Burmese territory. 'These men are disorganised, shelterless and hopeless,' he stated. 'The next step was to drive them out of Siam, Malaya and Sumatra.'

He reflected also on the enhanced reputation of the 14th Army. 'All of a sudden the people of Great Britain have become 14th army conscious. . . . one day the public was saying "oh yes" – Burma – must be awful out there – but can't say what goes on. The next day the cry goes up – "Tell us about South East Asia. What is the 14th doing?"' My father, in a further series of articles and broadcasts, was happy to oblige.

This work was later to be recognised in a treasured personal letter to him from General Slim, as we have noted, dated 17 August 1945. He wrote: 'I know it was entirely owing to you that the Fourteenth Army got such a very good showing from the press and the BBC and that all my arrangements went so smoothly and pleasantly.'[1] He added, 'I don't know if you are considering paying us another visit, but you will be very welcome indeed if you do come to this part of the world.'

But not all was good news. In a 'War Review' for the BBC's 'London Calling' programme, broadcast on June 28 and later relayed to their African, General Overseas North American and Pacific services, Gardner outlined both 'the bright side' and 'the reverse'. On the bright side, he said, 'hard military facts clearly show the inescapable end of Japan'. 'But why,' he declared, 'with the outlook so generally unhealthy and menacing for the Japanese, is it that so many competent observers put a period of another year or eighteen months or more as the duration of the Far East War?'

He continued:

> There are two main reasons. The first was the huge distances involved – the second the fanaticism of the Japanese soldier. The problem of distances was an obvious one . . . but on the second point there were large Japanese garrisons all over the Pacific and South East Asia, Garrisons which, cut off though some of them are, are well stocked and have large dumps and natural resources. They are contained but not defeated.

Meanwhile the build-up went on. By 23 July my father was reporting that, 'practically the whole of the British Navy strength is now deployed in the Far East, while the RAF's new giant Lincoln bombers and its load-hauling Lancasters are shortly to be used against the Japanese mainland.' He added, 'at the same time Admiral Mountbatten flies out to hold the first big inter-command conference with General MacArthur'.

And then everything changed – forever.

On 7 August, the Americans dropped the first atomic bomb on the Japanese city of Hiroshima. It killed nearly 130,000 people.

On the same day as the first explosion, Gardner wrote in one of his regular war commentaries: 'While the world speculates on the possible or probable collapse of Japan under the staggering impact of the atomic bomb, the Allied Commanders are getting quietly on with the arrangements which will make that collapse a certainty – though maybe not at such speed.'

Bearing in mind the news of the bomb was only a few hours old when he wrote this piece, he would not have known of its full impact and it is not surprising that he urged caution. He continued: 'During the last fortnight there has been much momentous news pouring out of the Far East theatre. There have been so many stories, statements and interviews that the only way to avoid mental indigestion when reading them is to rough-sort all the information into two piles – fact and speculation.'

But, concentrating on the speculation pile, he continued, 'This can go on Japanese reaction to the bomb, on Russia's possible role in the war, and all statements, both of Japanese and Allied origin about an invasion of Japan, especially those which suggest dates and places.' Later he added, 'There is no indication in the war zones that a realisation of an inevitable defeat has affected the morale of the Emperor's fighting troops or the defiant dispositions of the defenders of the homeland.'

On 8 August, Charles Gardner, now furnished with more details of the Hiroshima attack, wrote: 'The atomic bomb has burst on Japan. On August 5, 1945 (London time) the whole shape of the Far East war has changed – and indeed for all we know the whole pattern of civilisation.'

He continued:

> In the whole history of warfare no one side has ever held such an overwhelming advantage. A few days ago we counted the Allied superiority in mighty weapons, in terms of aircraft, ships and landing devices which had been the product of six years of 'hot-house' development in the European struggle. Today it may appear this giant power counts for little against the greatest secret of all time – the atomic bomb.

Two days later, on 9 August, the second bomb was dropped on Nagasaki with the same appalling results as at Hirishoma.

For the next 24 hours everyone took stock. The shock was felt around the world, most, of course, in Japan. But the Allies could not stand down completely, especially as many occupying Japanese troops in the region were still at battle stations and in some cases still fighting.

Six days later on 15 August the inevitable announcement of the Japanese surrender was made. After six years, the Second World War had at last come to an end. Designated VJ Day, there was great celebrations around the world and in the major cities there were scenes of great jubilation, especially in the United States which had borne the brunt of the fighting since the Japanese attack on Pearl Harbor in December 1941.

My father was not particularly a religious man, but I do remember on the evening of the Japanese surrender, he came home while we three children were still in bed. He asked us to get out, kneel down and pray for our self deliverance.

A day later he wrote in his Far East Commentary:

> By her surrender Japan escaped a number of unpleasant things. Two of these were obvious – the annihilation of her homeland by the Anglo-American bomb, and the beating of her untouchable armies in Manchuria by the Russians. A third disaster, less obvious, but still important was she missed, by the skin of her teeth, the great 'D' Day [landings] of South East Asia. When the news of peace came, a huge amphibious fleet was already assembled. The biggest single operation since June 1944 was mounted and ready to go.

It is interesting to note that my father referred to the 'Anglo-American bomb'. The secrecy around its development was so intense that very little was known, except he seemed to be aware that the British also had a nuclear capability and much of the original science came from Britain and was exported to the United States.

The job of SEAC now took on a new role – 'To repatriate all internees and prisoners of war from Japanese held territories in their region and to round up all Japanese troops in the territory.' By necessity they would also provide as much aid and help as possible to the beleaguered inhabitants. A fearful, and heart-breaking assignment.

Foremost in the minds of the British was Singapore. Two days after the surrender, in his Far East Commentary, Gardner wrote, 'Singapore was Britain's Pearl Harbour . . . the word Singapore stands for all the fiendish horror and atrocity which the Japanese have inflicted. But today now that victory has been achieved the first British troops – medical units – have parachuted into Singapore. The Royal Navy is anchored in the harbour.'

He continued, 'SEAC's immediate task is to get the Allied prisoners out and home. In Singapore there are about 30,500 of whom 7,000 are British.' As to their total task, he estimated there to be about 80,000 prisoners in the whole SEAC area. 'There are known to be 7,000 in Sumatra, including 1,200 British and many more in Siam and Java. Moutbatten has promised that the return of these people to their homes will be number one priority for the theatre.'

In early September Charles Gardner was promoted to Wing Commander, a significant move to a senior rank. In his first Far East Commentary following his welcome news, he returned to the increasing and worrying problems of rehabilitation and round-up of Japanese troops. By now the whole region had been split up amongst the Allies. 'At this moment Admiral Mountbatten is responsible to the United Nations for a bigger area than any one military commander of the war,' he stated. 'The countries for which he has to budget are – Burma, Siam, Malaya, Sumatra, Java, Borneo and part of Indo-China. All of these are now suffering from the economic and physical ruination of three and a half years of oppressive Japanese rule.'

One country that presented a particular and growing problem was the Indonesian island of Java, in the Dutch East Indies. My father devoted three Far East Commentaries to the extraordinary events which took place as the British tried to rehabilitate all prisoners and capture some 100,000 Japanese. However, when they landed in mid-September they were faced by a combination of Japanese troops and Indonesian nationalists who had banded together to repel the Allies with fierce resistance. The nationalists declared independence and possession of the land.

The trouble for the British had been exacerbated by a decision at the Potsdam Conference in August.[2] Gardner wrote:

> Java – which had been in the American theatre, was transferred to South East Asia and the British. It was at Potsdam that Admiral Mountbatten was first told of the plan for the liberation of Java and also to plan the machinery for the solution of its tangled affairs. Admiral Mountbatten had hardly had time to send a signal to Kandy telling his staff of the new responsibility when Japan surrendered.

By November my father wrote:

> In trouble-rent Java, help is gradually reaching the prisoners of war and internees. Through storm-ridden skies the Dakotas of the RAF fly daily to parachute food and medical supplies to island camps which can't be reached by road and jungle tracks. Columns of British and Indian troops fight their way forward through Indonesian and sometimes Japanese ambush to bring

back terrified and starving women and children to the safety of Allied protection.

It took many months for matters to be resolved with conciliatory negotiations between the Indonesians and the Dutch.

While the great nations were trying to sort out the human tragedy in so many countries, Charles Gardner took time out to record a history of the Burma campaign from the arrival of Mountbatten in 1942 to the final capture of Rangoon in May 1945. Much of this is reproduced in the next chapter. In summary he identifies three main reasons for the victory. The brilliance of the Army campaign and its ability to advance through treacherous country even in the monsoon; the air superiority that had been established to allow the constant supply to the troops on the ground, and the advanced medical care that had virtually eliminated malaria by the end of the campaign.

By October my father realised that his job for SEAC had run its course, although he kept filing reports up to the end of the month. Negotiations had already begun for his return to the BBC. But before leaving he was buoyed by a personal letter from Lord Mountbatten dated 18 October. The Supreme Commander wrote:

> I understand that you are likely to be demobilised in the near future and I am taking this opportunity to write and express my appreciation for the splendid work that you have done for South East Asia in London. It is due in large part to your efforts that this theatre is now one of the best publicised instead of being the 'forgotten front'.

My father replied:

> Your letter to me of the 18th will be my most highly regarded souvenir of the war. You addressed it to me personally – but if there is truth in what you say, any credit belongs equally to other people who worked without regard for office hours, time off, or leave for long periods in their attempts to help me put SEAC and the 14th Army over in this country and overseas.

After naming various staff members he added, 'I am happy to think we did some good – but if I may say without offence, on the eve of my bowler hat, I am prouder of having been on your staff than of anything.'

Mountbatten replied on 4 December:

I was very glad to get your letter of the 26th of October and to hear of all those from SEAC who have helped you so much in London. I fully realise that all you have accomplished could not have been done without an able staff, but the drive and initiative must, however, come from the top and this is what you supplied.

He then referred to honours. 'It is impossible for everyone to receive recognition in the New Year and Birthday Honours List but I expect you know that some time ago I obtained official approval for cards for good service to be issued in special cases. I have very great pleasure in sending you one for your good work.' At home we have a copy of the 'Card For Good Service' stating that 'Your devotion to duty has resulted in your name being brought to my notice.', signed by Louis Mountbatten, dated December 1945.

If my father was disappointed that this was the only recognition of his work he soon would not be so. In the Birthday Honours List of June 1946 he was awarded the OBE, 'for outstanding service'.[3] This was to go with a series of RAF campaign awards including the Atlantic Star, for active service in the Battle of the Atlantic, the Burma Star for operational service in the region, the Defence Medal for defending this country and the War Medal 1939–45 with clasp 'Mentioned in Despatches' – this referred to his Catalina experiences searching, finding and shadowing the Japanese fleet.

As he headed back to peacetime Britain and back to the BBC in December 1945, his association with Lord Mountbatten was not to end there. Indeed it was to be a personal matter for which Mountbatten called upon my father's assistance. We have preserved correspondence from him of an unusual request involving him in a sensitive royal secret. And nor did his return to the BBC run on smooth rails, as he had hoped.

Chapter Twenty-One

Reflection on the Burma Campaign

Although Charles Gardner's last written tribute to the campaign in Burma and its leader General Slim was in 1948, his more comprehensive account of their victory was written in 1946, as already noted, while their achievements were still fresh in his mind and acknowledged by the public at large. Extracts from this have already been reproduced in an earlier chapter.

At home, we have a copy of this concise, factual and absorbing short history of the campaign dated March 1946. We are not certain whether it was commissioned by a magazine or a BBC publication, but judging by its informal writing style and punctuation it suggest this was a broadcast script. I believe this history was put together by my father with the help of Army colleagues in the office. What I do know is that anybody interested in the Second World War should find it valuable as it describes the action from start to finish in detail, its locations and timescale and gives full credit to all the servicemen involved and their affiliations.

It should also be noted that this was written within ten months of the fall of the Japanese in Burma and was based on information to hand at that time. Since then there have been enormous changes in the region and many of the names of places have changed.

Since I have already recorded the events up to the successful defensive action at Imphal, I have therefore begun these extracts by recording the campaign after Imphal and leading to ultimate victory in Burma with the capture of Rangoon. I am doing so because today the 'Forgotten Army' has almost been forgotten. Dunkirk, the Battle of Britain, Alamein, the D-Day Landings and the Battle of the Bulge have continued to be foremost in describing the history of the war. Perhaps this reminder will help bring it back into some prominence, as it deserves.

History of the Burma Campaign from May 1944

The British defensive success from March to May 1944 laid the foundation for the Burma victory as the supply-less and starving Japanese reeled back into the jungle. The battles had been furious and the fighting possibly the stickiest of the whole war.

Mountbatten and his Allied Land C-in-C General Slim now took stock. In the north-east things were going well. Stilwell was now near B'hamo and had captured Kamaung, Mogaung and Myitkyira on the way. His road was nearly through and he had linked up with Chindits, which was now commanded by General Lentaigno following the untimely death of Wingate.[1] Japanese resistance was weaker and Chiang Kai-shek had despatched forces from his side to help the India–China link-up.

In the centre, the Japanese were disorganised, broken and starving and in Arakan the first fine weather (November) would see 15th Corps on the move again, this time with their objective Akyab an assured 'plum ripe for picking'.

In the air, EAC had a complete monopoly and valuable air supply lessons had been learned in Arakan and Imphal. Thus, the Japanese were unable to interfere with the Allies airborne supply line. On the debit side the monsoon had started – it was a 'drencher' – and the country ahead was frightening, and Rangoon was nearly 1,000 miles away.

There were many hectic and vital conferences, but the final decision suited the mood at the front. The order went out, 'Chase them through the monsoon'. It was a great opportunity.

Across the hills, down the valleys, the Japanese Army was broken but ever ready to stand and fight a 'do or die' rearguard action. Diseased and hungry, the enemy was short of everything it seemed except ammunition. Chasing after them, the East Africans took again the road through the dreaded Kabaw Valley, while the veterans of the 5th Indian Division under Major General Evans pursued them across the jungle track of the Chin Hills and down the road through Tiddim, which had seen our spring withdrawal. Each column had its path to follow and both led to the same spot – Kalewa. That was the way our armies had come out of Burma and that was the way they were going back.

Tiddim village was reached, a collection of huts with a few solid buildings. The Japanese, outwitted by 5th Division's astute flanking approaches, had left to stand and fight further down the road. With the 5th Division came tanks, which were winched up the steep slopes and once on the level were carried by transporters whose drivers accomplished miracles in negotiating the bends and turns of the precipitous road.

The tanks had their part to play at the feature which our men called the 'chocolate staircase' where the Japanese tried hard to halt the advance finally. There and at Kennedy Peak, a 9,000ft mountain where the enemy had dug innumerable strongpoints, the tanks were taken up the steep slopes to blast them out of their holes at point-blank range. From the Peak, where the tanks actually attacked from cloud cover, the going was swifter, although the Japanese was still full of fight and put on a determined rearguard action.

Kalemyo was reached, then on 14 November an Askari of 11 East African Division under Major General Demoline, met a Sepoy of the 5th Indian Division on the track that runs along the bank of the Myittha River from Kalemyo to the Chindwin River at Kalewa. On this track the Japanese were expected to stand firm, for there were defiles in which just a handful of men could hold up an army. But for some reason they failed to do so and the East Africans reached Kalewa and established a solid bridgehead on the east bank of the Chindwin River. The second great obstacle on the march back into central Burma was overcome.

For the Japanese left west of the river there was a plan. The country south of Tiddim, cleared of enemy units, was now turned over to the mixed force of troops and levies known as the Lushai Brigade. Fifth Division, earmarked for a great role in the final campaign, was pulled out for a well-earned rest.

From the East Africans, British Second Division took over the role of holding the Chindwin bridgehead. Already the engineers had laid across the great river a pontoon-borne Bailey Bridge. Great volumes of traffic were pouring across it night and day – this Bailey Bridge at 365ft long was the largest in the world.

For the first time in months the Japanese Air Force responded to the challenge and came across in strength to put out of action this vital link. They got a bloody nose and not a single hit on the bridge. The bridgehead was now expanded and 2nd Division under Major General Nicholson began to take the long road to Mandalay.

This January of 1945 was the time of great moment. The British were across the Chindwin, the monsoon was over and its horrors of mud and jungle defeated. Ahead was the mercifully clear and open plain of central Burma with its rivers and roads stretching south to Rangoon. There were now three whole months of fine weather and the aircraft for the world's biggest effort of air supply were standing ready.

In Arakan, 15 Corps had moved surely on to vital Akyab, and was heading for Ramree Island, from whose port-side airfields the Dakotas could bring food, water and bullets to the 14th all the way to Rangoon.

There was one snag – if the Army failed to reach Rangoon by early May, there would follow a disaster. In the rains the air supply line would not be operable and the whole 14th would be left out in the blue – in exactly the same position as the retreating Burma Corps of 1942. A land L of C (Left of Centre) nearly 2,000 miles long to Calcutta could never hope to supply Slim's forces in the rains – apart from the fact that stretches of it would be impassable anyway. Once launched, Slim's forces were embarked on a fixed course, 'Rangoon before the Monsoon' – 700 miles in six months. Failure in this might set the SEAC war back two years.

It was decided that the opportunity was too big to be lost. The 14th pushed on into central Burma on an air supply basis, while 15th Corps (now a separate command under the top-level co-ordination of General Leese) was taking Akyab (February 1944) and later Ramree. The air bases were secure.

From the north-east, too, came the cheering news that Stilwell had found his 'road back' and was through to China. The road, and its great oil pipeline, was not far behind the troops, and the siege of China was raised. After three years of dependence on airborne supplies over the rugged 'hump' of the Himalayas, Chiang and the 14th USAAF now had a land link again with the Allies.

Amid these happy omens, 4th and 33rd Corps went into the great attack of January 1945. Slim now had three months to make Rangoon, which was still 650 miles south.

Three divisions of 33 Corps (2nd British and 19th and 20th Indian) poured out of the North Burma Plain and enveloped Mandalay. This involved major crossings of the Irrawaddy River by each of the divisions at places where the river was three to four times as wide as the Rhine. The crossings were made, as Slim later said 'on a shoe-string and a bit of bamboo' but they were made, and all the bridgeheads were made against fanatical opposition. Gradually, the Japanese were forced back and day and night they were pounded from the air by the RAF tactical close-support dive-bombers.

Meanwhile from Arakan ports poured the loaded Dakotas, landing in central Burma on rough-hewn dirt strips, unloading and turning back again for more. At the peak of air supply (March 1945) these RAF, RCAF and USAAF Dakotas were flying 100,000 tons of men and equipment a month to the battle areas, a total which is so staggering that many civil aviation experts still hardly believe it possible.

In all something like 200 rough airstrips were built, used and abandoned in the Burma campaign to accept, near the moving firing line, the vital supplies which the Combat Cargo Task Force air-lifted to victory.

Under the powerful air umbrella of EAC, they took Mandalay before starting on the dramatic dash south. Five weeks to go, and 450 miles to Rangoon!

The Japanese drew up the remnants of their three armies below Mandalay to bar the road to the south. Slim then launched his key blow of the campaign. Three divisions of 4 Corps (5th, 7th and 17 Indian Divisions) secretly crossed the Irrawaddy at Pakokku and 17th Division made an 8-mile armoured dash across desert country at Meiktila, the key Japanese communications centre behind their lines. Meiktila fell after a week of fierce battles and the main Japanese forces thus had Slim's army both to the north and the south of them. They were cut up as the hammer and anvil came together and thousands of Japanese soldiers were killed.

This was the vital battle. In the first week of April the 5th and 17th Divisions set out from Meiktila on the final dash to Rangoon. There were 340 miles to go in thirty pre-monsoon days. By using motorised and airborne brigades astonishing progress was made. Toungoo, halfway mark, was reached by 22 April. By 1 May they were at St Pagu, 47 miles north of Rangoon. It was here that the monsoon rains began.

Mountbatten had foreseen that the rains might catch the offensive in its final stages and had an amphibious and airborne invasion ready. This was launched by 15 Corps on 2 May and Rangoon fell with virtually no opposition. Its Japanese garrison had moved north to defend Pagu.

The fall of Rangoon was virtually the end of the Burma campaign for, during the dash down from Meiktila, the 33 Corps had cleared the oilfield around Yenangya, and had turned south down the Irrawaddy River through Prome towards Rangoon. They were helped by the Burma National Army.

About 50,000 Japanese remained in isolated pockets or in the Shan Hills. They made many attempts to withdraw through enemy lines and there was furious fighting, particularly on the Toungoo–Mawchi road. In one of these engagements 11,000 Japanese were killed for an Allied loss of 73. This was done by the newly formed 12th Army (Lieuenant General Sir Montague Stopford).

When the Japanese surrendered, the South East Asia Command total of counted enemy killed reached 130,000 – 42 per cent of the total Japanese Army killed in the whole Far East War. Many more had been killed by the brilliant close-support of the air forces throughout the campaign, notably by 221 and 224 Groups of RAF.

At the time of peace SEAC was on the point of launching a great sea and air invasion of Malaya and Singapore, spearheaded by a new Corps – the 34th.

Thus was ended one of the most amazing campaigns of the war. An advance of nearly 700 miles in three months – all on the basis of air supply. In the north, Wingate had maintained his whole expedition on the same principle.

On the ground the 14th Army and 15 Corps, aided by Marines and by the great daring of the little ships of the Royal Navy and the Royal Indian Navy, the British, Indian Gurkha and African troops had overcome impossible obstacles of terrain, jungle and swamp.

Great imagination had played its part in the strategy – great fortitude and skill had carried out those plans.

Chapter Twenty-Two

A Royal Secret

From August 1945 to late March 1946 my father became involved in a royal secret about the then Princess Elizabeth's romance with Prince Philip, a serving officer with the Royal Navy. There had been rumours in the British press about its possible outcome, but Buckingham Palace could not confirm, comment or provide any information. Prince Philip was, of course, the nephew of Lord Mountbatten, who naturally took a very keen interest in developments, especially as some said he had brokered the marriage. As he was still in post as Supreme Commander South East Asia, he was 'out of touch' with news in London and he asked Charles Gardner at the Ministry of Information secretly to keep him briefed and send him relevant newspaper cuttings. This he did even after he had re-joined the BBC.

It says something of Mountbatten's trust in my father that he should be chosen as a confidant and the correspondence we have between the two is most enlightening, especially in the minute details of how to respond to press speculation. It should be remembered that such a marriage was of momentous importance to the history of this country and to the future of the royal family.

Although this correspondence was marked 'strictly personal' or by the adoption of a code name in later dealings, it took place over seventy years ago and because Prince Philip's origins are well-known, I have included relevant extracts as a matter of historic interest.

The letters concentrated mainly on the press handling of the rumours circulating at the time. These mostly surrounded Prince Philip, his family background in Greece, what he looked like, his naval career and most of all his suitability to be, one day, the Royal Consort of the Queen.

Mountbatten's main concern, as it transpired, was Prince Philip's looks, which were 'absolutely English', and his nationality, for he was still officially Prince Philip of Greece and Denmark. Furthermore, because a wartime embargo on foreigners obtaining British nationality had not yet been lifted, 'It is naturally not desired to make an exception in Prince Philip's case until this is done,' Mountbatten wrote.

Prince Philip, whose family line can be traced back to Queen Victoria, was in fact exiled from Greece as an infant but soon came to settle in Britain. He famously became a pupil at Gordonstoun School in Scotland, known for its harsh regime. He joined the Royal Navy aged 18 in 1939, and became a cadet at the Royal Naval College at Dartmouth. It was here he met, for the first time, the 13-year-old Princess Elizabeth, who was his third cousin. They began a correspondence that lasted throughout the war.

The first letter from Mountbatten to Charles Gardner was dated 8 September 1945. It was in response to my father's of 15 August (a copy of which we don't have) providing information and press cuttings about the rumours of a romance and the suitability of Prince Philip because of his nationality. Mountbatten was 'rather horrified' that the matter had been discussed among other officials before consulting Sir Alan Lascelles, who was the King's Private Secretary. He wrote:

> However, it is probably quite a good thing in the long run that everybody is now informed about this. I have had a very friendly letter from Sir Alan Lascelles, saying that he quite understands the position, and that 'no harm has been done' – in fact good, for, if and when the thing goes through, we shall now know exactly who to get hold of at the Ministry of Information. I have urged Sir Alan Lascelles whatever happens, to get in touch with the Ministry of Information [Charles Gardner] before the announcement is gazetted.

He then referred to two photographic negatives of Prince Philip and asked my father if he would get the necessary number of prints in anticipation of their being used:

> I do not know whether it would be better to let them gradually filter out, so that they were in the possession of the press before the announcement, and thus not make it appear to be a special handout; or whether they should go out with the handout, which might appear as though we were trying to do publicity propaganda, which we are not.

My father had already (on 5 September) sent more cuttings with a letter addressed to the Supreme Commander summarising the PR options open to him.

He wrote:

The fact that events have happened in a 'cart before the horse' order will undoubtedly mean that the Palace announcement if and when made, is bound to revive this rumour. It is obvious any mention at all of Prince Philip will merely add fuel to the whole business. Any attempt by any official P.R. organisation whether it be that of Buckingham Palace, or the Home Office or of the Admiralty to give Prince Philip the full credit for his naval career will be mis-read as a build up and so add to this rumour.

You might think it best to arrange it so that nobody in London knows anything about Prince Philip beyond the fact that he is a serving naval officer. If, however, you feel that this would be unfair to him, the steering of any press comment upon Prince Philip would have to be done sub rosa – i.e. a casual word dropped to a gossip writer in an accidental meeting at a club and so on. As I see it there can now be no possible suggestion of any career note or photograph being available even under pressure, from any source which is known to be connected with any official P.R. This would only be construed as a build-up.

Gardner then asked for further instructions and continued:

I suggest that the best help I can give in this matter when the Palace announcement is made, and when it is obvious that the press is taking this matter up again, is to get around fairly well on that day at the Press Club and other places to see one or two of our best friends in Fleet Street ostensibly about SEAC matters. The conversation could be drifted on to Prince Philip and I could work-in what I know of him from you as though it were a matter of personal knowledge. I do not think I would be suspect in any way and any casual information that I disclosed would probably bear fruit.

He concluded, 'You may, however, feel that the best method of handling the whole business is that there should be a complete official silence about the whole thing. The matter would then probably die down over night, as did the present rumour.'

On 27 October the now Wing Commander Charles Gardner was writing again to Mountbatten. By this time he was organising his departure from the MOI to re-join the BBC.

He wrote:

> The position with regard to Prince Philip is awaiting your decision as to whether the basic problem has been altered by the publication of stories to which your attention was drawn in a previous letter. Meanwhile prints have been made of the negative left in my charge, and these prints are held at this office. The prints were made circumspectly.

He then refers to a Mr Bamford, a career civil servant, 'who is au fait with your wishes, who appears to be remaining at the Ministry for the time being and could still act in accordance with the wishes of yourself and Sir Alan Lascelles'. He added, 'By the time that any action may be deemed necessary, I may have left the service, but I should be happy to do anything you may require in the way of "unofficial" guidance in any useful quarter to which I have access.'[1] He concluded, 'In accordance with your orders for secrecy, I have not put my No 2, Major Wynn Jones into the picture, but in the event of my leaving soon, I suggest that I be given permission to do so. He has many good contacts and is, of course, completely to be trusted.'

Mountbatten replied to my father in a 'Strictly Personal' note in which he confirmed that Major Wynn Jones should be 'put in the picture on condition that he discusses the matter with no one except Mr Bamford. I should like Wynn Jones to keep in touch with me about this, but not to take any action without prior reference to me,' he wrote. To ensure confidentiality, Mountbatten then refers to a code word, 'which in future will be operation NEPOT, which will enable Wynn Jones to telegraph me personally without giving the show away'.

The Supreme Commander also indicated there would be a delay before a formal announcement and continued: 'Do you think it would be a good idea to allow some of the prints [of Prince Philip] to filter out into newspaper offices at a time that there is no news value attached to Prince Philip, that is, when ridiculous rumours have died down?'

He concluded, 'I do not wish any action to be taken about this until you have given me your opinion, perhaps after consulting Mr Bamford and Wynn Jones. The alternative, presumably is to hold the prints until the announcement is made.'

194

By now my father had left the MOI and was fully absorbed in renewing his work as BBC Air Correspondent. However he was still kept in the loop and a letter headed 'Operation Nepot' addressed to his home at Eaves Cottage from Wynn Jones of 8 February 1946 brought him up-to-date. Wynn Jones reported there had been no change in the position but 'Bamford agrees entirely with my view that we do as Supremo suggests and allow some prints to filter out to the press would only have the effect of arousing curiosity and might well resurrect the rumour,' he wrote.

He continued, 'In view of experience on a previous occasion Bamford feels rather strongly that the subject is one for Buckingham Palace to handle. In view of the approaching fold up of the Ministry of Information, and presumably of this office, some definite drill should be laid down now for the handling of the operation.'

In his final letter to Mountbatten on 15 February my father agreed the prints should be held back. 'They should be issued in the normal way together with a simple career note which would be impressive by virtue of the facts.' Prince Philip who was known as Lieutenant Philip Mountbatten had an impressive war record and served both in the Mediterranean and Pacific fleets.

As far as distribution was concerned, Gardner wrote, 'My own inclination would be to have the pictures distributed by a government agency other than the Palace and I suggest the Admiralty. It would appear perfectly natural for the prints to come from that source as the affair is mainly a naval one.'

Mountbatten responded on 20 March saying he had discussed the matter with Brigadier Mike Wardell and Lieutenant Colonel Frank Owen.[2] 'The latter has undertaken to write up an article from the "hand out" which you hold, which he is kindly undertaking to publish in the Daily Mail and to try and get placed in other papers as a favour, as from within the Press rather than trying to plant it from outside from the Admiralty or the Palace.'

And there the matter rested as far as my father was concerned. For it later transpired that the King, when asked by Prince Philip for the hand of Princess Elizabeth, agreed to the proposal but he asked that it be delayed (and kept secret) to beyond her 21st birthday in April 1947. And so in July 1947 the official announcement of the engagement was made and four months later the wedding between Princess Elizabeth and Prince Philip Mountbatten took place to great acclaim in Westminster Abbey on 20 November 1947. Just before the marriage ceremony King George VI bestowed on Prince Philip the title of Duke of Edinburgh.

My father did meet Lord Mountbatten again on several occasions on news-related topics. Their last meeting was in 1954 at St John's School, Leatherhead, where he presented the prizes at speech day, the guest of Lord Montgomery the school's Chairman of the Governors.[3]

Chapter Twenty-Three

The 'Voice of the Air'

My father's return to the BBC as Air Correspondent in December 1945 coincided with a new era in British aviation, an era of over twenty years when Britain ruled the world. For by the end of the war, the British industry of over twenty-seven airframe companies and eight engine manufacturers had amassed huge technological knowledge, particularly with the jet engine, of which Britain was the principal pioneer.

New 'faster than the speed of sound' jet fighters, V bombers and the hugely successful Canberra jet bomber were now being developed, while in civil aviation, a whole new world of great potential was opening up. In just a few years Britain was to produce the world's first turbo-prop and pure jet airliners – the Viscount and Comet – and men began dreaming of a supersonic aircraft, which was to come in 1969 when the first Concorde took to the air.

Charles Gardner was to experience firsthand these exciting times both as a reporter and correspondent for radio, television and as the public address commentator at the Farnborough Air Show and other aviation events. He became known as the 'Voice of the Air'. As such he was very well-known to the public and industry alike. And it was through his contact with the designer of the new Viscount, George Edwards, that he was persuaded by Edwards to leave the BBC and join his company, especially to help promote sales in the United States of the Viscount.

His time with the company, then Vickers-Armstrongs Aircraft, was to be stimulating, for in addition to the successful sales of the Viscount, Edwards was building the first V bomber, the Valiant, and developing what would have been the first British Trans-Atlantic jet airliner, the V1000. Then came rationalisation of the industry and the formation of British Aircraft Corporation essentially to build the most ambitious fighter in the world – TSR2. The now Sir George Edwards, with Gardner still at his side, was pitched into the political battles to save that aircraft before further political controversy as the industry was, for a time, nationalised and TSR2 was cancelled. Meanwhile there was Concorde and all that went with the world's only supersonic airliner, while the huge costs entailed in such programmes brought about the age of collaboration, with the Jaguar (with France) and the Tornado (with Germany and Italy) leading the way.

My father's experience as a broadcaster and writer and later as a senior executive and author of the authorised history of the British Aircraft Corporation meant he was able to describe the intrigue and turmoil that surrounded this ever-changing industry. Today just two mighty companies remain, BAE Systems and Rolls-Royce. And they are still engaged at the highest level of building and developing aircraft and engines in the further advance of British aviation industry.

Charles Gardner continued to work for British Aircraft Corporation (BAC) until his retirement in 1977, as did his boss, the Chairman, Sir George Edwards. This coincided with the nationalisation of the company and the foundation of British Aerospace.

In retirement Charles wrote the complete and authorised history of BAC, which was published in 1981. For relaxation he sailed his boat with Eve from Bosham harbour in Sussex, played golf and watched cricket at Lord's.

In 1979, after forty years of living at Eaves Cottage in Fetcham, Charles and Eve moved to Topsham in Devon. However, Charles's retirement did not last long and in June 1983, aged just 71, he died. His obituary was carried in all the major national newspapers, covering his early days at the BBC, his commentaries at the Farnborough Air Show and particularly his Battle of Britain broadcast. His funeral was attended by many personalities in broadcasting, journalism and aviation. The address was given by Sir George Edwards.

Notes

Chapter One

1. Prior to the broadcast Gardner had been posted to France from 1939–40 from where he described activities of the RAF and the German Air Force, as we shall see in later chapters.

Chapter Two

1. Publishers of the *Nuneaton Tribune*.
2. We have two very full cuttings books dating from 1931.
3. Amy Mollison became the first person to fly solo in her Gipsy-Moth from England to Australia in 1930.
4. The Prince of Wales took delivery of a Vickers Viastra VIP version of a ten-passenger, twin-engined transport built at Weybridge, Surrey.
5. Eric Hollies is still fondly remembered at Warwickshire's home ground at Edgbaston, where a stand is named after him.

Chapter Three

1. We still have a copy of the BBC contract signed by my father in 1936.
2. Sir Ralph Murray is still considered one of the founding fathers of BBC news reporting. He later left the BBC to join the Foreign Office and became the British Ambassador in Rome.
3. We still have a copy of Lord Reith's memo.
4. We still have his air ticket for seat 6.
5. The DH Comet 88 was a two-seater, twin-engined aircraft designed in 1934 to compete in long-distance air races. This it did with great success winning the prestigious London to Melbourne race that year.

Chapter Four

1. Potter Heigham is one of the major boating centres on the Norfolk Broads.
2. My father always referred to his news reports as despatches which we have retained throughout the book, although 'dispatches' is more commonly used nowadays.
3. We have all three documents.
4. The cover of the *Radio Times* of 14 July 1939 has been retained.

Chapter Five

1. Among the British journalists assigned to the AASF in France who were with Charles Gardner were: Noel Monks (*Daily Mail*), his wife Mary Welsh (*Daily Express*), Ronnie Walker (*News Chronicle*) – a great friend known as 'Aunty Ronnie', Peter Lawless (*Daily Telegraph*), Godfrey Anderson (Associated Press), Reginald 'Groucho' Roland (*Exchange Telegraph*), E. Walling (Reuters), Thomas Fisher (British Movietone News), Lord Donegal (*Sunday Dispatch*), O.D. Gallagher (*Daily Express*) and Arthur Narracott (*The Times*).
2. The Maginot Line was a line of concrete fortifications and underground tunnels and bunkers constructed by the French in the 1930s. It ran along the French border with Germany from north to south and was designed with both defence and attack in mind. It was thought to be impregnable but proved ineffective as the Germans entered France through Belgium bypassing it. A few years ago my brother and I and some friends, on our annual war walk, visited these defences and found much of the fortifications and long tunnels intact.

Chapter Seven

1. We have the letter together with other correspondence from Hugh de Sellincourt, written in his distinctive small and precise hand.
2. The doctor was our local family doctor, Dr Waterfield. Dr Waterfield was a great help to my mother during the war as she struggled to bring up three children on her own. But he is best known as doctor to Barnes Wallis, and even appeared in the film *The Dambusters*. He visited Wallis's home in Effingham to treat his children and was in the film. While there he saw Wallis experimenting with models in tubs of water replicating the dams he was about to burst.
3. We have a copy of the *Radio Times*.

4. 'Cobber' Kain was to become one of two pilots to whom my father's AASF book was dedicated. The other was Flight Lieutenant Brian Kerridge.

Chapter Eight

1. Mary Welsh was clearly a very good friend. I had the privilege of meeting Noel Monks, who lived in Epsom, and Mary Welsh Hemingway in a chance encounter in New York with my father many years later.
2. The Dewoitine was a commercial twenty-four-seater monoplane airliner built by the French company SNCA.
3. We can only presume that he acquired his automatic pistol through a friend, probably in the RAF. It was not issued to him by the BBC.

Chapter Nine

1. The Dyle Line was a line of fortifications built by the Belgians and named after the River Dyle in the south of the country near the border with France. It consisted of a series of bunkers and barricades between the village of Koningshooikt and the city of Wavre.
2. The Maastricht bridges raid will be described in the following chapter.

Chapter Ten

1. My father's diary may have survived his time in France but, alas, did not survive the effects of time and was lost.
2. The Maastricht bridges had remained standing because the Dutch had failed to blow them up.
3. Ward and Stubbs were both appointed as war correspondents but shortly after Charles and Richard Dimbleby.

Chapter Eleven

1. His cuttings book is crammed with cuttings from all over the country. On the inside page there is the autograph on AASF paper of the famous New Zealand ace 'Cobber' Kain and another pilot from 73 Squadron.
2. Mary Welsh was at that time still married to Noel Monks of the *Daily Mail* but they were shortly to separate and she married Ernest Hemingway.

Chapter Twelve

1. We have both letters of appointment and joining instructions.
2. The reference to the logbook was his civil record. Alas that is missing but his RAF logbook is preserved.
3. His reference from the BBC addressed to 'To whom it may concern' was signed by the General Establishment Officer.

Chapter Thirteen

1. My father's home town was Nuneaton.
2. My brother has several photos of his group at Cranwell. As the oldest and most senior cadet he is sitting in the middle of the front row. This includes his passing out parade on 8 March 1941.
3. I have several photos of Sir John Barraclough in 2003 standing by a Catalina – the only one left in the UK which we used for making a video in support of the Coastal Command appeal.

Chapter Fourteen

1. The Atlantic Charter, signed on 14 August 1941, was a pivotal policy statement between the United States and Great Britain determining Allied goals for a postwar world. This was important because the United States was not in the war at that time.
2. We have the full transcript of Charles Gardner's 1941 broadcast about the Coastal Command operations in the North Atlantic.
3. The German Focke-Wulf Condor was a four-engined passenger airliner converted for 'recce' duties in the Atlantic and other areas.

Chapter Fifteen

1. Among the Hurricane pilots were Squadron Leader Peter Fletcher and Flight Lieutenant 'Teddy' Peacock-Edwards. Both were Rhodesians, both won DFCs for their gallant response to the Japanese attack and both were shot down and hospitalised. In later life Air Chief Marshal Sir Peter Fletcher, who wrote the foreword to the book *The Most Dangerous Moment*, retired to join British Aerospace as a director with special responsibility for the Airbus programme. He was well-known to the author. Peacock-Edward's son Rick became a friend through the RAF Club where he was Vice-Chairman.

Interestingly photographs of both my father, Teddy and Peter appear in Tomlinson's book.

2.   The belief by my father and the crew of Catalina 'L' that the navy was in the area was mistaken.

Chapter Sixteen

1.   Many years later I got to know Air Marshal Sir Charles Pringle, who was then the Director of the SBAC (Society of British Aircraft Companies) which ran the Farnborough Air Show. Sir Charles, who was an engineer, told me how he was responsible for servicing and looking after my father's Lysander in Ceylon. He had fond memories of my father and his flying experiences.

Chapter Seventeen

1.   The title DADPR carries executive rank within a large service-wide PR organisation.

2.   The US military designation for the Douglas Dakota is C-47 'Skytrain' while the RAF retained the Dakota name.

Chapter Eighteen

1.   The airstrip was at Gunnavarum.

2.   The 'Rear Echelon' was in fact set up within the Ministry of Information and not within the Air Ministry.

Chapter Nineteen.

1.   The 'Superfortress' was a heavy bomber built by Boeing and designated B-29. It was heavily involved in bombing operations in Europe and in the Far East from 1941.

2.   Sir William Slim was appointed Field Marshal and later took up the post of Governor General in Australia.

3.   HMS *Kelly* was famously commanded by Mountbatten, then a Captain in the Royal Navy and was lost in action in the Battle of Crete in 1941.

Chapter Twenty

1.   General Slim's reference to his arrangements referred to Gardner's visit to the 14th Army earlier in the year.

2. The Potsdam Conference from 17 July–2 August 1945 involved all the world leaders including Churchill, Stalin and Harry S. Truman, the new President of the United States.
3. Because of the numbers of military honours awarded at the end of the war, my father, along with many others, did not receive his medal from the King but it was sent to him together with a signed scroll and a personal letter, copies of which are in our possession together with the medal.

Chapter Twenty-One

1. General Wingate was killed in a plane crash having been caught in a thunderstorm on 24 March 1944.

Chapter Twenty-Two

1. Mr Bamford was later knighted as Sir Eric Bamford and became Chairman of the Inland Revenue.
2. Frank Owen returned to the *Daily Mail* after his service at SEAC where he was a friend and colleague of my father and edited the SEAC souvenir news.
3. My father was at St John's School as a parent. My family has a strong connection with the school – my brother and I were the first Gardners to attend, followed by my son Paul, by my brother's son Alexander and daughter Claire and now by his granddaughter Chloe. Since then my brother has been a governor for many years and both of us are still engaged in fundraising and 'Old Boy' activities.

Sources

Chapter One

BBC Recordings Library (housed in the British Library), London
Edward Stourton, *Auntie's War*, Doubleday, 2017
The BBC at War was a Fresh One Productions Dimbleby Partners in association with the BBC
Britain at War magazine, issue 44, December 2010

Chapter Two

Press cuttings, personal papers and correspondence

Chapter Three

BBC Written Archives, Caversham Park, Berkshire
Jonathan Dimbleby, *Richard Dimbleby*, Hodder and Stoughton, 1975, a biography
BBC, *Richard Dimbleby Broadcaster*, 1966, a tribute to Richard Dimbleby published a year after his death. My father was one of many contributors from which extracts have been taken, together with a *Sunday Times* feature on his life published in 1975. A photograph of a youthful Dimbleby and Gardner appeared in both
BBC Recordings Library
Personal papers and correspondence

Chapter Four

BBC Written Archives, Caversham Park, Berkshire
BBC, *Richard Dimbleby Broadcaster*

Stourton, *Auntie's War*
Janes's All the World's Aircraft, Sampson Low, Marston & Company
BBC Recordings Library
BBC Handbook, 1941, BBC
Press cuttings (the cutting referring to the loss of the *Thetis* does not contain
    the name of the newspaper)
Private correspondence and personal papers

Chapter Five

BBC, *Richard Dimbleby Broadcaster*, David Howarth's contribution
Radio Times, October 1939
BBC Handbook, British Broadcasting Corporation
Stourton, *Auntie's War*
Charles Gardner, *AASF*, Hutchinson & Co. (Publishers), London and
    Melbourne. No publishing date is given, probably for security reasons.
    My copy was the one my father gave to his parents for Christmas 1940.
    It is inscribed by his own hand to – 'My mother and father with love,
    Charles, 1940, RAF Cranwell'.
BBC Recordings Library
Personal letters, correspondence and filed despatches

Chapter Six

Gardner, *AASF*
British Recordings Library
Personal papers and correspondence

Chapter Seven

BBC Recordings Library
Gardner, *AASF*
Dimbleby, *Richard Dimbleby*
Personal papers and correspondence

Chapter Eight

Gardner, *AASF*
Stourton, *Auntie's War*
Personal correspondence and papers

Chapter Nine

Winston S. Churchill, *The Second World War*, 6 vols, Vol. II, Cassell & Co. Ltd, 1948
Gardner, *AASF*

Chapter Ten

Gardner, *AASF*
Stourton, *Auntie's War*
Churchill, *The Second World War*, Vol. II
BBC Recordings Library
Press cuttings and personal papers

Chapter Eleven

BBC Written Archives, Caversham Park, Berkshire
Stourton, *Auntie's War*
Britain at War Magazine, December 2010
Simon Elmes, *Hello Again*, Arrow Books, 2013

Chapter Twelve

Charles Gardner's papers

Chapter Thirteen

Flight Lieutenant Charles Gardner, *The Gen Book*, Hutchinson & Co. Ltd, 1942
Personal papers including a fourteen-page description written by my father of his joining up

Chapter Fourteen

Personal paper, BBC broadcast script

Chapter Fifteen

Michael Tomlinson, *The Most Dangerous Moment*, William Kimber, 1976
Churchill, *The Second World War*, Vol. IV

Personal papers including Gardner's sixteen-page typewritten report in our possession which was missing one page – the first

Chapter Sixteen

Personal paper, broadcast scripts

Chapter Seventeen

Broadcast scripts, despatches, correspondence and minutes of meetings in our possession

Chapter Eighteen

Broadcast scripts, despatches by Charles Gardner and other papers in our possession

Chapter Nineteen

Broadcast scripts and articles by Charles Gardner, personal papers and correspondence
Letters from Air Marshal Joubert and Lieutenant General Slim

Chapter Twenty

Broadcast scripts and articles by Charles Gardner, correspondence and letters from General Slim and Lord Mounbatten

Chapter Twenty-One

Charles Gardner, 'A History of the Burma War'

Chapter Twenty-Two

Personal correspondence between Charles Gardner and Lord Mountbatten and Major Wynn-Jones

Index